VIEN&NA
CHI&AGO
Friends or Foes?

*A Tale of Two Schools
of Free-Market Economics*

OTHER BOOKS BY MARK SKOUSEN

Playing the Price Controls Game

Economics of a Pure Gold Standard

The Structure of Production

Economics on Trial

Dissent on Keynes (editor)

Puzzles and Paradoxes in Economics
(co-authored with Kenna C. Taylor)

Economic Logic

The Making of Modern Economics

The Power of Economic Thinking

VIENNA & CHICAGO

Friends or Foes?

A Tale of Two Schools
of Free-Market Economics

by Mark Skousen

CAPITAL
PRESS

Cataloging-in-Publication Data on file with the Library of Congress

0-89526-029-8

Published in the United States by
Regnery Publishing, Inc.
One Massachusetts Avenue, NW
Washington, DC 20001

www.regnery.com

Distributed to the trade by
National Book Network
Lanham, MD 20706
Manufactured in the United States of America

10 9 8 7 6 5 4 3 2

Books are available in quantity for promotional or premium use.
Write to Director of Special Sales, Regnery Publishing, Inc.,
One Massachusetts Avenue NW, Washington, DC 20001,
for information on discounts and terms or call (202) 216-0600.

Cover design: Pitts•LaVigne Associates
Winter Park, Florida

Cover Photos:
Vienna photo © Copyright 2005 Thomas H. Wicky, www.ZoomVienna.com
Chicago photo by Jo Ann Skousen

Economists from left to right:
Ludwig von Mises and Friedrich Hayek (Austrian),
Milton Friedman and George Stigler (Chicago).

Dedicated to

members of the

Mont Pelerin Society,

friends of both the

Austrian and Chicago schools.

CONTENTS

ACKNOWLEDGEMENTS

Many individuals helped in the preparation of this book. I would like to thank the following. Among economists sympathetic to the "Austrian" school, I interviewed the following:

Roger Garrison (Auburn University)
Leland Yeager (Auburn University)
Peter Boettke (George Mason University)
Donald J. Boudreaux (George Mason University)
Llewellyn Rockwell, Mark Thorton, and Jeff Tucker
    (Mises Institute)
Walter E. Block (Loyola University)
Israel M. Kirzner (New York University)
Richard Ebeling
    (Hillsdale College, Foundation for Economic Education)
Lawrence H. White (University of Washington-St. Louis)
Jesus Huerto de Soto (Universidad Rey Juan Carlos)
Bruce Caldwell
    (University of North Carolina at Greensboro)
Edwin G. Dolan (Dartmouth College)
Dominick T. Armentano (University of Hartford)
Richard E. Wagner (George Mason University)
Erich Streissler (University of Vienna)
Karl Socher (University of Innsbruck)

Among economists leaning toward the "Chicago" school:

Milton Friedman (Hoover Institution)
Gary Becker (University of Chicago)
Robert Lucas, Jr. (University of Chicago)
Allan H. Meltzer (Carnegie-Mellon University)
Sam Peltzman (University of Chicago)
Anna J. Schwartz (National Bureau of Economic Research)
Larry T. Wimmer (Brigham Young University)

David I. Meiselman (Virginia Polytechnic Institute)
Stephen M. Stigler (University of Chicago)
Ronald H. Coase (University of Chicago)
David Friedman (Santa Clara University)
Richard Timberlake (University of Georgia)
Arnold C. Harberger
(University of California at Los Angeles)
Richard Thaler (University of Chicago)
Alan Ebenstein (Cato Institute)

Among members of the Keynesian and other schools:

Paul A. Samuelson (MIT)
Joseph Stiglitz (Columbia University)

I would also like to thank Roger Garrison, Peter J. Boettke, Larry Wimmer, Milton Friedman, and two anonymous referees for reading through an earlier draft of this manuscript, and making a number of corrections and suggestions. Appreciation goes to my wife, Jo Ann, who throughout my adult life has served as my editor par excellence. This book is immensely improved because of her extraordinary efforts.

AEIOU,

Mark Skousen

Mark Skousen
New York, New York
E-mail: mskousen@mskousen.com

The author interviewing Friedrich Hayek at his apartment in the Austrian Alps in 1985. It turned out to be his last interview.

The author with Milton Friedman at his home overlooking the San Francisco Bay in 1999.

Chapter One

INTRODUCTION
VIENNA AND CHICAGO,
A TALE OF TWO SCHOOLS

Yet the award [the 1974 Nobel Prize in Economics]
documented the beginning of a great shift toward ...
a renewed belief in the superiority of markets...
the eventual victory of this viewpoint was really
a tale of two cities—Vienna and Chicago.

—Daniel Yergin and Joseph Stanislaw (1998:96)

In late September, 1994, Henri Lepage asked me to address the Mont Pelerin Society in Cannes, France. The title was "I Like Hayek," an appreciation of the principal founder of the Society in 1947. I thought the subject would be well received, but I was mistaken. Over a dozen attendees lined up to take issue with my favorable comments about Hayek's capital theory and macroeconomic model of inflation and business cycles. It turned out that the critics were followers of Milton Friedman and the Chicago school.

Anyone who has ever attended a Mont Pelerin Society meeting will quickly attest that this international group of freedom-fighters are divided into two camps: followers of the Austrian school and followers of the Chicago school. I say "divided" guardedly because these two camps undoubtedly have more in common than disagreement. In general, they are devout believers in free markets and free minds. Yet they seem to relish the rivalry that exists regarding fundamental issues of methodology, money, business cycles, government policy, and even who are the great economists.

1

The first group is known as the Austrian or Vienna school, founded by Carl Menger, who taught economics at the University of Vienna in the late 19th century. Menger's disciples, Ludwig von Mises and Friedrich Hayek, left Vienna during the Nazi era and established an Austrian following in England and the United States. In 1974, a year after Mises died, Hayek received the Nobel Prize in Economics, the first one given to a free-market economist.

It was a long battle toward recognition. In 1947, Hayek invited a small group of classical liberals from around the world to a conference at the Hotel du Parc on the slopes of Mont Pelerin, Switzerland. Hayek was alarmed by the rapid advance of socialism in the post-war era, and decided to establish a society aimed at preserving a free civilization and opposed to all forms of totalitarianism. He dedicated the meeting in the spirit of Adam Smith and his "system of natural liberty." Among the 38 participants were the Austrians Ludwig von Mises, Fritz Machlup, and Karl Brandt. It also included the Americans Milton Friedman and George Stigler, who would become leaders of the market-oriented economics department at the University of Chicago. The quasi-market tradition at Chicago actually began earlier with the works of Frank H. Knight, Henry Simons and Jacob Viner. Friedman and Stigler were the second generation of free-market economists at Chicago. Both went on to win the Nobel Prize (Friedman in 1976, Stigler in 1982). Milton Friedman in particular has so dominated the department that Friedmanite economics has become practically synonymous with the Chicago or monetarist school. His prestige is felt on the campus even today, a generation after his retirement. The Chicago school has continued to have enormous influence, both in the United States and around the world. Friedman is considered one of the most eminent economists living today.

Points of Common Ground

As members of a free-market association, how could these two camps disagree so vehemently? The reality is that they don't disagree on most issues. Generally speaking, members of the Austrian and Chicago schools have much in common and, in many ways, could be considered intellectual descendants of laissez faire economics of Adam Smith, philosophical cousins rather than foes.[1]

- Both champion the sanctity of private property as the basis of exchange, justice, and progress in society.

- Both defend laissez-faire capitalism and believe firmly in Adam Smith's invisible hand doctrine, that self-motivated actions of private individuals maximize happiness and society's well-being, and that liberty and order are ultimately harmonious (Barry 1987:19, 29, 193).

- Both are critics of Marx and the Marxist doctrines of alienation, exploitation, and other anti-capitalist notions.

- Both support free trade, a liberalized immigration policy, and globalization.

- Both generally favor open borders for capital and consumer goods, labor, and money.

- Both oppose controls on exchange, prices, rents, and wages, including minimum wage legislation.

- Both believe in limiting government to defense of the nation, individual property, and selective public works (although a few in both camps are anarchists, such as Murray Rothbard and David Friedman).

1 Libertarian philosopher Norman P. Barry notes that although Mises and Friedman oppose each other on methodology and other issues, "they may both be called children of the Enlightenment" and their intellectual lineage goes back to Adam Smith and David Hume (Barry 1987:19, 45).

- Both favor privatization, denationalization, and deregulation.

- Both oppose corporate welfarism and special privileges (known as rent seeking or privilege seeking).

- Both reject socialistic central planning and totalitarianism.

- Both believe that poverty is debilitating but that natural inequality is inevitable, and they defend the right of all individuals, rich or poor, to keep, use and exchange property (assuming it was justly acquired). They do not join the chorus of pundits bashing the rich, although they frequently condemn corporate welfarism.

- Both refute the Keynesian and Marxist interventionists who believe that market capitalism is inherently unstable and requires big government to stabilize the economy.

- Both are generally opposed to deficit spending, progressive taxation, and the welfare state, and favor free-market alternatives to Social Security and Medicare.

- Both favor market and property-rights solutions to pollution and other environmental problems, and in general consider the environmentalist crisis as overblown.

Israel Kirzner rightly concludes, "It is important not to exaggerate the differences between the two streams.....there is an almost surprising coincidence between their views on most important policy questions....both have basically the same sound understanding of how a market operates, and this is responsible for the healthy respect which both approaches share in common for its achievements" (Kirzner 1967:102).

Speaking of achievements, both can claim separate victories in the battle of ideas during the past two centuries:

4

the Austrian school for introducing the subjective Marginalist Revolution in the late 19th century, and then dissecting the inevitable collapse of the Marxist/socialist central planning paradigm in the 20th century; and the Chicago school for mounting a successful counterrevolution to Keynesian macroeconomics and the "imperfect" or monopolistic competition model in microeconomics. Members of both schools have won Nobel prizes in economics, although the Chicago school has a clear lead. And both have sometimes been viciously attacked by their opponents, including Keynesians, Marxists, and institutionalists.

It is the thesis of this book that both the Austrian and Chicago schools played significant and largely successful roles in correcting the errors of classical economics and countering the critics of capitalism — socialists, Marxists, Keynesians, and institutionalists — during crucial times in the battle of ideas and events. The early chapters outline the focal points in history where the Austrian and Chicago economists played major roles in defending and advancing Adam Smith's system of natural liberty. Without their vital place, world history may well have been vastly different, and not for the better.

Then Come the Disagreements

Yet with so much to celebrate, where do they disagree? Surprisingly, on quite a few points. While they may be considered followers of Adam Smith's invisible hand of laissez faire, the descendants are divided into two wings of free-market economics. The Austrians and the Chicagoans differ in four broad categories:

First, methodology. The Austrians, following the writings of Ludwig von Mises, favor a deductive, subjective, qualitative, and market-process approach to economic analysis. The Chicagoans, following the works of Milton

Friedman, prefer historical, quantitative, and equilibrating analysis. Friedman and his followers demand empirical testing of theories and, if the results contradict the theory, the theory is rejected or reformed. Mises denies this historical approach in favor of extreme apriorism. According to Mises as well as his disciples Murray Rothbard and Israel Kirzner, economics should be built upon self-evident axioms, and history (empirical data) cannot prove or disprove any theory, only illustrate it, and even then with some suspicion.

Second, the proper role of government in a market economy. How pervasive are externalities, public goods, monopoly, imperfect competition, and macroeconomic stability in the market economy, and what how much government is necessary to handle "market failure"? The Austrians have consistently supported laissez faire policies while the Chicago school has shifted gears over the years. (One might say that both are "anti-statist" but the Austrians are more "anti-statist.") Is Adam Smith's system of natural liberty sufficiently strong to break up monopolies through powerful competitors, or is government necessary to impose antitrust policies when appropriate? The Austrians have always favored a naturalist, non-interventionist approach. On the other hand, the first Chicago school, led by Henry Simons, took a strong interventionist view, favoring the break-up of large utilities and other natural monopolies. The second generation at Chicago, led by George Stigler, initially supported Simons' interventionism, but ultimately reversed course in favor of a Smithian belief in the power of competition and non-interventionism.

According to Israel Kirzner, Peter Boettke and other Austrians, the difference between the two schools is even more fundamental: the Chicago school employs an "equilibrium always" pure competition model (what Chicago economists call an "as if" competition model) that assumes costless perfect information and the Austrians employ a more dynamic "disequilibrium" process model of market capitalism that takes into account institutions and decentralized decision making (Kirzner 1997, Boettke 1997). The debate over the most appropriate competitive model also spills over into issues of political economy, public choice, law and economics, and the efficiency of democracy.

Third, sound money. What is the ideal monetary standard? Both schools favor a stable monetary system, but they differ markedly on the means. Most Austrians prefer a gold standard, or more generally, a naturally-based commodity standard created by the marketplace. Some go further and demand "free banking," a competitive system whereby private banks issue their own currency, checking accounts and credit services with a minimum of government regulation. The Chicago school, on the other hand, rejects the gold standard in favor of an irredeemable money system, where the money supply increases at a steady or neutral rate (the monetarist rule). Both ideally desire 100% reserves on demand deposits as a stabilizing mechanism, though here again, there is a difference—the Austrians want demand deposits backed by gold or other suitable commodity, the Chicagoans by fiat money.

Fourth, the business cycle, capital theory, and macroeconomics. Mises and Hayek developed the "Austrian" theory of the business cycle, maintaining that expanding the fiat money supply and artificially lowering interest rates create an unsustainable, unstable boom that must eventually collapse. Friedman and his colleagues reject most aspects of the Mises-Hayek theory of the business cycle in favor of an aggregate monetary model. The Chicagoans praise Hayek's political theory in *The Road to Serfdom* and *The Constitution of Liberty*, but they reject much of his capital theory and Austrian macroeconomics. (Thus, they took issue with me after my speech in 1994.) Friedman contends that a steady increase in the money supply equal to the average economic growth rate will provide a sustainable non-inflationary environment for

7

the economy. But the Austrians dissent and maintain that a given rate of monetary inflation is never sustainable, whatever the level. Many Austrians also deny the validity of "macroeconomics" and aggregation (such as national statistics or price indexes) as useful pedagogical tools. Austrians and Chicagoans argue over the cause and cure of the Great Depression of the 1930s, what level of aggregation is appropriate in macroeconomic model building, and even disagree at times on their views of Keynes and Keynesians, Adam Smith and classical economists, and other schools of thought. They even differ on their goals and how far they should reach out to influence the intellectual community and the public.

This book will analyze all these issues, deciding which camp has the most convincing arguments for each. At the end of each chapter, I'll give my opinion as to which school has the upper hand, concluding with either "Advantage: Vienna," or "Advantage: Chicago." After reviewing the differences between the two schools, the final chapter will assess if there are any gains in trade, to quote Chicago economist Sherwin Rosen. How far is Chicago from Vienna? Over time and dialogue, the answer will be clearer. Hopefully through this book, the reader may see the intellectual distance narrow, although by the very nature of the argument (as I shall try to show) the separation is not likely to disappear completely, nor should it. In the final chapter, I outline my own views as to the direction both schools should go to benefit the profession and the cause of economic science.

My Travels to Vienna and Chicago

I am in an unusual position to analyze each school, having studied the two philosophies thoroughly for many years and developed close friendships with leaders of both camps. My first introduction to free-market economics was through the Austrians in the 1960s. My father's library contained dozens of books about anti-communism and free-market capitalism. Among them was a copy of *Human Action*, by Ludwig von Mises, although I found it long and heavy-going for a teenager. I was soon reading Henry Hazlitt's *Economics in One Lesson*, monthly issues of *The Freeman*, and bi-weekly issues of William F. Buckley's *National Review*.

When I took my first college course in economics at Brigham Young University in the mid-1960s, the textbook was Paul Samuelson's *Economics*. I was surprised, given the university's conservative bent. Recognizing the textbook's Keynesian bias (espousing the paradox of thrift, deficit spending, progressive taxation, and welfare state), I asked Larry Wimmer, one of my professors, for alternative readings. As a recent graduate from the University of Chicago, he recommended Milton Friedman. I read *Capitalism and Freedom* from cover to cover, and found it to be a powerful antidote of interventionism, although his analysis of Keynesian economics seemed incomplete. (Friedman's views on Keynes have always been controversial—see chapter 8.)

It was at this point, in the early 1970s, that I discovered the libertarian economist Murray Rothbard, who introduced me to a whole new vision of Austrian economics. He was the first "American" Austrian economist who could write in clear, persuasive prose, as opposed to the often heavy, pedantic writings of Mises. I was especially impressed with his readable booklets, *What Has Government Done to Our Money?* and *The Essential Mises*. I read with great interest *America's Great Depression*, an introduction to the Austrian theory of the business cycle as it applied to the Great Depression of the 1930s. Rothbard's works were a life-changing eye-opener. Discovering Rothbard was, in my mind, similar to how Paul Samuelson must have felt reading Keynes. I devoured everything Rothbard had to say. I read his magnum opus, *Man, Economy and State*; its sequel, *Power and Market*; and all his other writings. In short, I was hooked on Austrian economics.

My passion for Austrian economics continued throughout my college days. My doctoral thesis at George Washington University was partially financed by my employer. Published initially as a book by the Mises Institute and later by the Foundation for Economic Education, *The Economics of a Pure Gold Standard* was deeply influenced by Rothbard's support of a 100% gold reserve standard. When I left the CIA to work for Robert D. Kephart and his financial newsletter empire in the mid-1970s, I developed a close relationship with Rothbard and other Austrian economists such as Peter Boettke, Richard Ebeling, Roger Garrison, Hans Sennholz, and Walter Block.

In 1985, Gary North and I spent three hours in a formal interview with Professor Hayek at his summer home in the Austrian Alps.

It was the last extensive interview he gave before his death in 1992.[2] I never met Ludwig von Mises. I've spent many hours with economists sympathetic to Mises, including Henry Hazlitt, Benjamin Rogge, John Chamberlain, Israel Kirzner, and Mises's wife Margit. I became involved with the Mises Institute and helped finance conferences at Harvard University and the University of Vienna. In the 1980s, I spent half my time researching and writing an updated macro model of the economy based on the Austrian time-structure of the economy, culminating in *The Structure of Production*, which was published by New York University Press in 1990. (Mises taught at New York University for decades and Israel Kirzner, one of his students, has been a mainstay at NYU until his retirement in 2001.)

Shifting Ground

By the 1990s, my views had become more eclectic as I expanded my horizons and spent more time researching other

2 Extensive quotations of this interview can be found in *Hayek on Hayek* (1994). Strangely, we were never given credit for these interviews, which represented half—over forty percent—of the interview exchanges in *Hayek on Hayek*. They were attributed to the "W. W. Bartley III audiotape archive, 1984-88" (Ebenstein 2003).

schools of economics, including supply-side, public choice, and the Chicago traditions, for my text on the history of thought, *The Making of Modern Economics* (M. E. Sharpe, 2001). During the process I learned to appreciate the value of these parallel universes and, in some cases, I've changed positions. For example, I have come to the conclusion that empirical work, which the Chicago and supply-side schools emphasize, has done much good in converting the world to the free market and rejecting socialism. There is no question in my mind that Milton Friedman and Anna J. Schwartz's *A Monetary History of the United States* did more than any other work to dispel the conventional wisdom that unfettered capitalism was responsible for the business cycle, and especially the Great Depression. Friedman produced compelling evidence that it was the government's monetary policies, not the free market, that caused the business cycle, and that the Federal Reserve blundered repeatedly and caused the collapse of the banks and the economy in the 1930s. Granted, the Vienna school blamed government, too, for the Great Depression, but did so in a qualitative way without relying on empirical evidence; Friedman and Schwartz told the story in a way that convinced many non-believers.

Many other statistical works conducted by free-market economists have changed the minds of scholars and government officials regarding the application of market economics to policy decisions. One of the most interesting studies is the annual survey of economic freedom conducted by Florida State's James Gwartney and others, demonstrating that the more a nation adopts liberalized market reforms, the higher their standard of living becomes. Such studies have done more to reverse the tide from socialism to capitalism than a thousand books in deep philosophy. In the 1990s I have broadened my perspective by attending meetings sponsored by the Mont Pelerin Society, the Foundation for Economic Education, the Cato Institute, and numerous other think tanks. At the same time, I have studied the works of Milton

Friedman, George Stigler, Gary Becker, Thomas Sowell, Allan Meltzer, Armen Achian, Roger LeRoy Miller, and other members of the Chicago school. I have spent many hours with Milton Friedman, Gary Becker, and other Chicagoans, both in correspondence and personal meetings, regarding the Chicago viewpoint.

The Author's Biases

Where do I stand on the great issues dividing the Austrians and the Chicagoans? Perhaps a story will best illustrate. When I became president of the Foundation of Economic Education in 2001, I had an interesting encounter at my first board meeting. After the meeting, Bettina Greaves, a long time FEE employee and devoted Misesian, approached me privately and said, "I support you in every way as the new president of FEE, but may I make a suggestion? You need to be more critical of Milton Friedman!" I nodded my head and thanked her for her support. Then, no less than half hour later, Muso Ayau, past president of the Mont Pelerin Society and founder of the Universidad Francisco Maroquin in Guatemala, pulled me aside to give me some advice as the new president. He whispered in my ear, "I support you in every way as the new president of FEE, but could you do me a favor? Please stop being so critical of Milton Friedman!"

I have come to appreciate the Hegelian method, that truth is achieved through conflict. Some dislike the intellectual arguments. I enjoy them, as long as they generate more light than heat. Regretfully, sometimes the disagreements have become personal and vindictive, resulting in some colleagues not talking to each other for years. But for the most part, the result of the debate has been closer understanding and sometimes a change of heart. I personally have shifted ground over the years as I have listened and read intently the various controversies and the evidence.

References

Barry, Norman P. 1987. *On Classical Liberalism and Libertarianism*. New York: St. Martin's Press.

Boettke, Peter J. 1997. "Where did economics go wrong? Modern economics as a flight from reality." *Critical Review* 11:1 (Winter), 11-64.

Ebenstein, Alan B. 2003. *Hayek's Journey: The Mind of Friedrich Hayek*. New York: Palgrave Macmillan.

Hayek, F. A. 1994. *Hayek on Hayek*, eds. Stephen Kresge and Leif Wenar. Chicago: University of Chicago Press.

Kirzner, Israel M. 1967. "Divergent Approaches in Libertarian Economic Thought," *Intercollegiate Review* (January-Febrary), 101-08.

Kirzner, Israel M. 1997. "Between Mises and Keynes: An Interview with Israel M. Kirzner." *Austrian Economics Newsletter* 17:1 (Spring).

Yergin, Daniel and Joseph Stanislaw. 1998. *The Commanding Heights*. New York: Simon & Schuster.

Chapter Two

OLD AND NEW VIENNA
THE RISE, FALL AND REBIRTH
OF THE AUSTRIAN SCHOOL

No book since Ricardo's Principles has had
such a great influence on the development of economics
as Menger's Grundsätze.

—Knut Wicksell (1958:191)

Mises and Hayek articulated and vastly enriched the
principles of Adam Smith at a crucial time in this century.

—Vernon L. Smith (1999:208)

The Austrian and Chicago schools were born in the midst of crises in economic theory, at times when the classical laissez-faire model of Adam Smith faced unprecedented challenges from the critics of capitalism. The Austrians rescued classical economics from the socialist/ Marxist threat in the late 19th century, while the Chicago school countered the Keynesian challenge of the 20th century. Let's begin by examining the roots of the Austrian school.

Adam Smith and the
Origin of Classical Economics

Classical economics, led by Adam Smith, J.-B. Say, David Ricardo, and John Stuart Mill, revolutionized and transformed Western civilization in the 18th and 19th centuries. The classical economists introduced the principles and policies of the enlightenment within the field of political economy. Rejecting the old mercantilist policies of protectionism, state monopolies, and colonialism, they proposed a radical change favoring free trade, limited government, balanced budgets, the gold standard, and laissez faire; in short, maximum economic freedom.

Adam Smith (1723-90), a student of the Scottish enlightenment and founder of the classical model, built a "system of natural liberty" in his magnum opus, *The Wealth of Nations*. Published in 1776, *The Wealth of Nations* was a declaration of economic independence against the prevailing doctrines of protectionism and state interventionism.[1] Very little progress had been achieved over the centuries in Europe because of the entrenched system known as mercantilism. The commercial and political powers believed that wealth was finite and thus one nation grew only at the expense of another. Consequently, they favored government-authorized monopolies at home and supported colonialism abroad, sending agents and soldiers into poorer countries to seize gold and other precious commodities. Smith carefully delineated the host of high tariffs, duties, quotas, and regulations that aimed at restraining imports, production, and employment.

A former Professor of Moral Philosophy at Glasgow University, Adam Smith denounced high tariffs and other restraints of trade as counterproductive. Trade barriers hurt the ability of both countries to produce, he said. For example, by expanding trade between Britain and France, traditional enemies, both nations would gain. "If a foreign country can supply us with a commodity cheaper than we ourselves can make it, better buy it of them" (Smith 1965 [1776]:424).

---

1 Adam Smith was the most famous classical liberal to advocate economic freedom, but not the first. Other predecessors, including the Spanish Jesuit priest Juan de Mariana, the Irish banker Richard Cantillon, and French official A. R. J. Turgot advocated free markets and often elucidated economic principles more consistently than Smith. In some ways, Abbe Etienne Bonnot de Condillac's book, *Commerce and Government*, published in the same year as Smith's (1776), is a more consistent exposition of sound economics.

Smith favored a controversial solution, the free movement of labor, capital, money, and goods. Milton Friedman states, "Adam Smith was a radical and a revolutionary in his time—just as those of us who preach laissez faire are in our time" (Friedman 1978:7). Critics contended that Smith's radical idea would lead to economic disaster and instability. To the contrary, Smith promised that the dismantling of state regulations of trade, prices and employment would lead to "universal opulence which extends itself to the lowest ranks of the people" (Smith 1965 [1776]:11).

His eloquent advocacy of natural liberty fired the minds of a rising generation. His book literally changed the course of politics over the next hundred years, dismantling the old mercantilist doctrines of protectionism and human bondage. It was a perfect companion to the American Revolution of 1776 and precursor to the Industrial Revolution of the 19th century. "The Invisible Hand" (Smith 1965 [1776]:423) has come to represent Adam Smith's model of economic freedom. In *The Wealth of Nations*, Smith argues that if individuals are left to their own devices, pursuing their own self interest, they will generate a self-regulating and highly prosperous society. George Stigler calls Smith's invisible-hand doctrine the "crown jewel" of economics. "Smith had one overwhelmingly important triumph: he put into the center of economics the systematic analysis of the behavior of individuals pursuing their self-interests under conditions of competition" (Stigler 1976:1201).

The French Advance Adam Smith's Model

The French laissez-faire school of Jean-Baptiste Say (1767-1832) and Frederic Bastiat (1801-1850) advanced the classical model of Adam Smith by championing the boundless possibilities of open trade and a free entrepreneurial economy. J.-B. Say, known as "the French Adam Smith," developed in particular Say's law of markets, which became the fundamental principle of classical macroeconomics. Say's law, often simplified as "supply creates its own demand," focuses on the notion that savings, capital investment, and entrepreneurship — all elements of the supply-side of the economy — are the keys to economic growth, and that rising consumption is the effect, not the cause, of prosperity.

Bastiat, a brilliant French journalist, was an indefatigable advocate of free trade and laissez-faire policies, a passionate opponent of socialism, and an unrelenting debater and statesman. Bastiat was unrivaled in exposing fallacies, condemning such popular cliches as "war is good for the economy" and "free trade destroys jobs." In his classic essay, *The Law* (1850), Bastiat established the proper social organization best suited for a free people, one that "defends life, liberty, and property....and prevents injustice." Under this legal system, "if everyone enjoyed the unrestricted use of his faculties and the free disposition of the fruits of his labor, social progress would be ceaseless, uninterrupted, and unfailing" (Bastiat 1998:5).

The British economists Thomas Robert Malthus (1766-1834), David Ricardo (1772-1823), and John Stuart Mill (1806-73) continued the classical tradition in supporting the virtues of thrift, free trade, limited government, the gold standard and Say's law of markets. In particular, Ricardo vigorously and effectively advocated an anti-inflation, gold-backed British pound sterling policy as well as a repeal of both the Corn Laws, England's notoriously high tariff wall on wheat and other agricultural goods; and abolishing the Poor Laws, England's modest welfare system.

Classical Economics Takes a Wrong Turn

Yet there was a problem. Classical economics after Adam Smith suffered from a serious theoretical flaw that provided ammunition to Marxists, socialists and the critics of capitalism.

Smith himself supported an optimistic model favoring the harmony of interests and universal prosperity. However, Smith's disciples, especially Malthus, Ricardo, and Mill, promoted an antagonistic model of capitalism that gave classical economics a bad reputation, leading English critic Thomas Carlyle to label it "the dismal science." Instead of focusing on Smith's positive view of wealth creation and harmony of interests, his British disciples emphasized the distribution of wealth, the conflict of interests, and a labor theory of value.

In his famous *Essay on Population* (1798), Robert Malthus asserts that pressures on limited resources would keep most workers close to the edge of subsistence. His thesis underlines the gloomy and fatalistic outlook of many scientists and social reformers who forecast poverty, death, misery, war, and environmental degradation due to an ever-expanding population and "unbridled" economic growth. Malthus remained true to Smith's laissez-faire roots by opposing government programs to alleviate poverty and control population growth, but he failed to comprehend the role of prices and property rights as an incentive to ration scarce resources. He also misunderstood the dynamics of a growing entrepreneurial economy through technological advances. Medical breakthroughs, the agricultural revolution and economic growth have postponed the Malthusian Armageddon, perhaps indefinitely.

David Ricardo, apart from his many positive contributions to technical economics, created an alternative "distribution" model, wherein workers, landlords, and capitalists fought over the economy's desserts. He endorsed a Malthusian "iron law of wages," where wages are constantly under pressure from an excess supply of labor. In his classic work, *On the Principles of Political Economy and Taxation* (1817), he proposes a labor theory of value: "with few exceptions the quantity of labor employed on commodities determines the rate at which they will exchange for each other" (in de Vivo 1987:193). In Ricardo's fatalistic system, wages tend toward subsistence levels, profits decline long term, and landlords reap unjust returns. Karl Marx and the socialists exploited Ricardo's hostile system of class conflict and labor theory of value, concluding that all interest and profit obtained by capitalists must be treated as "surplus" value, unjustly extracted from the "whole product" created by the working class.

John Stuart Mill perpetuated the Ricardian system in his *Principles of Political Economy* (1884 [1848]), the standard textbook until Alfred Marshall's *Principles of Economics* (1890). In his favor, Mill wrote eloquently in support of Say's law, free trade, the gold standard, and individual liberty, especially in his classic work, *On Liberty* (1859). Yet his textbook, thoroughly steeped in Ricardian economics, preaches that prices are determined by labor costs, wages and profits vary inversely, and long-run wages tend toward subsistence levels. Most significantly, Mill separated the "immutable" laws of production from the "arbitrary" rules of distribution, which led intellectuals to support grandiose tax and confiscation schemes aimed at redistributing wealth and income, convinced that such radical measures could be accomplished without disturbing economic growth (Mill 1884 [1848]:155). For this reason, Friedrich Hayek comments, "I am personally convinced that the reason which led the intellectuals to socialism, was John Stuart Mill" (in Boaz 1997:50).

Adam Smith recognized that economic freedom and limited government would create "universal opulence," but the founder of classical economics struggled to develop a sound theoretical framework (other than the division of labor) with which to explain how consumers and producers work through the profit-and-loss system to achieve this "universal opulence." Ricardo and the British disciples took Smith's parenthetical statements (such as his labor theory of value in a crude economy, and his criticism of landlords) and created a model of class struggle rather than one of harmony of interests; the iron law of subsistence wages instead of universal economic growth. They viewed the economy as if it were a large cake, where a larger dessert for capitalists and landlords could only mean a smaller piece for workers.

Using the famous diamond-water paradox, Smith and the British economists separated production "in use" and production "in exchange." Why is a useful commodity like water so cheap and of little value in price, while an impractical commodity like diamonds is so expensive and treated with such high value in the marketplace? This puzzler gave rise to the socialist complaint that in the marketplace capitalists are more interested in "making profits" than providing a "useful service," as if profitable exchange is unrelated to consumer use. In short, the classical economists may have supported laissez faire policies, but their economic theories undercut laissez faire and gave ammunition to the socialist/Marxist causes of redistribution, nationalization, and state central planning. As Murray Rothbard observes, "Economics itself had come to a dead end...having thus given hostage to Marxism..." (Rothbard 1980:7-8).

The flaw in the classical model had a serious impact. Economics as a science reached a point of stagnation in England. The French abandoned Say and Bastiat, and embraced socialism. Germany rejected the very idea of economic theory. "Under the onslaughts of the [German] Historical School," Friedrich Hayek writes, "not only were the classical doctrines abandoned—but any attempt at theoretical analysis came to be regarded with deep distrust" (Hayek 1976:13).

Meanwhile, the Industrial Revolution of the 19th century had catapulted England and the West into a new world of wealth and capital, and clearly all classes, including workers, were making advances. Average real wages rose between 0.6%

and 1.5% a year during the 19th century, and the average workers enjoyed a gradual increase in their standard of living.

If capitalism was to survive and prosper, it would require a breakthrough in economic theory. The classical economists desperately needed a new model that could explain how all classes gain and all consumers benefit, a theory that could conform to their laissez faire policies. But where would it come from?

Old Vienna: The Setting of a Revolution

By the 1870s, the political economy of the classical school was ripe for a revolution. That revolution developed in a surprising place—old Vienna, the capital of the Austro-Hungarian empire. The Austro-Hungarian Empire covered the territories of today's Austria, Hungary, the Czech Republic, Slovakia, and parts of Poland, Ukraine, Romania, Bosnia, Serbia, Yugoslavia, and Italy. It was the crossroads between East and West, North and South, witness to invasions from the Celts, Romans and Turks. The empire's aristocratic leaders, the Habsburgs, ruled Eastern Europe with an iron fist for over 400 years. But why would the land of the Habsburgs serve as the nesting ground for a revolution in economic thought?

It was a gradual process. The rise of Protestantism divided the region into Lutheran and Catholic sects, with the Catholic monastic orders (Franciscans, Dominicans, and Jesuits) moving into Austrian lands, and along with them, a great flow of art, architecture, and ideas. This set the stage of Vienna as the center of art and intellectual thought. Under Leopold I (1658-1705), Vienna became the European center of music and theater. Travel became more common and explorers brought home fantastic tales. Rulers all over the world, including Peter the Great, and Louis XIV, were interested in sharing ideas, art, and architecture. In the Golden Age of Baroque, the nobility built magnificent summer palaces.

The First Holy Roman Empress

The most significant Austrian monarch, however, was not an emperor but an empress—Maria Theresa (1740-80), a mighty Holy Roman Empress who produced 16 children, including Marie Antoinette. It was said that men expanded territories, while women improved living conditions. Maria Theresa abolished serfdom and torture, and established public education and public parks. She built the Imperial Theatre, the Schonbrunn Palace rivaling Versailles, and hosted 40 balls a year. Her son, Joseph II, was emperor at the time of Mozart.

After the Turkish wars ended, the people had time and money to spend on culture, and music thrived. It was a status symbol to have a resident composer and orchestra for after-dinner entertainment and chamber music. The Viennese had an insatiable desire for Italian composers, especially opera. When William Gluck (1714-87) returned from Italy, he developed uniquely German operatic forms that laid the groundwork for Wagner and the post-romantics. Later the Viennese composers developed operetta, combining French humor and Viennese wit with stirring music. As the 19th century approached, a period of revolution was in the air. It was the age of Joseph Haydn (1732-1809), the classical Viennese composer; Wolfgang Mozart (1756-91), child prodigy who played before Maria Theresa at the Schonbrunn Palace, and returned at age 27 for his most creative nine years; Ludwig van Beethoven (1770-1829), a native of Bonn who came to Vienna at age 22 and flourished as never before; Franz Schubert (1797-1828), a brilliant native Viennese compuser who died prematurely; Johannes Brahms (1833-97), spiritual father of Vienna Philharmonic Society; and Johann Strauss (1804-49) and Johann Strauss, Jr. (1825-1899), the father and son famous for their waltzes and operettas, which would encourage the Operetta craze, culminating in Franz Lehar's "The Merry Widow" in the early 1900s.

Then came the most significant figure in modern Austria, Franz Josef (1848-1916), and his 68-year reign. He was famous for his mutton chops and stern authoritarian manner. His brother was the emperor of Mexico. His only son, Prince Rudolf, was tutored by Carl Menger, founder of the Austrian school. And his nephew, Archduke Ferdinand, heir to the throne, was assassinated in Sarajevo, Yugoslavia, by a Serbian patriot, on June 28, 1914.

Why Vienna as the birthplace of a revolutionary idea? Vienna offered a great flourishing of architecture, art, music, and education. The Habsburgs established Vienna as the political, cultural and intellectual center of Eastern Europe. Vienna, located on the beautiful Danube River, became the third-largest city in Europe, next to London and Paris, famous for its magnificent museums, palaces, parks, opera houses and cafes. Most significantly, in 1867, Austria, in alliance with Hungary, established a constitutional government that expanded economic and political freedom. Early in the 19th century, until 1820, Austria prohibited books by Adam Smith, John Locke, Rousseau, and Hobbes; after 1867, Austria, under constitutional democratic reforms, flourished economically. For half a century, from the 1870s until World War I, there occurred an extraordinary intellectual flowering within the Austro-Hungarian empire. Vienna attracted some of the world's most creative musicians, scientists, philosophers and economists. The philosopher Ludwig Wittgenstein and the psychologist Sigmund Freud lived and worked in Vienna.

Carl Menger Founds the Austrian School

In the 1870s, the University of Vienna was considered one of the largest and most prestigious schools of learning in Europe. It was there, during the reign of Franz Josef, that Carl Menger (1840-1921), the founder of the Austrian school, began his groundbreaking work. A man of extraordinarily impressive appearance, Carl Menger (sometimes spelled Karl) graduated from the University of Vienna in 1860 and worked as a lawyer, journalist and civil servant. But it was as a reporter on economic conditions and the stock market that he discovered a startling breakthrough that would herald a revolution in economics. The result was a book, *Grundsätze der Volkswirthschaftslehre*, published in 1871 (translated into English as *Principles of Economics* in 1950).

His purpose was highly ambitious: At the youthful age of 31, Menger sought to replace the classical model of Adam Smith with an entirely new theoretical framework that would more clearly define Adam Smith's system of "universal opulence." He was no Karl Marx; he wished no harm to the great founder of classical economics, but solely to restore the theoretical soundness of Smith's "system of natural liberty." Menger shared Smith's belief in maximum freedom. And like Smith, Menger's great interest was economic growth, "the causes of progress in human welfare." But the classical economists' price theory was defective and needed repair, if not outright replacement. Menger saw it as his duty "to set himself the task of countering the theories of Adam Smith which he saw to be erroneous" (as his son put it). He wrote furiously in "a state of morbid excitement" (Skousen 2001:175, 181n).

The outcome was a book of monumental achievement. His primary goal was to demonstrate to his colleagues, and especially his German counterparts, the leaders of the German historical school, that universal principles of economics do exist. The German historical school contended that there could be no scientific economic laws separate from politics, customs, and the legal system (Streissler 1990). Menger wished to prove otherwise. To do so, he did things differently than Smith and his disciples. The classical economists had focused on the distribution of wealth and income between classes (landlords, workers, and capitalists), which gave ammunition to the socialists and Marxists in promoting an economics of class warfare and inequality. Ricardo and Mill in particular separated production from distribution, and developed a divisive conflict of interests. For example, they maintain that if profits or rents increased, they did so only at the expense of workers' wages.

In sharp contrast, Menger introduced a new approach. He focused on individual behavior and how people achieve a higher standard of living as measured by the quantity, quality, and variety of goods and services. Rather than focusing on the average wage or salary earned by one group or another, Menger stressed the utility or maximum benefit enjoyed by each individual according to the value and utility of goods and services produced and consumed. In his first chapter, he began by focusing on goods, not classes. In "The General Theory of the Good," he showed how landlords, workers, and capitalists — the factors of production — had to cooperate in order to transform unfinished commodities into final useful goods and services through the stages of production. By doing so, Menger reestablished Smith's "harmony of interests."

In developing this "general theory of the good," he uncovered a new theory of price. Using tobacco as an example, he demonstrated that prices are determined by the subjective valuations of final users, thus rejecting the Ricardian chimera of labor units as "the invariable measure of value." What would happen if people stopped smoking, Menger asked (a question that sounds modern). He concluded that it doesn't matter how much labor is put into the production of cigarettes; the price of cigarettes, tobacco, and tobacco seeds would fall to zero. Using the tobacco example, Menger also discovered the principles of marginal utility and opportunity cost. He noted that farm land used to grow tobacco doesn't fall to zero, but is valued according to its next best, or marginal, use, such as growing wheat or raising cattle. Thus, Carl Menger is one of the founders of the Marginalist Revolution and co-discoverer, with William Stanley Jevons in England and Leon Walras in Switzerland, of the marginal utility/cost principle.

The Marginalist Revolution solved another quagmire in economic theory: Menger taught a new generation of economists that production and distribution could once again be linked together. The demand of consumers ultimately determines the final prices of consumer goods, which in turn sets the direction for productive activity. Final demand establishes the prices of the cooperative factors of production — wages, rents, and profits — according to the value they add to the production process. In short, income is not distributed, it is produced, according to the value added by each participant. Under this new brand of microeconomics, profits and use are directly connected through their marginal utility. Prices reflect the consumer's most highly valued (marginal) utility, and profit-driven production seeks to meet those needs.

It was a brilliant move, and Menger's *Grundsätze* solved many problems in classical economics, reversing the Marxist/socialist broadside against the capitalist system. It restored Adam Smith's harmony of interests and the benefits of his "system of natural liberty." Neo-classical economics became a science that integrated the Austrian principles of marginal utility, opportunity cost (next best use), and subjective consumer demand. After publishing his *Grundsätze*, Menger was offered a position at the University of Vienna, and a few years later, became the tutor to Crown Prince Rudolf of Austria. At the youthful age of 33, Menger became a professor of law and political science at the prestigious University of Vienna, based in part on the publication of his magnum opus written in 1871.

Menger and the Marginalist Revolution

Menger introduced and popularized the Marginalist Revolution in economics. Menger is usually listed third, behind Britain's William Stanley Jevons and France's Leon Walras, as the co-discoverer of the principle of marginality, but in truth, Menger was the chief protagonist of subjective marginal analysis. Jevons, though first to write about marginal utility, ran up against Ricardian orthodoxy in England, and Walras was largely ignored because his writings were mathematically obtuse.

What determines prices? In his book, Menger broke away from the classical school. Smith, Ricardo and Mill claimed that exchange prices of goods and services are unrelated to their practical uses; yet they were unable to explain adequately the value of those goods and services. They failed to resolve the diamond-water paradox referred to earlier. Why is the value of a diamond so high when water is essential to life? Menger answered this question definitively a hundred years after Smith raised it. He showed that the value of goods is determined by their marginal utility rather than by their total utility. In other words, diamonds are more expensive than water because, given their relatively scarcity, an extra diamond generally has far greater utility than an extra bottle of water. That is, the greater the quantity, the lesser the marginal value. Thus price is determined by marginal or extra use. Water is cheap because it is plentiful: diamonds are expensive because their supply is so limited. All prices, whether for shoes, real estate or stocks, are determined by the marginal buyers and sellers at any given moment.

Finally, Carl Menger formulated the basis of Austrian capital theory and macroeconomics by emphasizing the critical role of time and interest rates in economic activity. In his masterpiece, Menger noted that all consumer goods, from automobiles to food on the table, go through many stages of production, from raw materials to final products. The process may take months or even years, depending on the product. It may also take months or years to use up or consume a product. This time structure forms the basis for a correct understanding of macroeconomics and how the economy operates as a whole. Menger divided the economy into consumer goods (called "first order" or "lower order" goods) and producer goods (called "higher order" goods). But he did not simply lump all producer goods into a single homogeneous category called "investment," the standard approach in neoclassical economics. Menger noted that there are many stages in the production process, and that once capital is converted into an array of capital goods, capital becomes heterogeneous. Once produced, capital goods are specific in use and cannot easily be switched to another use, as labor and land often can. Menger's time-oriented heterogeneous capital theory would play a vital role in the Austrian theory of the business cycle later developed by Mises and Hayek.

Menger retired from teaching at the University of Vienna in 1903 and died in 1921, following World War I. He was disillusioned at the end of his life because the Great War left his beloved country in chaos and under the control of socialists, where the capital was known as "Red Vienna." In my judgment, Carl Menger is the greatest economist of the 19th century because by correcting the theoretical errors of Adam Smith and the classical economists, he established the marginalist/subjectivist revolution in microeconomics, and by formulating a time-structural capital-using model, he identified the correct vision of modern macroeconomics. Few economists can claim breakthroughs in both micro and macro economics.

Böhm-Bawerk Takes on Marx, and Introduces a Non-Marxist Theory of Capitalism

Eugen Böhm-Bawerk (1851-1914), a pupil of Carl Menger, advanced economics further as Marxists came on the scene with talk of exploitation, alienation, and crisis. Böhm-Bawerk made contributions to the theory of capital, interest and economic growth. He was Menger's most illustrious student and became the most famous economist on the European continent at the turn of the century. He is the only Austrian economist well-known in his native country, with his face appearing on the Austrian 100 Schilling currency (before the Euro currency was issued). Böhm-Bawerk was Austria's finance minister three times in the 1890s, and helped restore Austria to the gold standard. After retiring from government, he became a professor of economics at the University of Vienna. He died suddenly in 1914 right before the beginning of World War I.

Böhm-Bawerk's theory of capital and interest has had a major impact on economic growth theory, and his critique of Marx's exploitation theory is considered so devastating that Marxian economics never really took hold of the economics profession as it did in other fields. He demonstrated that entrepreneur/capitalists deserve the fruits of their labor because they take greater risks than workers fulfilling a vital creative use in the market system. His most significant work, *The Positive Theory of Capital*, published in 1889 and almost immediately translated into English, forms the basis of the modern theory of economic growth. Building on Menger's stages of production, Böhm-Bawerk argues that individuals and firms adopt more roundabout processes of production in order to achieve economic growth and a higher standard of living. By "roundabout," Böhm-Bawerk means the sacrificing of current consumption to produce more capital goods, adopt new technology, and institute longer processes of production, which in turn lead to greater consumption in the future. For example, it may take two days for a worker to sew a dress by hand. But suppose she builds a sewing machine (or buys one, which also involves sacrifice of time and money) that could allow her to sew five dresses a day. The building of a sewing machine may take six months — a long roundabout process — but once manufactured, it would increase productivity tremendously. Or, if she buys a sewing machine, she may need to postpone consumption and save up for six months to purchase the machine.

The Positive Role of Saving

Böhm-Bawerk was the leading defender of savings and investment during a period of increasing antipathy toward the traditional virtue of thrift. Böhm-Bawerk contended that increasing savings and postponing consumption did not hurt business, but was simply a more effective form of spending. Savings paid dividends indefinitely into the future if the funds were well spent on new businesses, technology and capital formation. Thus, capital formation is *sine qua non* to economic growth.

Following Böhm-Bawerk's lead, the Austrian school has persistently argued that a high level of voluntary saving, both individually and nationally, is the key to rapid economic growth. Austrians criticize Keynesian economists who denigrate savings and promote a high-consumption society, as well as monetary activists who emphasize the money supply as a key ingredient to economic growth. Austrians argue that more voluntary saving by individuals and retained earnings by firms are the key to long-term prosperity, not more monetary inflation, more consumption, or more government. By the same token, the Austrians have also criticized efforts by centralized governments to promote "forced saving" plans which artificially raise the investment rate. To be most efficient, all saving and consumption should be voluntary, based on the free desires of individuals to determine their own time preference.

Wieser and the "Great Man" Theory

Friedrich von Wieser (1851-1926) became Böhm-Bawerk's brother-in-law when his sister married Böhm-Bawerk. They went mountain climbing together, a hobby common to many Austrian economists of the older generation, and they were best friends. Wieser was appointed a professor at the University of Vienna in 1884, and in 1903 he succeeded Menger as chair of economic theory. Böhm-Bawerk, Menger and

Wieser served as members of the Austrian House of Lords. In 1917, Wieser became the Minister of Commerce. He died in 1926, outliving both Böhm-Bawerk and Menger.

Wieser's *Natural Value*, published by Macmillan in English in 1893, introduced the world to the subjectivist philosophy of the Austrians. Wieser's *Theory of Social Economy* (1918) was the standard Austrian textbook for many years. He invented modern terms such as "marginal utility," "economic planning," and "opportunity cost." Marginal utility led to mathematical prowess and economics as the "queen of the social sciences," and, it might be noted, Weiser's interpretation of marginal utility analysis provided a scientific justification for a progressive income tax (Caldwell 2004:142). Opportunity cost, the value of an alternative product or activity, is an extremely important concept in economics, finance, and business. Economic Value Added, or EVA, as a way to determine if a firm achieves real profit or valued added in an economy.

But perhaps the most significant concept in Professor Wieser's repertoire was his recognition of the importance of the creative individual in commerce, industry, education, religion, and government. He was especially impressed with the contributions of inventors, pioneers, capitalists and entrepreneurs — individuals willing to take risks, sometimes big risks, to accomplish their lofty goals.[2] In the world of business, who are the creative individuals? They are the inventors, superior money managers, independent investment advisors who can beat the market, the chief executive officers who turn a company around, and the political leaders who adopt sound economic policies and lead their countries to a new destiny. Of course, sometimes the leader is a malevolent dictator who takes the nation down the road of destruction and

2 In the spirit of Wieser, Ayn Rand, an admirer of Ludwig von Mises and other Austrian economists, created supreme individualists and high achievers in her novels. As Howard Roark declares in *The Fountainhead*, "Throughout the centuries there were men who took first steps down new roads armed with nothing but their vision."

chaos. (Recall Friedrich Hayek's chapter 10, "Why the Worst Get on Top," in *The Road to Serfdom*.) Leaders can make a difference, for good or for evil. Interestingly, Wieser loved the German word *Führer* and flirted with early German Nazism in the last few years of his life. Hero worship can work both ways.[3]

Ludwig von Mises, Founder of Modern Austrian Economics

Ludwig von Mises (1881-1973) represents the third generation of Austrians. He brought Austrian economics into the 20th century and is regarded as the father of the modern Austrian school. Mises taught economics at the University of Vienna, and was chief economist at the Vienna Chamber of Commerce. However, the Nazi takeover of Austria forced Mises to leave his beloved native land and eventually emigrate to New York in 1940, where he and his wife, Margit, lived the remainder of their lives. For a variety of reasons, Mises was a virtual exile in America; he was "visiting" professor of economics at New York University for several decades, with his salary subsidized by friends and the Volker Fund. He spent most of his time writing books and articles that went counter to the conventional wisdom of socialist and Keynesian thinking, but contributed little in developing technical economics.

Mises was an outspoken and dogmatic defender of laissez faire capitalism who often lashed out at his critics and his friends who disagreed with him (see chapter 9 on the problems these *ad hominem* disputes have created). Yet despite personal disagreements and intransigence, Mises made major contributions to economics in the 20th century. Mises came on the scene just as economists were debating the role of money in

3 Mises did not consider Wieser a true believer: "Wieser was not a creative thinker and in general was more harmful than useful. He never really understood the gist of the idea of subjectivism in the Austrian School of Thought, which limitation caused him to make many unfortunate mistakes. His imputation theory is untenable. His ideas on value calculation justify the conclusion that he could not be called a member of the Austrian School, but rather a member of the Lausanne School (Leon Walras et al and the idea of economic equilibrium" (Mises 1978:36; cf Huerto de Soto 1998:93).

the economy, and what should be the ideal monetary standard. With his book *The Theory of Money and Credit*, published originally in 1912 and translated into English in 1934, he became the first economist to apply Austrian theories to money and the business cycle. In addition, he wrote the first systematic economic critique of socialist central planning in his book *Socialism* (1922), which argues that central planning can never work efficiently and will ultimately collapse.

Mises's magnum opus is *Human Action: A Treatise on Economics*, a massive volume published in 1949 by Yale University Press and revised in 1966. A novice might better begin with *Planning for Freedom*, a compilation of speeches and articles, or *Economic Policy*, a series of lectures Mises gave in Argentina in 1960. *Human Action* establishes many key principles of Austrian economics—methodological indi- vidualism, rational human action, dualism between nature and man, subjectivism in value, uncertainty in economic behavior, sound money, and the case of limited government. One of Mises's major points is that human action is always purposeful and rational. Therefore, for every cause, there is an effect. The price of every commodity or security is based on the rational buying and selling by individuals. Prices are never random, even though price patterns may appear to be. Another Misesian concept is methodological dualism, the idea that social science (praxeology, the science of human action) is distinct from the physical and biological sciences. According to Mises, human beings think, adopt values, make choices, are conscious, make mistakes and learn from the past. In short, they act purposefully. On the other hand, the actions of animals and inert matter are essentially mechanical and predictable. They are acted upon. Mises states, "Reason and experience show us two separate realisms: the external world of physical, chemical and physiological phenomena, and the internal world of thought, feeling, valuation and purposeful action. No bridge connects — as far as we can see today — these two spheres" (Mises 1966:18).

In scientific experiments with animals, plants and physical elements, the results are often exact and repeatable. Not so with human action, which is often unpredictable and unreliable. In essence, Mises argues that human beings have free will, while animals and objects do not. Does this mean that the future is completely unpredictable? Can economic analysts make an educated guess about the direction of the economy and the markets? This is a hotly debated topic in the academic world. Some economists argue that the future of the economy and the markets are unknowable and no one can predict the future. Even some of the Austrian economists, such as Ludwig Lachmann, fit into this camp, known as "radical subjectivists."[4]

Mises was also famous for his uncompromising attack on socialism and central planning by communist regimes such as the Soviet Union. As early as 1920, Mises argued that, without prices and competitive bidding, a centrally planned totalitarian state could not operate an efficient, progressive economy. He followed his paper with a full-length book entitled *Socialism* (1922). He used the example of a bridge to prove his point. Where should it be built? What materials should be used? Without considering prices and costs, it would be impossible to know for sure.

Led by Oskar Lange, Paul Samuelson, and Robert Heilbroner, among others, the economics profession scoffed at Mises, but ultimately Mises was proven correct nearly twenty years after his death. In fact, Heilbroner admitted in 1989, when the Soviet union was near collapse, that the 50-year-old debate was over: Mises had been right; capitalism had won over socialism. "Capitalism organized the material affairs of humankind more satisfactorily than socialism" (Heilbroner 1989:98).

4 They argue that the markets are in such constant disequilibria and are so complex, it is virtually impossible to predict their direction (Lachmann 1977:190). Gerald O'Driscoll and Mario Rizzo wrote an entire book devoted to this kind of subjectivism in a book entitled *The Economics of Time and Ignorance*, in which they state: "A world in which there is autonomous or creative decision making-making is one in which the future is not merely unknown, but *unknowable*" (O'Driscoll and Rizzo 1985:2). British economist G. L. S. Shackle compared this state of uncertainty to a kaleidoscope, where every new scene is distinct (Shackle 1974).

Hayek, the Great Depression, and *The Road to Serfdom*

Mises's most famous student[5] was Friedrich A. Hayek (1899-1992), who received two doctorates at the University of Vienna and worked under Mises as director of the Austrian Institute of Economic Research. In 1974, Hayek was the first free-market economist to receive the Nobel Prize in economics for his work on business cycle theory and the importance of knowledge in the economy. He is the only Austrian to win the prize.

World attention was drawn to Mises and Hayek when they forecasted the cataclysmic events of the 1930s. The 1929 stock market crash and subsequent worldwide depression took the mainstream economics profession by surprise. None of the top professors of the day foresaw the collapse of the world economy—not Frank Taussig at Harvard, Irving Fisher at Yale, or John Maynard Keynes at Cambridge. Fisher and Keynes, in particular, suffered heavy personal losses. On the other hand, Mises and Hayek anticipated serious trouble, although they never attempted to pinpoint the time of the crash. Austrian economics had first come to the forefront under Menger and Böhm-Bawerk. Now, a generation later, the Austrian school gained notoriety under Mises and Hayek. Lionel Robbins, chairman of the economics department at the London School of Economics, was impressed with Friedrich Hayek and invited him to lecture at LSE to help counter the growing influence of Keynes and his interventionist doctrines. Hayek and his family moved to England upon his appointment as the Tooke Professor of Economics at LSE.

Hayek's explanation of the depression in *Prices and Production* (1935 [1931]) was based on Mises's earlier work, but this time with diagrams called Hayekian triangles. Together

---

5 Some Austrians dispute this, noting that Hayek never attended any of Mises's classes at the University of Vienna. He worked for Mises at the Austrian Chamber of Commerce, but was never his student. However, Hayek did attend Mises's private seminars in Vienna, and regarded Mises, eighteen years his senior, as his mentor in economics.

Mises and Hayek developed what is known today as Austrian macroeconomics and the Mises-Hayek theory of the business cycle. It draws from Böhm-Bawerk's capital theory, Swedish economist Knut Wicksell's natural interest rate hypothesis, and the Ricardo-Hume specie-flow mechanism (see chapter 6). Essentially, the Austrian theory emphasizes how monetary inflation by the central banks artificially distorts the structure of the economy, causing an unsustainable boom that must end in a bust. Mises and Hayek demonstrated the non-neutral impact of money on relative prices, income and business activity. That is, when the government inflates the money supply or artificially lowers interest rates below their "natural" rate (Wicksell's term for the natural time preference), certain individuals and businesses benefit while others lose, and capital and labor are "misallocated." "Easy money" does not simply raise prices, but disrupts the economy and creates winners and losers. As Roger Garrison summarizes, "Padding the supply of loanable funds with newly created money [by the government] holds the interest rate artificially low and drives a wedge between saving and investment....The credit-induced artificial boom is inherently unsustainable and is followed inevitably by a bust, as investment falls back into line with saving" (Garrison 1996:114).

According to Mises and Hayek, increasing the money supply and lowering interest rates below the natural rate misdirects resources into "higher order" producer goods. However, this boom cannot last and eventually must collapse when the money supply stops growing or interest rates return to their natural rate, creating a "cluster of business errors." According to the Austrians, the government's monetary policy, not free-market capitalism, is primarily responsible for the boom-bust pattern of Western economies and market instability. In short, the Austrians argue that even in the monetary sphere there is no free lunch, a famous phrase borrowed from science fiction writer Robert Heinlein by Milton Friedman. An expansion in the money supply can only create a destabilizing business cycle, not genuine long-term prosperity. As we shall see in chapter 6, Friedman and the Chicago economists agree with much of this analysis, but not all. The Austrians and the Chicagoans differ, sometimes strongly, in their interpretation of the business cycle.

Hayek's macro theory and business cycle explanation of the crash and depression took the profession by storm in the early 1930s, rivaling Keynes's theories. But when the world economy failed to recover quickly, as Mises and Hayek had predicted, economists and government officials looked elsewhere for explanations and cures, and ultimately switched allegiance from Hayek and the Austrians to Keynes and the Keynesians.

After the Keynesian revolution, Hayek became disillusioned with the economics profession and turned to philosophical and political interests. During World War II, he wrote a classic on political philosophy, *The Road to Serfdom* (1944), warning that the world's movement toward welfare statism and national dictatorship could lead countries down a dangerous "road to serfdom" and the loss of political and economic freedom. His book became a bestseller after *Reader's Digest* condensed it. Hayek followed this book with a seminal article, "The Use of Knowledge in Society," broadening his critique of socialist central planning. The article explains that prices communicate vital information to consumers and producers, and that specialized knowledge, vital to economic growth, is decentralized and local, and thus cannot be duplicated by industrial planners and technocrats. As Hayek states, "To assume all the knowledge to be given to a single mind....is to disregard everything that is important and significant in the real world" (Hayek 1984 [1948]:223). Hayek saw the market economy more as an organism that coordinates activities, which differed significantly from Keynes and most other economists who saw the economy as a machine that has broken down from time to time (Caldwell 2004:10).

Engaged in a bitter divorce and new marriage to his childhood sweetheart, Hayek left the London School of Economics and, in 1950, joined the faculty at the University of Chicago as a member of the Committee on Social Thought. There he wrote *The Constitution of Liberty* (1960), an extremely important work outlining his support for a written constitution that limits arbitrary power and preserves individual rights. Hayek debunked labor unions, progressive taxation, rent controls, and inflation, warning that even a "moderate degree of inflation is dangerous" (Hayek 1960:338). However, he surprised his libertarian friends by endorsing local building codes and a minimal "safety net" welfare state (1960:285-86, 354-57). In 1962, he left Chicago for the University of Freiberg, where he continued to work on a three volume work, *Law, Liberty, and Legislation* (1973-79). After winning the Nobel Prize, he began writing once again on economic issues—socialism, inflation, and monetary reform, culminating in his final book on a lifetime theme, *The Fatal Conceit: The Errors of Socialism* (1988).

Schumpeter and "Creative Destruction"

One Austrian economist who maintained his stature throughout the 20th century is Joseph Schumpeter (1883-1950). Born the year Marx died, Schumpeter studied under Wieser and Böhm-Bawerk at the University of Vienna, spent a year as Austria's finance minister, and left Europe for good in 1932 when he accepted an invitation by Frank Taussig to teach at Harvard University. A year after he became president of the American Economic Association, he died suddenly in 1950. Schumpeter is regarded as the *enfant terrible* of the Austrian school. He dressed impeccably, but was personally arrogant and unpredictable. He engaged in outrageous behavior, was an infamous womanizer, and once declared his personal goals to be the world's best horseman, best lover, and best economist. He said he accomplished two out of the three.

Schumpeter's economics were unpredictable. He defended socialist economics, forecast the demise of capitalism, and rejected the Mises-Hayek theory of the business cycle. Yet he was hostile to and professionally jealous of Keynes. "We all like a sparkling error better than a trivial truth," he wrote in his diary. Schumpeter, like Mises and Hayek, always maintained that the depression should run its course without interference from the federal government. He despised the New Deal of Franklin Delano Roosevelt. His writings are imbued with dynamic disequilibrium, entrepreneurism, and other Austrian themes, yet he named Leon Walras, not Carl Menger or his teacher Eugen Böhm-Bawerk, as the "greatest of all economists" for discovering general equilibrium analysis.

Schumpeter was prolific, and two of his books have achieved classic status: *Capitalism, Socialism and Democracy*, published in 1942 and updated in 1950, and *History of Economic Analysis*, published posthumously in 1954. *Capitalism, Socialism and Democracy* goes far beyond economics into political science and sociology, and has been translated into sixteen languages. It is a tortuous work sprinkled with brilliant gems and colorful concepts. Schumpeter writes eloquently about the dynamics of global capitalism and how the disruptive forces of technology undermine equilibrium conditions. Sometimes his phrasing, such as "creative destruction," sounds Marxian in tone. Borrowing from his Viennese teacher Wieser, he saw the entrepreneur as the central catalyst in the dynamics of the market system. Capitalism never can be stationary. The industrial process "incessantly revolutionizes the economic structure *from within,* incessantly destroying the old one, incessantly creating a new one" (Schumpeter 1950: 82-83). Schumpeter contradicted modern-day orthodoxy by defending big business. He rejected the Chamberlin-Robinson model of "perfect competition," standard fare in today's textbooks, as naive and wrong-headed. In Schumpeter's view, competition is a process constantly reinventing itself, not a point of static equilibrium. He concludes, "Now a theoretical construction which neglects this essential element of the case....is like *Hamlet* without the Danish prince" (Schumpeter 1950:86).

Monopolistic firms in their embryonic growth stages are highly innovative and require enormous risk capital. Schumpeter would not be surprised to see Microsoft overtake IBM, or Toyota surge ahead of Ford, or WalMart surpass Sears. "Leap frogging," as Benjamin Rogge called it, is a common feature of the competitive process. Schumpeter was pessimistic about the long-term survival of capitalism because he feared that bureaucracy would dominate the entrepreneurial spirit in the corporate world. Large multi-national corporations are always vulnerable to oversized bureaucracy, but so far competition has countered this trend, and global capitalism has remained vibrant.

The Austrian Revival in America

It is a startling fact that in less than fifty years Austrian economics went from being perhaps the most influential school at the turn of the century to its virtually disappearance from the academic scene at the end of World War II. Austrian concepts such as marginal utility analysis and opportunity cost were integrated into mainstream economics, but its four distinctive contributions of the 20th century — capital theory, business cycle theory, entrepreneurship and the dynamic market process, and the economic theory of socialism — had been vanquished by the profession. As noted in this chapter and elsewhere in this book, Austrian capital theory was attacked by John Bates Clark and Frank Knight; its business cycle theory was eviscerated by Keynesians Piero Sraffa and Nicolas Kaldor; and Mises's critique of socialism was buried by Oskar Lange (Blaug 1992). Since then, Austrian economics had made a slow and painful recovery.

The recovery began with the establishment of the first free-market think tank in 1946 by Leonard E. Read, a Chamber of

Commerce executive. Ludwig von Mises became FEE's resident scholar and remained so until his death in 1973. FEE attracted a small number of students and business people from around the world and enjoyed a virtual monopoly as a libertarian economics organization in the 1950s and the 1960s. FEE's monthly publication, *The Freeman*, contained essays by Mises, Henry Hazlitt, Hans Sennholz, Gary North, Percy Greaves and other Austrian-oriented economists and business people. FEE also published and promoted many free-market books, including Frederic Bastiat's *The Law* and Leonard Read's *Anything That's Peaceful*, and his famous essay, "I, Pencil." They distributed Henry Hazlitt's bestseller, *Economics in One Lesson*, and other free-market books with an Austrian bent.

Mises, Hayek, and Schumpeter were pessimistic about the future of freedom and capitalism. But the next generation, led by Americans Henry Hazlitt, Murray N. Rothbard and Israel Kirzner, were more upbeat. Hazlitt befriended Mises in New York, wrote for *The Freeman*, and was closely aligned with the Austrians throughout his career in New York. Rothbard and Kirzner, students of Mises's private seminar in New York City, led a revival of Austrian economics in the post-war period, primarily in the New York area. Henry Hazlitt (1894-1993) was a modern-day Bastiat, a journalist who wrote editorials for *The New York Times* and *Newsweek*. In 1946, he wrote a bestseller, *Economics in One Lesson*, a book based on Bastiat's parable of the broken window. His theme: "The art of economics consists in looking not merely at the immediate but at the longer effects of any act or policy; it consists in tracing the consequences of that policy not merely for one group but for all groups" (Hazlitt 1979 [1946]:17).

Modern Austrian economics was resurrected in 1974, when Friedrich Hayek won the Nobel Prize, and a meeting of some fifty Austrian scholars was held near Royalton College in South Royalton, Vermont (Vaughn 1994:104-05). Sponsored by the Institute of Humane Studies, the meeting attracted such luminaries as Murray Rothbard, Israel Kirzner, Ludwig Lachmann, Gerald P. O'Driscoll, Sudha Shenoy, and Roger Garrison. It culminated in an edited volume, *The Foundations of Modern Austrian Economics* (Dolan, 1976). Kirzner (1930-), a British-born professor at New York University, focused almost exclusively on Austrian microeconomics, with his most successful book, *Competition and Entrepreneurship* (1972). For years the Austrian Economics Graduate Program at New York University, organized by Kirzner, allowed graduate students to pursue an advanced degree in economics. Kirzner, a rabbi, retired from NYU in 2002, but the program continues under the guidance of Mario Rizzo and David Harper, though now under the less descriptive name "Program on the Foundations of the Market Economy."

Murray Rothbard and Libertarian Economics

Murray N. Rothbard (1926-1995) was the inspiration of many young economists and libertarians following the radical sixties. Raised in New York City by secular Jewish parents, Rothbard earned his Ph. D. in economic history in 1956 at Columbia University, and immediately proceeded to write prolifically on Misesian economics, especially a treatise called *Man, Economy, and State* (1962) and *America's Great Depression* (1963). These scholarly works broadened Austrian themes into a full-scale alternative to standard neo-Keynesian economics. *Man, Economy, and State* is often called an Americanized version of Mises's *Human Action*. It dissected Keynesianism and then introduced an Austrian version of micro and macro economics. *America's Great Depression* exposed the fallacies of Keynesian explanations of the 1929-33 collapse, and introduced the Austrian theory of the business cycle as a plausible explanation, fully elucidated by a history of the events that led up to the crisis. Rothbard's book was published in the same year as Milton Friedman and Anna J. Schwartz's *A*

Monetary History of the United States (1963). This is significant in the long-standing quarrel between Friedman and Rothbard because they took virtually opposite views of the cause of the Great Depression. While Friedman argued that the Federal Reserve during the 1920s acted benignly ("the high tide of the Reserve System") and then reacted ineptly in permitting the deflationary policies of 1929-32 to destroy the economy, Rothbard claimed that the Federal Reserve's inflationary policies during the 1920s planted the seeds of an inevitable Great Depression, and that the deflationary forces were beneficial in cleansing the system. (For more details about this debate, see chapter 6.)

In the 1972 (second) edition of *America's Great Depression*, Rothbard asserted that neither the Keynesian nor monetarist schools could properly explain the new phenomenon of inflationary recession; moreover, the Austrian theory of the business cycle had a clear explanation of stagflation, arguing that consumer price inflation is "a general and universal tendency in recessions." That is to say, "the prices of consumer goods always tend to rise, relative to the prices of producer goods, during recession," only this time, in the early 1970s, government inflationary policies were so strong that consumer prices rose "absolutely and visibly as well" (Rothbard 1972: xii).

Short, headstrong, and bright, Rothbard took on the Keynesians, Marxists, and socialists of all stripes, and later on, the Chicago monetarist school. His lucid, powerful polemics attracted a large number of libertarians, gold bugs, and free-market economists. His pamphlet, *What Has the Government Done to Our Money?* (1964), touched the hearts of followers as much as *The Communist Manifesto* had affected the minds and hearts of Marxists. Rothbard was the next Mises, without the heavy German rhetoric. His essay on money was something every intelligent layman could comprehend. The mystery of money was no more.

I first encountered Rothbard's writings in an anthology entitled *Views on Capitalism*. The "conservative" view was represented with writings by Adam Smith, Friedrich Hayek, Milton Friedman, and Murray Rothbard. The editors introduced Rothbard in colorful language: "Rothbard represents an extreme right-wing mini-faction whose critique of present American society reveals astonishingly close kinship with that of many radicals, closer in fact than with his fellow conservatives. Although he is strongly committed to a defense of laissez faire as other conservative figures..., his support of black power and his characterization of American foreign policy as 'imperialistic' would be eagerly assented to by many thinkers usually associated with the political 'left.'" There followed a short essay, "The Great Society: A Libertarian Critique." I shall never forget the impact this little essay had on my thinking. Rothbard cited Franz Oppenheimer's *The State*, which outlined two, and only two, paths to the acquisition of wealth. "One route is the production of a good or service and its voluntary exchange for the goods or services produced by others. This method—the method of the free market— Oppenheimer termed 'the economic means' to wealth. The other path, which avoids the necessity for production and exchange, is for one or more persons to seize other people's products by the use of physical force. This method of robbing the fruits of another man's production was shrewdly named by Oppenheimer the 'political means'" (Rothbard 1970:87). I had never thought of government in this light—it came as a shock to me. I was hooked on Rothbard and his version of Austrian economics, and devoured all of Rothbard's economic and political writings. Libertarian students finally had a star to worship.

The best introduction to Rothbard can be found in his essays and short books. In addition to those listed above, "The Essential von Mises" (published in *Planning for Freedom* by Ludwig von Mises) is especially elucidating and forthright on how Mises advanced free-market economics and the theory of money. Economics majors and serious students of Austrian economics look to Rothbard's major works, *Man, Economy, and State; Power and Market; America's Great Depression;* and *The Mystery of Money,* for insights. The Mises Institute continues to publish Rothbard's articles and books in new editions.

Rothbard, always more than an economist, wrote extensively on political theory, ethics, and libertarian politics. He helped create the Cato Institute in 1977 and the Ludwig von Mises Institute with Lew Rockwell in 1982, and stamped his own brand on Misesian economics. He and his wife Joey spent most of their life in New York, where he was professor of economics at the Brooklyn Polytechnic Institute, an engineering school. (They had no children.) In 1985, he moved to the University of Nevada at Las Vegas. While working piecemeal on his history of economic thought (only half finished when he died of a heart attack in 1995), he became embroiled in libertarian politics. He rejected Mises's belief in limited government and advocated "anarcho-capitalism." But like Mises, he had a poison pen and often engaged in *ad hominem* in-fighting and bitter rivalries. Today Murray Rothbard is better remembered for his economic writings and ideas.

The Austrian School Today

The Austrian school has made a significant comeback in academia since Hayek won the Nobel Prize in 1974. Traditionally, the longest standing program is the Austrian Graduate Program at New York University, mentioned earlier. George Mason University in northern Virginia has gained prominence as a place for undergraduate and postgraduate studies under the tutelage of Peter Boettke, a major contributor to Austrian economics who studied under Hans Sennholz at Grove City College and Israel Kirzner at NYU. Boettke has written extensively on the collapse of Soviet socialism and central planning (Boettke 1993, 2001), organized the well-received *Elgar Companion to Austrian Economics* (1994), and edits *The Review of Austrian Economics*. Most importantly, he is the primary author of the late Paul Heynes's updated edition of his popular textbook, *The Economic Way of Thinking* (2003). Other major contributors to Austrian and libertarian economics at GMU include Walter Williams, Don Boudreaux, Bryan Caplan and Tyler Cowen. GMU is eclectic. It offers affiliated fields, such as the Center for Public Choice under Gordon Tullock and James Buchanan, experimental economics under another Nobel laureate Vernon Smith, and constitutional economics under Richard Wagner. Buchanan and Smith consider themselves "fellow travelers" with the Austrians.

The faculty of Auburn University in Alabama has included several well-known Austrian economists, such as Roger Garrison, Mark Thorton and Leland Yeager (recently retired). But note that Auburn recently discontinued its Ph. D. Program. Garrison is considered the most lucid proponent of Austrian macroeconomic theorizing today. His popular advanced text, *Time and Money*, creatively compares and contrasts Austrian with Keynesian and monetarist macroeconomics (Garrison 2001). My own work aims to rebuild a time-structural model of the economy in *The Structure of Production* (1990), and my textbook, *Economic Logic* (2000) is the first attempt to create a modern college textbook based largely on Austrian principles.

The Foundation for Economic Education, now under the able leadership of Richard Ebeling, continues publishing *The Freeman* and other Austrian-oriented publications and seminars, but has fallen behind in influence and size compared to other educational foundations. The Mises Institute, next door to Auburn University, is in the forefront of advancing Austrian economics. Under the direction of founder Lew Rockwell, the Mises Institute enjoys a large budget and a new building, where it publishes books, journals, and a variety of essays on its website. It publishes *The Quarterly Journal of*

Austrian Economics, and many other publications, including electronic materials in the tradition of Mises, Rothbard, and other Austrians. It holds numerous conferences on Austrian themes, including the annual Mises University, a weeklong series of classes. Other schools that offer strong Austrian ties include Hillsdale College in Michigan, which hosts the annual Ludwig von Mises lecture series; Grove City College near Pittsburgh, where Hans Sennholz was long-time chairman of the economics department; and Walsh College of Accountancy and Business Administration in Troy, Michigan, where chairman Harry Veryser has created a master's degree in Austrian economics. In California, Santa Clara University has an Austrian/libertarian bent and California State University at East Bay employs labor economist Charles Baird. Lawrence H. White, a specialist in free banking, is the first F. A. Hayek Professor of Economic History at University of Missouri-St. Louis, where a number of teachers are sympathetic to Austrian thinking.

How many economists are Austrian-oriented? Ohio University professors Richard Vedder and Lowell Gallaway guess that less than 2% fit into this category. (One might be tempted to say the founders of marginal analysis have been marginalized.) See figure 2.1 below. "Even in its resurrected state," conclude Vedder and Gallaway, "only a very small proportion of economists today consider themselves Austrian" (Vedder and Gallaway 2000:33), probably because Austrians stress non-mathematical modeling in an age of high theory and econometric performance. "The more overly Austrian the paper is, the greater the probability of rejection" (2000:35). This is no doubt due to the Austrians' aversion to participating in the mainstream of modern economics: Keynesianism, econometrics and statistical analysis, and Walrasian general equilibrium analysis (Caldwell 2004:4; Kirzner 1997).

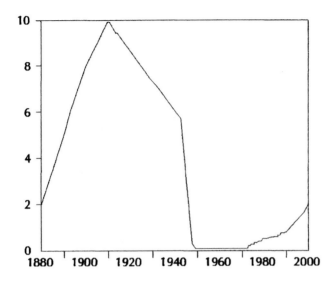

Figure 2.1—"Percent of Economists Who Are "Austrian": 1871-2000
Source: Vedder and Galloway 2000:33

In writing *Economics on Trial* (1993), I estimated the various schools' influence in the textbooks, based on the combined references to specific theories and their leaders in the name and subject indexes. Figure 2.2 shows the results.

School	Index Frequency
Keynes and Keynesianism	442
Friedman and Monetarism	252
Marx and Marxism	131
Laffer and Supply Side	95
Austrianism	67
Galbraith and Institutionalism	53

Figure 2.2. Schools of Influence in Economics
Source: *Economics on Trial* (1993:275-76)

However, since this time, the references to Mises, Hayek, Schumpeter and other Austrians may have increased. For example, prior to the sixth edition, University of Houston professors Roy Ruffin and Paul Gregory made no mention of Mises and Hayek in their popular textbook, *Principles of Economics*. Since then, however, they cite these Austrians in reference to a "defining moment" in economic history—the rise and fall of socialism, and Schumpeter is highlighted in the "defining moment" of the Great Depression and the Welfare State (Ruffin and Gregory 2001:7-8). In addition, Peter Boettke and David Prychitko have introduced many Austrian concepts in the new edition of the late Paul Heyne's *The Economic Way of Thinking* (2003). More may be on the way.

What about the University of Vienna today? Since Mises and Hayek left Austria, the economics department in old Vienna has gradually lost its Austrian roots. Today most professors would consider themselves "Austro-Keynesian." Erich Streissler is one of the few Viennese economists who has maintained an interest in the Austrian tradition, having written extensively on the works of Menger, Hayek, and Schumpeter. In a recent correspondence, Karl Socher, professor at the University of Innsbruck, comments, "Once, in the seventites, when economists in Vienna had been Keynesians, one of the Austro-Keynesians, Hans Seidel, said to me, Innsbruck is 500 km nearer to Chicago than Vienna (because we in Innsbruck were no Keynesians). I answered: No, we are still nearer to Vienna than to Chicago, but to the old Vienna. And Vaclav Klaus, after lectures in Linz and Vienna, when he discovered that Austrian Economics is not known any more in Austria, said: "'Because you have forgotten the Austrian School, we will take it and revive it in Prague'" (private correspondence, May 28, 2005).

References

Bastiat, Frederic. 1998 [1850]. *The Law*. New York: Foundation for Economic Education.

Blaug, Mark. 1992. "Commentary" in Bruce J. Caldwell and Stephan Boehm, ed., *Austrian Economics: Tensions and New Directions*. Boston: Kluwer Academic Publishers, 31-33.

Boaz, David. 1997. *Libertarianism: A Primer*. New York: Free Press.

Boettke, Peter J. 1993. *Why Perestroika Failed: The Politics and Economics of Socialist Transformation*. New York: Routledge.

Boettke, Peter J., ed., *Elgar Companion to Austrian Economics*. Hants, England: Edward Elgar.

Boettke, Peter J. 2001. *Calculation and Coordination*. New York: Routledge.

Böhm-Bawerk, Eugen. 1891. *The Positive Theory of Capital*. London: Macmillan.

Caldwell, Bruce. 2004. *Hayek's Challenge: An Intellectual Biography of F. A. Hayek*. Chicago: University of Chicago Press.

Dolan, Edwin G., ed. 1976. *The Foundations of Modern Austrian Economics*. Kansas City: Sheed & Ward.

Friedman, Milton. 1978. "Adam Smith's Relevance for 1976," in Fred R. Glahe, ed. 1978. *Adam Smith and the Wealth of Nations: 1776-1976. Bicentennial Essays*. Boulder: Colorado Associated University Press, 7-20.

Friedman, Milton and Rose. 1998. *Two Lucky People*. Chicago: University of Chicago Press.

Friedman, Milton and Anna J. Schwartz. 1963. *A Monetary History of the United States, 1867-1960*. Princeton: Princeton University Press.

Garrison, Roger W. 1996. "The Austrian Theory: A Summary," in Richard Ebeling, ed., *The Austrian Theory of the Business Cycle*. Auburn, AL: Mises Institute.

Garrison, Roger W. 2001. *Time and Money: The Macroeconomics of Capital Structure*. London: Routledge.

Glahe, Fred R., ed. 1978. *Adam Smith and the Wealth of Nations: 1776-1976. Bicentennial Essays*. Boulder: Colorado Associated University Press.

Hayek, Friedrich A. 1935 [1931]. *Prices and Production*, 2nd ed. London: George Routledge.

Hayek, Friedrich A. 1944. *The Road to Serfdom*. Chicago: University of Chicago Press.

Hayek, Friedrich A. 1960. *The Constitution of Liberty*. Chicago: University of Chicago Press.

Hayek, Friedrich A. 1973-79. *Law, Legislation and Liberty*. Chicago: University of Chicago Press.

Hayek, Friedrich A. 1976. "Introduction, Carl Menger," in Carl Menger, *Principles of Economics*. New York: New York University Press.

Hayek, Friedrich A. 1984 [1948]. "The Use of Knowledge in Society," in Chiaki Nishiyama and Kurt R. Leube, eds., *The Essential Hayek*. Stanford: Hoover Press, 211-24.

Hazlitt, Henry. 1979 [1946]. *Economics in One Lesson*. New York: Arlington House.

Heilbroner, Robert. 1989. "The Triumph of Capitalism," *The New Yorker* (January 23).

Heynes, Paul, Peter Boettke, and David Prychitko. 2003. *The Economic Way of Thinking*. 10th ed. Upper Saddle River, NJ: Prentice Hall.

Huerto de Soto, Jesus. 1998. "The Ongoing Methodenstreit of the Austrian School." *Journal des Economistes et des Etudes Humaines* 8:1 (March), 75-113.

Kirzner, Israel M. 1972. *Competition and Entrepreneurship*. Chicago: University of Chicago Press.

Kirzner, Israel M. 1997. "An Interview with Israel M. Kirzner," *Austrian Economics Newsletter* 17:1 (Spring), 1-13.

Lachmann, Ludwig M. 1977. *Capital, Expectations and the Market Process*. Kansas City, Kansas: Sheed Andrews and McMeel.

Malthus, Thomas Robert. 1985 [1798]. *An Essay on the Principle of Population*. New York: Penguin.

Menger, Carl. 1950. *Principles of Economics*. New York: New York University Press.

Mill, John Stuart. 1989 [1859]. *On Liberty and Other Writings*. Cambridge: Cambridge University Press.

Mill, John Stuart. 1884 [1848]. *Principles of Political Economy*, edited by J. Laurence Laughlin. New York: D. Appleton.

Mises, Ludwig von. 1981 [1936]. *Socialism*. Indianapolis: Liberty Classics.

Mises, Ludwig von. 1953 [1912]. *The Theory of Money and Credit*. New Haven: Yale University Press.

Mises, Ludwig von. 1966 [1949]. *Human Action*, 3rd ed. Chicago: Henry Regnery.

Mises, Ludwig von. 1978. *Notes and Recollections*. South Holland, IL: Libertarian Press.

Mises, Ludwig von. 1980. *Planning for Freedom.* Spring Hill, PA: Libertarian Press.

O'Driscoll, Gerald P., Jr. and Mario Rizzo. 1985. *The Economics of Time and Ignorance.* Oxford: Basil Blackwell.

Oppenheimer, Franz. 1997. *The State.* New York: Fox and Wilkes.

Rothbard, Murray N. 1970. "The Great Society: A Libertarian Critique," in Richard Romano and Melvin Leiman, eds., *Views on Capitalism.* Beverly Hills, California: Glencoe Press, 85-95.

Rothbard, Murray N. 1962. *Man, Economy and State.* Princeton: Van Nostrand.

Rothbard, Murray N. 1972 [1963]. *America's Great Depression.* 2nd ed. Los Angeles: Nash Publishing.

Rothbard, Murray N. 1980 [1973]. *The Essential Von Mises.* Auburn: The Mises Institute.

Rothbard, Murray N. 1983. *The Mystery of Money.* New York: Richardson and Snyder.

Ruffin, Roy J. And Paul R. Gregory. 2001. *Principles of Economics.* 7th ed. Boston: Addison Wesley.

Schumpeter, Joseph A. 1950 [1943]. *Capitalism, Socialism, and Democracy.* New York: Harper and Row.

Schumpeter, Joseph A. 1954. *History of Economic Analysis.* New York: Oxford University Press.

Shackle, G. L. S. 1974. *Keynesian Kaleidics: The Evolution of a General Political Economy.* Chicago: Aldine Publishing Co.

Skousen, Mark. 1990. *The Structure of Production.* New York: New York University Press.

Skousen, Mark. 1993. *Economics on Trial.* Homewood, IL: Business One Irwin.

Skousen, Mark. 2000. *Economic Logic.* Washington, DC: Capital Press.

Skousen, Mark. 2001. *The Making of Modern Economics.* New York: M. E. Sharpe.

Smith, Adam. 1965 [1776]. *The Wealth of Nations.* New York: Modern Library.

Smith, Vernon L. 1999. "Reflections on Human Action After 50 Years," *Cato Journal* 19:2 (Fall).

Stigler, George J. 1976. "The Successes and Failures of Professor Smith." *Journal of Political Economy* 84:6 (December), 1199-1213.

Streissler, Erich W. 1990. "The Influence of German Economics on the Work of Menger and Marshall." In Bruce Caldwell, ed., *Carl Menger and His Legacy in Economics.* Durham, NC: Duke University Press.

Vaughn, Karen I. 1994. *Austrian Economics in America: The Migration of a Tradition*. Cambridge: Cambridge University Press.

Vedder, Richard and Lowell Gallaway. 2000. "The Austrian Market Share in the Marketplace of Ideas, 1871-2025," *Quarterly Journal of Austrian Economics* 3:1 (Spring), 33-42.

Vivo, G. de. 1987. "David Ricardo," *The New Palgrave: A Dictionary of Economics*. London: Macmillan. Vol. 4, 183-98.

Wicksell, Knut. 1958. *Selected Papers on Economic Theory*. London: Allen and Unwin.

Wieser, Friedrich von. 1927 [1914]. *Theory of Social Economy*. New York: Greenberg.

Chapter Three

THE IMPERIALISTIC CHICAGO SCHOOL

*There is no center of intellectual ferment like the
University of Chicago any place in the world.*

—James Buchanan

*The cold war is over and the
University of Chicago has won.*

—George F. Will

Like the Austrians, the Chicago school was born out of crisis, a second crisis in economics. The first crisis, as you will recall, was resolved with the marginalist/subjectivist revolution of the late 19th century. The works of Eugen Böhm-Bawerk in Austria, Alfred Marshall in Britain, and John Bates Clark in the United States, among others, successfully countered the defective labor theory of value and other socialist/Marxist claims. They recognized that prices were not determined by their labor input, but grounded in the quantity available and the intensity of consumer demands at the margin. In a competitive market economy, free of restraint, workers are not exploited but paid their discounted marginal value—what they contribute to the productive process of goods and services. According to the neo-classical model, the key to higher wages is an increase in productivity, although most economists supported labor union activity that prevented abuses. Similarly, capitalists and landlords are legitimately rewarded for their contributions if they are not subsidized or restrained by coercive government.

On the macro level, the neo-classical economists endorsed economic liberalism and the positive role of saving and capital formation in maximizing the wealth of nations. J.-B. Say's law of markets was almost universally accepted as the classical macroeconomic model: increased capital, technology, and productivity in a "system of natural liberty" (Adam Smith's term) lead to rapidly rising living standards for all. The international gold standard, where gold and silver coins circulated, banknotes and demand deposits were backed by specie, and national currencies were defined as various weights of gold bullion, was accepted by most economists as the ideal anti-inflationary monetary system under which economic liberalism could flourish. They understood the Hume-Ricardo specie flow mechanism and the quantity theory of money, that excessive inflation (often during war time) resulted from going off the gold standard and expanding the money supply beyond its commodity backing. The neo-classical model seemed to have overcome all obstacles, and a dynamic capitalism catapulted the West into the 20th century, providing new products and a higher standard of living never before imagined. By the 1920s, Irving Fisher and other standard bearers of the new model of capitalism hailed it as a "New Era" of unbounded prosperity.

The Great Depression: Capitalism Faces Its Greatest Challenge

Then came the second crisis in capitalism: The Great Depression of the 1930s, the most traumatic economic event of the 20th century. In the United States, industrial output fell by 30 percent and nearly a third of the commercial banks failed. The unemployment rate soared to 25 percent. Stocks lost nearly 90 percent of their value. Europe and the rest of the world faced a similar fate. The capitalist system of natural liberty so carefully crafted and refined came under siege. The classical virtues of thrift, balanced budgets, limited government, the gold standard, and Say's law — staples of laissez faire — were attacked as never before. The house that Adam Smith built was threatening to collapse.

Most neo-classical economists were at a loss to explain the collapse. Irving Fisher, the Yale professor who had spent a lifetime studying cycles and the quantity theory of money, was completely surprised by the 1929 crash and subsequent depression. The "Oracle of Wall Street," worth $10 million at the height of the market, lost everything and eventually went bankrupt. Harvard's Frank Taussig and Cambridge's John Maynard Keynes fared little better. Keynes, noted for his financial acumen, failed miserably to anticipate the crash and lost three-fourths of his capital. Later he admitted he had been misled by stable price indices in the 1920s. Unlike Fisher, however, Keynes recovered remarkably in the 1930s and made a second fortune (Skousen 1992:161-69).

In Vienna, Ludwig von Mises and Friedrich Hayek were among the few who "called the crash." For a time in the early 1930s, they were the darlings of the economics profession. Having predicted the crash, they were called upon to forecast the end of the Depression. Mises and Hayek advocated a laissez faire solution: let the market run its course and the economy would quickly recover on its own. But when the slump persisted year after year, policy-makers and students looked elsewhere for answers. The Austrian school was moribund, at least for another half century. The length and severity of the Great Depression caused most of the Anglo-American economics profession to question classical laissez-faire economics and the ability of a free-market capitalist system to correct itself. In an era of fear—fear of losing one's job, fear of hunger, and fear of war looming ominously—many intellectuals turned to radical Marxism. Socialist central planning was on the rise. Marxism was all the rage on college campuses. Most of Keynes's students at Cambridge were Marxist, despite the protests of Keynes, who detested Karl

Marx and *Das Capital*. Keynes had visited Russia in 1925 and hated it. "How can I adopt a creed which, preferring the mud to the fish, exalts the boorish proletariat above the bourgeois and the intelligentsia who, with whatever faults, are the quality in life and surely carry the seeds of all human achievement?" (Keynes 1931:298-300)

Unfortunately, the socialists had contemporary history on their side. They could point to Nazi Germany and the Soviet Union as examples of centrally-planned economies with full employment and economic superiority. After all, had not Sidney and Beatrice Webb, Fabian socialists and founders of the London School of Economics, returned from a tour of the Soviet Union brimming with optimism and firm in their belief that Stalin had inaugurated a "new civilization"? Was not full-scale socialism the only alternative to an unstable, insecure capitalist world?

Keynes to the Rescue

Who would save capitalism from Marxism, Nazism or some other extreme ism in the 1930s? That voice was to be John Maynard Keynes (1883-1946), elitist leader of the new Cambridge school. Keynes would be the moderate candidate, a man who "did not overthrow the system but saved it" (Galbraith 1975:136). He became the theoretical spokesman for Big Government and the Welfare State, a half way house between laissez faire and totalitarianism. He prescribed a middle way that would preserve personal liberty (which he cherished) without destroying the foundations of Western civilization.

In his revolutionary 1936 book, *The General Theory of Employment, Interest, and Money*, Keynes rejected the invisible hand doctrine of Adam Smith. Capitalism, he said, was inherently unstable and had no tendency toward full employment. But to get an imperfect market back on track, he refused to join the Marxists and socialists in calling for totalitarian control of the economy; all that is necessary, he argued, is for government to take control at the macro level. How? Not by slashing prices and wages—the classical approach—but by deliberately running federal deficits and by spending money on public works that would expand demand and restore confidence. Once the economy is back on track and reaches full employment, he wrote, the government will no longer need to run deficits, and the classical model of free markets can then function as before. Keynes called his general theory "aggregate effective demand management." Government could expand or contract aggregate demand as conditions required. During a recession, it could run deficits, and during an inflationary boom, it could run surpluses, thus eliminating the cycle inherent in capitalism without destroying capitalism itself. Keynes rejected the socialist demands to nationalize the economy, impose price-wage controls, or interfere with the micro foundations of supply and demand.

Keynes and *The General Theory* took the profession by storm in the late 1930s and early 1940s. It was like a flash of light on a dark night. As John Kenneth Galbraith reported, "Here was a remedy for the despair....It did not overthrow the system but saved it. To the non-revolutionary, it seemed too good to be true. To the occasional revolutionary, it was. The old economics was still taught by day. But in the evening, and almost every evening from 1936 on, almost everyone discussed Keynes" (Galbraith 1975:136). The Keynesian model of aggregate demand management convinced the profession faster than the marginalist revolution, especially after World War II seemed to vindicate the benefits of deficits and massive government spending. It wasn't long before most intellectuals abandoned Marxism. Everywhere college professors, under the guidance of Alvin Hansen, Paul Samuelson, Lawrence Klein, and other Keynesian disciples, began teaching students about the consumption function, the multiplier, the marginal propensity to consume, the paradox of thrift, and C + I + G. It was a strange, new, intoxicating doctrine.

Free-Market Responses to Keynes

Keynes may have offered a plausible cure for the depression and kept the West from needing radical surgery, but his theories also championed the welfare state and boundless faith in big government. His disciples promoted deficit spending, creeping inflation, and progressive taxation and attacked the virtues of thrift, limited government, the gold standard, and laissez faire. To free-market economists, Keynes's *General Theory* "constitutes the most subtle and mischievous assault on orthodox capitalism and free enterprise that has appeared in the English language" (Hazlitt 1977:345).

Unfortunately, the Austrian counterattack on Keynesian economics was almost completely ineffectual (see Skousen 1992: 9-34). Mises wrote only short dismissive articles on Keynes. Hayek, the leading anti-Keynesian of the 1930s, thought that *The General Theory* was merely a "tract of the times" and ignored it, a decision he later regretted. After the war, he devoted most of his time to political philosophy. William H. Hutt, a professor at the University of Cape Town, wrote a lengthy rebuttal entitled *The Keynesian Episode* (1979 [1963]), but his book was difficult to follow and not well received. In the late 1950s, Henry Hazlitt, a journalist and author of *Economics in One Lesson*, complained of a "great dearth" of anti-Keynesian books and articles. He took up the task himself by writing a page-by-page critique of *The General Theory* in a book called *Failure of the New Economics* (1959). Hazlitt made a penetrating, scholarly, and intelligent dissection of every page of *The General Theory*, but he became mired in Keynes's esoteric terminology and, consequently, his book ended up gathering dust on the shelves of conservatives and business people while being ignored by the profession.

Murray Rothbard probably spent more effort than any "American Austrian" in dissecting Keynesian theories, in two books, *Man, Economy and State* (1962) and *America's Great*

Depression (1963). Earlier, he wrote, "It is a mistake to dismiss [Keynesianism] brusquely, as many conservative economists have done....but failure to deal with its fallacies in detail and in depth has left the field of ideas open to Keynesianism to conquer" (Rothbard 1960:150). Yet, notwithstanding these valiant efforts, Rothbard's words, published outside the mainstream, appealed only to his libertarian audience. Despite having a doctorate degree from Columbia University, he refused to join the American Economic Association or to contribute to the professional journals. He wrote books published by little known publishers, Van Nostrand and Nash Publishing, and taught at low-tier universities, Brooklyn Polytechnic Institute of Brooklyn and University of Nevada at Las Vegas.

Milton Friedman, The Chicago School, and the Monetary Counter-Revolution

If the Austrian school was not going to dethrone the Keynesian model in the academic world, who would step up?

The answer came ultimately from an exceptional figure, an individual who almost single-handedly engineered a "counterrevolution" in macroeconomics, demolished the Keynesian monolith, and helped restore the classical model of Adam Smith. Milton Friedman (1912-) was able to dethrone Keynesianism through a brilliant two-step strategy. First, he used his impeccable credentials in technical economics to pursue his goals. Like Rothbard, he earned his Ph. D. from Columbia University, but unlike Rothbard, he wrote for the National Bureau of Economic Research (NBER) and major professional journals. His books were published by Princeton University Press and other prestigious academic publishers. He won the highly sought after John Bates Clark Award (given to the brightest economist under the age of 40). He became a member of a major academic institution, the University of Chicago. He not only joined the American Economic Association (AEA), but in 1967, he was elected its president, and in 1976, he won the highest honor of the profession, the Nobel Prize. In short, he succeeded within the profession.

Secondly, Friedman focused relentlessly in his early career on scholarly technical work. Specifically, he engaged in rigorous quantitative methods of research to support his theories, and to test empirically the Keynesian model and the quantity theory of money. Theory, even brilliant sophisticated logic, would not be enough to dislodge the Keynesian hegemony, as the Austrians discovered. One needs reliable data, quantitative analysis, and sophisticated mathematical skills to test various theories in economics, to separate good from bad economics. Friedman learned the value of solid empirical work from Simon Kuznets, Wesley Mitchell, and other researchers at the National Bureau of Economic Research in the 1930s. According to Gary Becker, another Chicago Nobel laureate, rigorous testing of theories with empirical data is Friedman's most important contribution to technical economics.[1] It turned out to be a remarkably fruitful enterprise.

Friedman was linked to Chicago from an early age. He grew up in New York, the only son of eastern European Jewish immigrants, and attended Rutgers University. In 1932, at the depths of the depression, he won a scholarship to study economics at the University of Chicago. There he met George Stigler, who became his lifelong colleague, friend, and counterpart, known as "Mr. Micro" in combating the Cambridge model of imperfect competition. Friedman wrote later of Stigler, "He was a delightful office companion, a stimulating conversationalist, a highly constructive critic, and, like myself, lived, breathed, and slept economics" (Friedman

---

1 When I asked his reaction to Gary Becker's statement, MIT's Paul Samuelson cited some young econometricians who were "a bit dismissive about the net Chicago effect" and suggested that all schools tend to "exaggerate" the importance of their scholarly work. "When I was a Chicago undergraduate, I believe both ante-dating and post-dating Friedman's main graduate study period, only Paul Douglas and Henry Schultz did serious statistical work. Generally, Viner, Knight (and the leading graduate students who were, like me, Knight groupies) were pretty derisive of those Douglas measurements....Schultz, who was a little insecure, did respectable pioneering work but was looked down on by Allen Wallis and George Stigler" (private correspondence with Samuelson, 19 August 2003).

1998: 149). It was at Chicago that Friedman also met his future wife, Rose Director, sister of economist Aaron Director. In 1938, Milton and Rose married. They have been partners and coauthors ever since.

After working in the war years for the Treasury in Washington, D. C., and the Statistical Research Group at Columbia University, where he earned his Ph. D., Friedman returned to the University of Chicago, and began his storied success. It was a few years after his appointment that Friedman "swiftly took over the intellectual leadership" and created a distinct "Chicago school" (Reder 1982:10).

"My Kind of Town, Chicago Is"

Chicago is the quintessential American city, a place where the market-oriented economics of Milton Friedman and the Chicago school could flourish. It is the epitome of open wild-west capitalism, the "City of the Big Shoulders," in the words of poet Carl Sandburg. Chicago is an unpretentious, productive city that grew from 30,000 inhabitants in 1850 to become the world's sixth largest urban center forty years later. Today it is the epicenter of manufacturing and agriculture, the foundation of industrial America. Trucks and railroad cars transport more goods in and out of Chicago than any other city in the United States. Like Texas, Chicago does things in a big way. It houses the nation's tallest building, the largest grain market and commodity trading center, the busiest airport, and the nation's most spectacular architecture. "Chicago symbolized the global ability of capitalism to generate markets from nowhere," states Robert Leeson (2000:1).

The University of Chicago was founded by the world's richest man, John D. Rockefeller, who contributed $35 million to establish the university in 1890, and thus earned its early nickname, The Standard Oil University. Yet since its inception it has attracted some of the most impressive scholars, scientists, and teachers from around the world, including physicist Enrico Fermi, inventor of the nuclear reactor; philosopher Leo Strauss; and Robert Maynard Hutchins and Mortimer Adler, creators of the Great Books series (Shils 1991). Because of Rockefeller's connection, Chicago has always had a distinctive pro-business tradition, beginning with the appointment of its first director of the Chicago Department of Economics, J. Lawrence Laughlin. However, it would be unfair to characterize the department as purely libertarian. In fact, Chicago has long housed an eclectic group of economists, including institutionalists such as Thorstein Veblen, first editor of the *Journal of Political Economy*; Oskar Lange, the Polish socialist; and Paul Douglas, a social activist United States senator.

It was during the 1930s, known as the golden age at the university, that a Chicago tradition can be traced to a group of influential pro-market economists, especially Jacob Viner, Henry Simons, Lloyd Mints, and Frank Knight. This foursome of Chicago economists motivated a distinctive group of students in the mid-1930s, including Milton Friedman, Rose Director Friedman, George Stigler, and Aaron Director. (Paul Samuelson was also a student at Chicago during the 1930s, but went on to Keynesian fame.)

Viner, Simons, Mints, and Knight supported free trade, stable money, and uncontrolled wages and prices. Jacob Viner (1892-1970) was an academic theorist, long-time editor of the *Journal of Political Economy,* and historian of economic and religious thought. In his demanding price theory class, he stressed market tools that served as a powerful engine to analyze economic problems. It was Viner's approach that Milton Friedman labeled "the distinctive feature of 'Chicago economics'" (Friedman 1998:204). Friedman was impressed with the "coherent, logical whole" of sound economic theory. "That course was unquestionably the greatest intellectual experience of my life," he recalled (Briet and Spencer 1982:83). Undoubtedly Friedman's and Stigler's popular price theory textbooks were greatly affected by Viner's insightful course.

Henry Simons (1899-1946), whom George Stigler called "the Crown Prince of this theoretical Kingdom," was more vocal than Viner or Knight in crusading for causes. In his book *Economic Policy for a Free Society* (1948), Simons emphasized a government policy of "rules over authorities" in monetary policy, an idea that Friedman later endorsed. Like Yale's Irving Fisher, Simons and Friedman advocated 100% reserves on demand deposits as a way of avoiding ruinous runs on banks and economic depression.

Some observers consider Frank H. Knight (1885-1972) the most influential teacher at Chicago (Nelson 2001:114-15). The author of *Risk, Uncertainty, and Profit* (1921) and inventor of the circular-flow diagram ("wheel of wealth," as Knight called it), Knight spent most of his career at Chicago and served as president of the AEA in 1950. He was skeptical about everything and disdainful of rank and authority, especially anything coming from the nation's capital. Knight inspired the next generation to "challenge everything" and to reject any idea that lacked logic or empirical support, which may explain in part why Chicago economists are often irreverent and sometimes inconsistent in their support of free markets (Buchanan 2001:13). He regarded individual freedom as a basic value and expressed concerns about representative democracy infringing on those rights. Knight was a radical critic of Roosevelt's New Deal, Keynesian-inspired macro-management of the economy, and socialist interventionism.[2] He denied a belief in strict laissez faire, opposing big business and labor unions as monopolists and advertising as wasteful (Patinkin 1981:37). Nevertheless, Knight declared, "I believe that individualism must be the political philosophy of intelligent and morally serious men....It is my conviction that any great extension of state action in economics is incompatible with political liberty, that 'control' will call for

2 However, in the 1930s, after a decade of depression and the imminence of world war, Knight declared publicly that liberal society had failed to provide stability in times of crisis and therefore communism may provide a necessary though regrettable social order. When Knight was asked years later to reprint these lectures, he replied, "I wish I could unprint them" (cited in Boettke 1995, note 17)

more control and tend to run into complete regimentation....and finally into absolutism, with or without a destructive struggle for power" (Knight 1948:li-lii).

At an AEA meeting in the 1950s, Knight bluntly told a group, "If there's anything I can't stand it's a Keynesian and a believer in monopolistic competition."

"What about believers in the use of mathematics in economic analysis, Frank?" asked a colleague.

"Can't stand it either," he replied firmly (Samuelson 1977:886-87).

Stigler recalled the four economists of the early Chicago school: "Knight was a great philosopher and theoretician, almost in a Marxist sense; Viner was steadfastly non-dogmatic on policy views; Mints was a close historical student of money and restricted himself to that field; Simons was the utopian" (Stigler 1982:170).

Keynesians Before Keynes: The Chicago School of the 1930s

Yet the early Chicago school was never doctrinaire in extolling its laissez faire philosophy. Surprisingly, Viner, Simons and Knight advocated large and continuous deficit spending throughout the early 1930s to combat mass unemployment and deflation. In a 1932 letter to Congress, a dozen Chicago economists warned of "tremendous losses, in wastage of productivity capacity, and in acute suffering" (Davis 1968:477). They encouraged Congress to favor "fiscal inflation" during the Depression, including deficit spending financed by new money. Viner supported a Keynesian-style countercyclical fiscal policy, operating surpluses in boom times and deficits in bad times. During prosperous times, the cardinal principles of finance were to tax heavily, spend lightly, and redeem the debt. During a depression, government should do the opposite: tax lightly, spend heavily, and borrow more. Simons emphasized the need to restore business confidence by advocating deficit spending and tax cuts. According to Milton Friedman, "There is great similarity between the views expressed by Simons and by Keynes—as to the causes of the Great Depression, the impotence of monetary policy, and the need to rely on fiscal policy" (Davis 1968:476). Simons also blamed poor economic performance on corporate monopoly and labor union power, and advocated nationalization of railroads, utilities and all other "uncompetitive" industries, as well as highly progressive taxation on the rich, in his book ironically called *Economic Policy for a Free Society* (Simons 1948; cf. Patinkin 1981:4; Block 2002). Yet it would be wrong to characterize the early Chicago school as Keynesian outside the extreme conditions of the Great Depression. Knight and Viner, for example, considered Keynes's notion of "equilibrium at less than full employment" as an "unacceptable innovation" (Reder 1982:18). Most of the time, they opposed state regulation and artificial stimulation, especially after the Chicago school gathered influence under of Milton Friedman and George Stigler.

How Friedman Converted the Profession

Friedman took an entirely different road than the Austrians. Instead of ignoring Keynes and building a separate theoretical apparatus, he worked within the Keynesian system, and used his statistical skills to examine the veracity of Keynes's "new economics." Keynesianism and its new-fangled tools were ubiquitous within the discipline, but it suffered from a flaw, perhaps an Achilles' heel. Keynes's "general theory" was theory only; he did no empirical work to test its validity. He left empirical work up to his disciples to measure the marginal propensity to consume, the size of the expenditure multiplier, and fluctuations in the velocity of money. The Keynesians did precisely that in the 1940s and 1950s. Simon Kuznets in the United States and Colin Clark in

England were instrumental in advancing national income accounting, including Gross National Product (now Gross Domestic Product), a Keynesian measure of "aggregate effective demand," and Lawrence Klein tried to determine the size of the government multiplier. These were heady times.

There was no reason to believe Friedman to be an anti-Keynesian when he published his exhaustive study, *Theory of the Consumption Function* (1957). After all, it was a NBER study, the kind many Keynesians were doing. It used Keynesian language and tools; Friedman, as we shall see, in fact had expressed considerable sympathy toward Keynes earlier in his career. Yet Friedman's conclusions undermined Keynes in several crucial ways. First, Friedman demonstrated that the Keynesian consumption function did not fit the historical evidence. Crucial to the Keynesian case for increased government spending to bring about full employment is the consumption function—the notion that there is a stable short-term relationship between household consumption spending and household current income. According to the Keynesian model, government spending would increase household incomes through a leveraged multiplier effect. However, using a massive study of consumption data in the United States, Friedman showed that households adjust their expenditures only according to long-term or permanent income changes, and pay little attention to transitory patterns. Therefore, the Keynesian consumption function was fundamentally flawed and any leveraging of government expenditures through the multiplier would be much smaller than expected. Friedman's diligent and comprehensive work set a new high standard of empirical scholarship, and later research by Franco Modigliani, James Tobin, and other Keynesians confirmed this "life-cycle" or "permanent income" hypothesis of consumption. Further studies over the years validated Friedman's conclusion that the expenditure multiplier is closer to 1 than the textbook version of 4 or 5.

Friedman wasn't the only one who cast doubts on Keynes's theories. He verified Simon Kuznets's studies at NBER denying Keynes's "psychological law" that the "marginal propensity to save" increases with income (Keynes 1973 [1936]: 31, 97), at least on a countrywide level. Kuznets, who later won a Nobel Prize, showed that since 1899 the percentage of income saved has remained steady despite a substantial rise in real income. This discovery was all the more important because the Keynesians used the idea of an increasing propensity to save by the wealthy to justify highly progressive income and estate taxes as a way to encourage a high-consumption society and avoid stagnation. According to the Keynesians, consumption was the key stimulant to short-term economic performance and progressive taxation would raise a country's propensity to consume. Now, under the weight of historical evidence, the Keynesian prescription appeared impotent.

Does Money Matter?

But the more serious blow to Keynesian economics came in 1963 with the publication of Friedman's magnum opus, *A Monetary History of the United States, 1867-1960*, co-authored by Anna J. Schwartz. Another NBER study published by Princeton University Press, it was a direct assault on Keynesian monetary theory and a confirmation of the classical quantity theory of money. In the post-war era, political policy makers and economists accepted the Keynesian idea, coming out of the Depression, that "money doesn't matter," that somehow an aggressive expansion of the money supply during a recession or depression would not have an effect. Monetary policy is like a string, they said; you can pull on it but you can't push on it. Central banks can stop a boom, but are incapable of igniting a recovery. According to the early Keynesians, open-market operations and easy money policies would only lead to hoarding or a build-up of cash reserves at banks due to what Keynes called a "fetish for liquidity" (Keynes 1973: 155). Only an aggressive fiscal policy—deficit spending and tax cuts—could stimulate spending and recovery.

Recall the quantity equation invented by Irving Fisher: MV=PT, where money (M) multiplied by velocity (V) equals prices (P) multiplied by the volume of transactions (T). Prior to the Depression, Fisher's quantity theory of money was widely accepted. Velocity was considered highly stable and short-term fluctuations in the economy and price inflation reflected changes in the quantity of money (changes in M, given V, resulted in changes in PT, or nominal income). This view completely changed after the Depression. Keynes claimed that velocity is a will o' the wisp and highly volatile. In a downturn, if the quantity of money goes up, the velocity of money will simply go down, and nothing will happen on the other side of the equation to either prices (P) or transactions (T). The quantity of money is therefore relatively impotent, and only "autonomous spending" by the government could stimulate output and income. Moreover, in recent times, prices are relatively rigid. The Great Depression was caused by a collapse of "effective demand" for capital investment, and only a positive program of direct spending by government could reverse the tide.

By the 1950s, the general consensus regarding monetary policy was reflected in Paul Samuelson's popular textbook, *Economics*. "Today few economists regard federal reserve monetary policy as a panacea for controlling the business cycle" (Samuelson 1955:316). Monetary policy was reduced to a permanent "cheap money" policy to keep interest rates as low as possible to accommodate government borrowing. The burden of controlling the business cycle fell largely on fiscal policy, by varying the rate of government spending and taxation. Finally, inflation was largely viewed as a cost-push phenomenon, and an "incomes policy" (wage/price controls) might be helpful in controlling inflation.

Friedman proved otherwise. He and Schwartz spent years painstakingly gathering a wide variety of statistics on money, credit, interest rates, and the policies of federal monetary authorities since the Civil War. This mass of statistics culminated in a monumental three-volume work that could not be ignored by the profession. First, Friedman showed time and time again that monetary policy was effective in both expansions and contractions. As Friedman explains, "Empirically, however, it turns out that the movement of velocity tend to reinforce those of money instead of offset them. When the quantity of money declined by a third from 1929 to 1933 in the United States, velocity declined also. When the quantity of money rises rapidly in almost any country, velocity also rises rapidly" (Friedman 1991:10).

Friedman's View of the Great Depression

Second, Friedman and Schwartz revealed that, contrary to the conventional view, monetary policy was devastatingly effective, in a negative way, on the economy during 1929-33. In the most important chapter, "The Great Contraction," of *A Monetary History*, the authors discovered how damaging the Fed had been: "From the cyclical peak in August 1929 to the cyclical trough in March 1933, the stock of money fell over a third" (Friedman and Schwartz 1963:299). For thirty years, an entire generation of economists had been in the dark about the Fed's impact on the Great Depression. According to the official apologia, the Fed has done its best to avert disaster, but was powerless to stop the collapse. It provided liquidity (high-powered money), and still a third of the commercial banks failed as customers tried to convert their deposits into currency. Yet the indictment of the Fed is unmistakable: "....it is crystal clear that at all times during the contraction, the Federal Reserve had it within its power to prevent the decline in the quantity of money and to produce an increase" (Friedman 1991:10). Furthermore: "The Great Contraction is in fact a tragic testimony to the importance of monetary forces" (Friedman and Schwartz 1963:300). On another occasion, Friedman explains, "Far from being testimony to the irrelevance of monetary forces in preventing depression, the early 1930s are a tragic testimony to their importance in producing depression" (1968:78-79). They government had acted "ineptly" in turning a garden-variety recession into the worst economic calamity of the century.

One of the reasons for this ignorance about the power of monetary policy is that the Fed did not publish money supply figures until Friedman and Schwartz developed M1 and M2 aggregates in their book. As Friedman states, "If the Federal Reserve System in 1929 to 1933 had been publishing statistics on the quantity of money, I don't believe that the Great Depression could have taken the course it did" (Friedman and Heller 1969:80).

Thus, Friedman concludes, "The fact is that the Great Depression, like most other periods of severe unemployment, was produced by government mismanagement rather than by any inherent instability of the private economy" (1982 [1962]:38). Furthermore, he writes, "Far from the depression being a failure of the free-enterprise system, it was a tragic failure of government" (1998:233). From this time forward, thanks to the profound work of Friedman and Schwartz, the textbooks would gradually replace "market failure" with "government failure" in their sections on the Great Depression.

Friedman Faces a Hostile Climate During the "Age of Keynes"

A Monetary History was published in 1963, when Keynesian theory was at its peak in prominence. A year earlier, he wrote *Capitalism and Freedom*, his first book written for the general public. It was a slow seller. Friedman, like other free-market economists, was on the defensive, was often ignored, and was frequently derided as an "extremist" and "Neanderthal" during the Keynesian "new economics" of the 1960s. During the "dark ages of the Keynesian despotism," as Harry Johnson called it, economics departments around the country were often hostile to Friedman's message (Johnson 1975:103). During this time, for example, Duke University library refused to carry his books. Friedman himself described the hostile intellectual climate at the time: "Those of us who were deeply concerned about the danger to freedom and prosperity from the growth of government, from the triumph of the welfare state and Keynesian ideas, were a small beleaguered minority regarded as eccentrics by the great majority of our fellow intellectuals" (Friedman 1982:vi).

Meanwhile, the Kennedy-Johnson tax cut was passed in 1964. Walter Heller and other economic advisors to President Kennedy argued in favor of running a deliberate deficit by cutting income tax rates, thereby reversing the 1961 recession. Sure enough, the economy rebounded. Despite protests from Friedman, Keynesians proclaimed victory. Friedman insisted that the tax cut did not validate Keynesian theory because the money supply grew rapidly during this period. It was not a fair test. Moreover, in a debate with Heller, Friedman startled the audience by declaring, "the state of the budget by itself has no significant effect on the course of nominal income, on inflation, on deflation, or on cyclical fluctuations" (Friedman and Heller 1969:47). He did sound extreme!

Debunking the Phillips Curve: Friedman Makes a Bold Prediction

Rising prices and cost-push inflation became a persistent issue in the sixties, especially during the Vietnam War. Friedman, grounded in his quantity theory of money, refused to blame inflation on labor unions, corporate monopoly power, or expensive imports. Rather, he declared his famous dictum: "Inflation is always and everywhere a monetary phenomenon" (Friedman 1968:105).

The Keynesians relied on the Phillips Curve to downplay the threat of inflation. It was an important empirical tool in their tool kit. Australian economist A. W. Phillips had published a milestone article in 1958 suggesting a trade-off between inflation and unemployment. His study showed a century-long inverse relationship between unemployment and wage inflation in the United Kingdom (Phillips 1958). In *Barron's*, Paul Samuelson called the Phillips Curve trade-off "one of the most important concepts of our time" (Leeson 2000:89). He and Robert Solow, among others, suggested that unemployment was a more serious problem than inflation, and that if the choice came down to more inflation or more unemployment, the Federal government should opt for more inflation. Using the Phillips Curve to justify a liberal fiscal policy, inflation could be tolerated and even encouraged if it meant lower unemployment. Equally, a restrictive fiscal policy (surpluses) or monetary policy (tight money) to fight inflation would be costly in terms of job loss and should be resisted.

Stagflation of the 1970s and the Rise of Rational Expectations

In his famous 1967 AEA presidential address, "The Role of Monetary Policy," Friedman introduced the "natural rate of unemployment" concept (similar to Wicksell's natural rate of interest idea) to counter the Phillips Curve and Keynesian policy. He contended, "there is always a temporary trade-off between inflation and unemployment; [but] there is no permanent trade-off." Any effort to push unemployment below the "natural rate" must lead to an accelerating inflation. Moreover, "the only way in which you ever get a reduction in unemployment is through unanticipated inflation," which is unlikely. Friedman warned that any acceleration of inflation would eventually bring about higher, not lower, unemployment. A year earlier Friedman had predicted in his *Newsweek* column (17 October 1966), "There will be an inflationary recession." This forecast was greeted with scorn by the Keynesians. But when it came true in the early 1970s, it evicted the Keynesians from their high position in political influence, and, equally important, caused the textbooks to include discussions of the natural rate of unemployment hypothesis. The debate now is not over the existence of the natural rate, only the level.

By the late 1970s, Friedman — Nobel Prize in hand — was proven right about the power of monetary policy and the shaky relevance of fiscal policy. The Phillips Curve became unrecognizable as inflation and unemployment rose together. In a famous statement, British prime minister James Callaghan confessed in 1977, "We used to think you could spend your way out of a recession....I tell you, in all candor, that that option no longer exists; and that insofar as it ever did exist, it only worked by injecting bigger doses of inflation into the economy followed by higher levels of unemployment at the next step. That is the history of the past twenty years" (Skousen 2001:404).

Out of this Phillips Curve controversy arose a whole new "rational expectations" school, led by Robert Lucas, Jr., another Chicago economist who won the Nobel Prize in 1995. Rational expectations undermine the theory that policymakers can fool the public into false expectations about inflation. Accordingly, government policies are frequently ineffective in achieving their goals.

Friedman's Impact on Government Policy

It would be folly to declare that "Keynes is dead" as a result of Friedman's multi-level assault, however. In many ways, Keynesian economics is very much alive in the halls of Congress, the ivory tower of academia, and the Wall Street media. The development of Aggregate Supply and Demand analysis (AS-AD) in the textbooks revitalized new Keynesian theory by offering a plausible explanation for stagflation. In the words of G. K. Shaw, modern Keynesian theory "not only resisted the challenge but also underwent a fundamental metamorphosis, emerging ever more convincing and ever more resilient" (Shaw 1988:5). The remaining Keynesian precepts became a "permanent revolution."

The era of big government is far from over. Governments still run deliberate deficits during a recession. In today's conventional wisdom, Keynes's law (demand creates supply) reigns over Say's law (supply creates demand). The media assails the virtue of thrift in a downturn. When Congress passes a tax cut, financial commentators regularly warn, "If consumers save the tax rebate, it won't help the economy," and newspapers editorialize, "Save the Economy: Spend Your Tax Rebate!" Under the Keynesian banner, consumer spending — not saving, productivity, or entrepreneurship — drives the economy in the short run.

Yet, Friedman had changed the way economists and government officials viewed the world. Naive or crude Keynesianism is largely dead. Friedman's influence has been felt in the following ways:

1. **Fiscal vs. monetary policy**: Friedman's work has largely cast doubt on the effectiveness of fiscal policy in fighting recessions or inflation. New Keynesians emphasize an "activist" monetary policy. The battle has been fought, not so much in terms of fiscal vs. monetary policy, but "activism" (Keynesian) vs. "rules" (monetarists). In the 16th edition of his textbook, Paul Samuelson writes, "Fiscal policy is no longer a major tool of stabilization policy in the United States. Over the foreseeable future, stabilization policy will be primarily handled by Federal Reserve monetary policy" (Samuelson 1998:655). This statement, which in many ways is an admission of defeat, has been the same in recent editions.

2. **Anti-inflation policy**: As the quantity theory of money is once again accepted as sound policy, checking inflation has become a major goal of central banks of all major industrial nations. Both monetary growth and price inflation have been

substantially tempered since the mid-1980s. I call it the Friedman Effect.

It should be emphasized that Friedman is strongly opposed to "incomes policies," efforts by government to restrain inflationary pressure through wage-price-rent controls and guideposts. Under a competitive marketplace, all prices, wages, and interest rates should be free to rise or fall according to supply and demand. Friedman rejects Irving Fisher's and Henry Simons' price stabilization schemes, although the ultimate objective of Friedman's monetarist rule is to match the long-term growth rate of the economy and stabilize the price level. In the quantity theory of money, controlling M (money) is the key, not P (price level). "A rule in terms of the quantity of money seems to me far superior for both the short term and the long-term, than a rule in terms of price-level stabilization" (Friedman 1969:84).

3. **Monetarist Rule:** Friedman has little faith in an activist monetary policy. "Any system which gives so much power and so much discretion to a few men that mistakes—excusable or not—can have such far-reaching effects is a bad system" (Friedman 1982:50). As a result, Friedman favors Simons's approach of "rules" over "authorities," specifically a steady rise in the broad-based money supply (such as M2) equal to the long-run growth rate (and thus keeping prices relatively stable). In fact, according to Friedman, the Federal Reserve should be abolished and replaced by a computer. As we shall see in chapter 6, however, Friedman does suggest exceptions to this rule, such as Japan, where he supports "printing more yen" to jump start the Japanese economy in the short run. (In the long run, Friedman denies that monetary stimulus can affect output.)

4. **Decontrolling interest rates:** Friedman opposes central bank manipulation of the interest rates. The money supply should be controlled, but interest rates should fluctuate according to supply and demand, without regulation.

Friedman would close the discount window and the Fed policy of targeting short-term rates. Friedman initially won the debate when, on October 6, 1979, Fed chairman Paul Volcker announced that he was going to control monetary reserves, not interest rates. As a result, interest rates skyrocketed to 21% in the early 1980s, and broke the back of inflationary expectations in the U. S. However, gradually interest-rate manipulation has again become the focal point of stabilization policy, and it would be wrong to suggest that the Fed and other central banks now focus primarily on monetary targets rather than interest-rate targets. Given the uncertainty of velocity, and the difficulty in measuring the money supply, central banks have turned more to targeting short-term interest rates. As Joseph Stiglitz states, "monetarism [the Friedman idea that the central bank should be passive] has been discredited," and a monetarist rule is not likely to be adopted in the future. When a central bank is given power, it is likely to exercise it.

Friedman the Crusader

Since the 1960s, Friedman has taken a stronger interest in public debates, starting with *Capitalism and Freedom*, and writing a *Newsweek* column from 1966 to 1984. *Capitalism and Freedom*, based on a series of lectures given in the late 1950s at Wabash College, was published in 1962. This book is considered by most observers as his best book outlining a laissez faire philosophy and basic economic beliefs. It introduces some of his most controversial policy recommendations—flexible exchange rates, school vouchers, the negative income tax, and a list of 14 government programs that should be abolished (the draft is the only one abandoned so far).

It should be noted that George Stigler, Friedman's long-time colleague at Chicago in the 1960s and 1970s, differed when it came to crusading for causes. "The great economists...have not been preoccupied with preaching," he writes (Stigler 1982:5).[3] Rather Stigler believed more in minding the store, arguing that the key to long-term success is to change the minds of the intelligentsia, while Friedman campaigned to change the thinking of politicians, business leaders, and the general public.

Chile and the Chicago Boys

When Friedman received a Nobel Prize in 1976, he was greeted by protesters in Stockholm who were angry about his involvement in Chilean politics. He was regarded as the intellectual architect and unofficial advisor to the team of Chilean free-market economists known as the "Chicago Boys." These were Chilean economists mostly from the Catholic University of Chile who had been trained at the University of Chicago under a long-standing scholarship program with the guidance of professor Arnold C. Harberger. Chile had suffered a major economic crisis in the early 1970s under the first democratically elected Marxist, Salvador Allende. Allende's socialist policies of nationalization, high wages, and price controls created an economic disaster, and the military, led by General Augusto Pinochet, staged a coup d'etat in September 1973. Allende committed suicide. When the global inflationary recession made things worse in Chile, General Pinochet called in the Chicago Boys to reorganize the economy. They urged drastic cuts in government spending, denationalization, tax reform, expanded trade, and strict control of the money supply. Later, during the copper collapse of 1982, they recommended the first highly successful privatization of social security.[4] Because they were associated with a military regime

3 Stigler took a controversial position later in life that government programs under stable democracies were "efficient" like market economies, a view Friedman and other Chicagoans would not subscribe to (Stigler 1992). See chapter 7 for a discussion of this recent debate between Austrians, Chicagoans, and public-choice economists.

4 According to Harberger, the idea of privatization originated from the teacher's annuity plans, known as TIAA-CREF, or Teachers Insurance and Annuities Association/College Retirement Equities Funds, at the University of Chicago, where faculty were offered a choice of stock and bond funds. Chilean graduates and professors saw how well the teacher's annuities worked, and adopted the idea in Chile in the early 1980s, when the state pension system went bankrupt. (Private interview with Arnold C. Harberger at the Mont Pelerin Society meetings in Salt Lake City, August 18, 2004.)

known for its human-rights violations, critics labeled the economic policies of the Chicago Boys (and Friedman, by association) "draconian" and "anti-progressive." Nevertheless, Chile recovered and achieved an economic miracle of high economic growth, low inflation, and a booming export market. Under the direction of the Chicago Boys, Chile has become the new economic model for Latin America.

One of the characteristics that distinguished Friedman from other free-market proponents is his willingness to dialogue and debate his critics. In January 1980, Milton and his wife, Rose, produced a television miniseries broadcast on the Public Broadcasting System (PBS) called "Free to Choose," aimed at spreading free-market ideas to the general public. The Friedmans called the ten-part series "the most exciting venture of our lives" (Friedman 1998:471). Each program began with a public lecture by Friedman, followed by a lively debate among advocates and dissenters. Topics included "Who Protects the Consumer?", "Who Protects the Worker?" and "How to Cure Inflation." The programs had an international flavor, with filming and commentary in the United States, Europe, and Asia. Hong Kong was presented as a showcase of the benefits of free markets under the most adverse circumstances. Over three million Americans viewed "Free to Choose," and their book of the same name eventually sold over a million copies.

Friedman retired from the University of Chicago in 1977, accepting a position at the Hoover Institution at Stanford University in California. He and Rose have been actively involved in the Mont Pelerin Society and various public causes, including tax limitation. Friedman acted as an informal advisor to President Ronald Reagan, as he had previously done with President Richard Nixon and presidential candidate Barry Goldwater. In the late 1990s, he established the Milton and Rose D. Friedman Foundation to promote the use of school vouchers as a means of improving public education, especially among disadvantaged families. "Schooling is one of the technically most backward of our major industries," Friedman states (1998:349).

Milton's Paradise: The Invisible Hand of Liberty

In sum, Milton Friedman's whole body of work has focused on dismantling the "house that Keynes built" and leading economists back to the foundations of Adam Smith and his "system of natural liberty." Shorn of government mismanagement, capitalism is not inherently unstable or irrational, as the Keynesians and Marxists allege. As Friedman himself declared after he wrote *A Monetary History*, "It is now widely agreed that the Keynesian proposition is erroneous on the level of pure theory.....[T]here always exists in principle a position of full employment equilibrium in a free market economy" (Friedman and Meiselman 1963:167).

There is no better example of the influence of Friedman than the shift back to the classical model in the textbooks, as exemplified by the popular textbooks of Harvard's Gregory Mankiw. In his textbook *Macroeconomics*, written in the early 1990s, Mankiw surprised the profession by beginning with the classical model and placing the Keynesian model at the end, reversing the standard Samuelson approach. In essence, he contradicts Keynes. Now the classical model is the "general" theory, and the Keynesian model a "special" case for the short term. In the preface, Mankiw justifies his new pedagogy, stating that "in the aftermath of the Keynesian revolution, too many economists forgot that classical economics provides the right answers to many fundamental questions" (Mankiw 1994:preface). Mankiw's textbook shows that, under the classical model, which he dubs "the real economy in the long run," government spending crowds out private capital; saving and capital formation rather than government programs serve as the key determinant of economic growth; excessive unemployment is caused by state interference with the "natural" rate; and inflation is a monetary phenomenon—all Friedmanite themes.

Perhaps Lawrence Summers, Harvard economist who served as chairman of President Bill Clinton's economic team, best reflects the attitude of his former critics when he writes, "He [Friedman] was a Devil figure in my youth...Only with time have I come to have large amounts of grudging respect. And with time increasingly ungrudging respect" (Stanislaw 2004:10).

George Stigler and the Adam Smith Model of Competition

Friedman was not alone in doing battle with the critics of capitalism. At Chicago, he had a partner. Friedman was known as "Mr. Macro," and George Stigler (1911-91) was known as "Mr. Micro." While Friedman studied money, credit, and macroeconomics, Stigler emphasized price theory, industrial organization, and microeconomics. Friedman and Stigler were opposites physically, yet saw eye to eye politically, although Stigler was never a crusader or reformer like Friedman is. In the early 1950s, Friedman began his famous Money and Banking Workshop; when Stigler came over from Columbia University to join the Graduate School of Business and the economics department at Chicago, a joint appointment in 1958, he began the Industrial Organization Workshop.[5]

As noted at the beginning of this chapter, the attack on free-market capitalism had been two-fold in the 1930s: on the macro side, Keynes accused the market economy of being inherently unstable and created a "countercyclical stabilization" model to offset the boom-bust cycle of capitalism. On the micro side, Edward H. Chamberlin in *The Theory of Monopolistic Competition* (1933) and Joan Robinson in *Economics of Imperfect Competition* (1933) independently challenged the classical model of competition, arguing that the modern industrial economy was defective and that most market conditions were "imperfect" and "monopolistic." Both the Keynesian and

5 The Money and Banking Workshop is still in operation today at University of Chicago; the Industrial Organization Workshop was recently merged into an Applied Economics Workshop within the business school. The Center for the Study of the Economy and the State, reflecting Chicago political economy, was established by George Stigler in 1977 and named the George J. Stigler Center in 1991. The latest addition is the Initiative on Chicago Price Theory, headed by Steven D. Levitt.

Chamberlin-Robinson theories captured the imaginations of the profession and have been an integral feature of textbooks ever since.

While Friedman took on the Keynesians, Stigler responded to the Robinson-Chamberlin "imperfect" competition model. This "Cambridge model," so called because Chamberlin taught at Harvard in Cambridge, Massachusetts, and Robinson taught at Cambridge University in England, has strong policy implications. They claimed that, since laissez faire is defective and cannot ensure efficient competition under market conditions, the government has an obligation to intervene through controls and antitrust measures to curtail the natural monopolistic tendencies of big business.

In the early 1950s, while at Columbia, Stigler was a firm defender of the Cambridge model and antitrust laws, just as Friedman had been sympathetic to Keynesian thinking in the early 1940s war years. Even Henry Simons had, at Chicago, taught that big business posed such a serious problem in the United States that he advocated the nationalization of railroads, utilities, and all other "uncompetitive" industries and placing severe "limitations upon the squandering of our resources in advertising and selling activities" (Simons 1948:51, 57). Stigler moved in a different direction, advocating the breakup of "concentrated" big businesses and punishing companies engaged in collusion. He appeared before Congress in 1950 advocating that U. S. Steel Corporation be dismantled.

However, influenced by the work of Joseph Schumpeter at Harvard and Aaron Director, creator of "law and economics" courses at the University of Chicago, Stigler shifted gears after moving to Chicago in 1958. Using the Chicago-style empirical approach, he and other colleagues, including Harold Demsetz and Sam Peltzman, amassed considerable data to demonstrate surprising price flexibility and competition among large companies, concluding that industry concentration did not necessarily lead to monopolistic pricing. Stigler concludes, "Competition is a tough weed, not a delicate flower" (Stigler 1988:104). As a result, the enthusiasm for antitrust legislation has diminished over the years, and Stigler's views evolved into what might be called "the Chicago school of anti-monopolistic competition." He writes, "What is still more embarrassing is that I no longer believe the economics I was preaching" (Stigler 1988:99). Today, due to the dominant influence of Stigler, a consistent Chicago technique has developed into what has been called the "Tight Prior Equilibrium Model" or the TP model, where equilibrium is virtually assumed in the marketplace. This style of reasoning is universally applied to any and all markets, including the political arena (Reder 1982:11-15).

Stigler was a pioneer in the economics of information. He noted that the unemployed are as much information seekers as job seekers, now known as "search unemployment" theory. He rejected Simons's attack on advertising. The overwhelming evidence compiled by Stigler recognized advertising "to be an extremely efficient way of conveying much...information" (Stigler 1988:164). In a seminal work published in the early 1970s, he developed his "capture theory" of regulation, demonstrating that producers capture the regulatory agency and use it to prevent competition (Stigler 1971).

Stigler's empirical work did not go unobserved. He became president of the AEA in 1964 and won the Nobel Prize in 1982 for his work on industrial organizations, the effects and causes of regulation, and the vital role of information seeking. Stigler's *Theory of Price* (1987 [1946]) was the most popular intermediate micro textbook, going through numerous editions (I learned microeconomics from the third 1966 edition). On a broader scale, the whole work of Friedman and Stigler was in a sense a reaffirmation of Adam Smith's "invisible hand" doctrine and a rejection of the political arm of government, on both a macro and micro level. Today a portrait of George Stigler hangs in the business school building at Chicago, with Stigler holding a copy of Adam Smith's *Wealth of Nations.*

May a Thousand Flowers Blossom: The Imperialism of the Chicago School

The Chicago school of Friedman and Stigler has spread its wings to the far reaches of academia and the halls of state power. As a result, economics is no longer the dismal science, but a new imperial science invading like an army the new frontiers of politics, law, crime, religion, sociology, history, and Wall Street. The combination of Chicago price theory and empirical research are powerful and immensely appealing weapons. The University of Chicago has dominated the Nobel Memorial Prize in economic science since its inception in 1969, much to the consternation of Keynesians, Marxists, and even Austrians. More than half the prizes were awarded to Chicago economists in the 1990s, including Ronald Coase, Gary Becker, Robert Fogel, and Robert Lucas, Jr.

The department of economics at Chicago has been responsible for several new schools developing over the years. Let's review the most prominent ones.

New Classical and Rational Expectations Theory

Friedman (and Mises earlier) raised the possibility that workers can't be fooled indefinitely by inflation, and that they would eventually demand higher real wages when inflation is anticipated. Under the works of John Muth, Thomas Sargent, and Chicago economist Robert Lucas, Jr. (winner of the Nobel Prize in 1995), most economists now recognize that government policies are frequently anticipated in the economy, thus making activist policies less effective, or even perverse. Thus the new classical school of "rational expectations" was born.

The rational expectations revolution has had broad influence in the policy arena, raising doubts about the efficacy of inflationary policies by central banks, the stimulating business-cycle effect of public works projects and tax cuts, and the ability of institutional money managers to outperform in an efficient market setting. Lucas demonstrated the futility of the Phillips curve, denying that creating higher inflation could in any way permanently increase employment, and shows the benefits of tax cuts in bringing about long-term economic growth rates (Lucas 1997 [1995]:233-34, 246-65).

Robert Fogel and the Birth of Cliometrics

One of the first academics to combine economics with history through rigorous quantitative methods was Chicago's Robert W. Fogel. Under the influence of Simon Kuznets and Fritz Machlup, Fogel applied advanced statistical analysis to a variety of economic issues, such as the railroads and slavery. He showed that railways, for example, were not the driving force behind American economic growth, and in his most controversial work, *Time on the Cross* (1974), coauthored with Stanley Engerman, he used painstaking research to demonstrate that large-scale plantation agriculture with its use of slave labor was more efficient than small-scale family farms in the North. Fogel was accused of being a racist, but finally felt some vindication for his revisionist work upon winning the Nobel prize in 1993, which he shared with historian Douglass C. North. (As noted in chapter 4, Austrians as well as other historians take strong exception to Fogel's findings on the profitability of the slavery system.) Recently Fogel has led a team of researchers at the University of Chicago compiling and interpreting a vast quantity of data on height by age and average nutritional status, taken from military records, in an effort to shed new light on measuring the quality of life beyond per capita income (Atack and Passell 1994:xvi-xviii).

Gary Becker and Socio-Economics

Gary Becker has been instrumental and daring in applying Chicago "rational choice" theory to human behavior, such as racial discrimination (his dissertation), crime, and marriage. His book titles reflect the broad scope of his work: *The Economics of Discrimination* (1957), *The Economic Approach to Human Behavior* (1976), and *A Treatise on the Family* (1981). Becker identifies his method as one involving the "combined assumptions of maximizing behavior, market equilibrium and stable preferences, used relentlessly and unflinchingly" (Becker 1976:5). He called a recent book, appropriately, *The Economics of Life* (1997). Many of his case studies involve the application of common sense market principles, such as "behavior responds to incentives." For example, in state welfare programs, higher unemployment benefits tends to increase the unemployment rate. "The offer of alms increases the supply of beggars" (Reder 1982:28). Becker applies the incentive principle to show that increasing the cost of crime through stiffer jail sentences, quicker trials, and higher conviction rates effectively reduces the number of criminals who rob, steal, or rape. "According to the economic approach, criminals, like everyone else, respond to incentives" (Becker 1997:143).

For his pathbreaking work in nontraditional areas, Becker won the Nobel Prize in 1992. In his Nobel lecture, he summarized the universal applications of his rational choice model:

"The analysis of discrimination includes in preferences a dislike of — prejudice against — members of particular groups, such as blacks or women. In deciding whether to engage in illegal activities, potential criminals are assumed to act as if they consider both the gains and risks — including the likelihood they will be caught and severity of punishments. In human capital theory, people rationally evaluate the benefits and costs of activities, such as education, training, expenditures on health, migration, and formation of habits that radically alter the way they are. The economic approach to the family assumes that even intimate decisions like marriage, divorce, and family size are reached through weighing the advantages and disadvantages of alternative actions. The weights are determined by preferences that critically depend on the altruism and feelings of duty and obligation toward family members (Becker 1997 [1992]:51).

Approval from other economists and social scientists was long in coming. "This work was not well received by most economists," Becker states, and his critics were "sometimes very nasty" (Becker 1997:3). George Stigler recalls, "I attended the conference at which Becker's paper [on the economics of having children] was presented in 1960. I still remember the tone of outrage with which a Harvard economist complained at the propriety of comparing babies with refrigerators and other durable consumer goods" (Stigler 1988:197). As a result of the works of Becker, Ronald Coase, Aaron Director, and other Chicago economists, a whole new discipline has developed in economics and the law. What are the financial consequences of gun control, drug laws, landlord restrictions, comparable worth rules, welfare, social insurance, and environmental regulations? Again, Chicago economics has been in the forefront of the process of analyzing the economic effects of civil and criminal law, with major contributions by Judge Richard Posner and law professor Richard Epstein, among others.

Under the influence of Gary Becker, a new research center called the Initiative on Chicago Price Theory was established in the fall of 2004. The first director of the center is Steven D. Levitt, co-author of the bestselling book *Freakonomics*, which applies price theory to the "riddles of everyday life, from cheating and crime to sports and child rearing," much in the tradition of Becker's work. According to Levitt, the center will soon be named after Becker. Founding members of the Initiative on Chicago Price Theory are Gary Becker and another protégé, Kevin M. Murphy, who applies microeconomic principles in the areas of inequality, unemployment, wages, health care and longevity. Interestingly, all three members of the new center—Becker, Murphy, and Levitt—are winners of the John Bates Clark Award, given to the brightest economists under the age of 40.

The Coase Theorem: "Eureka!"

One of the most influential Chicago economists is Ronald Coase, who won the Nobel Prize in 1991 for two articles, "The Nature of the Firm" (1937) and "The Problem of Social Cost" (1960), considered the most cited article in the history of economics. His seminal articles have given rise to the whole "law and economics" field. Coase rejects the traditional view, reflected in British economist Arthur C. Piguo's welfare economics and later in biologist Garrett Hardin's "tragedy of the commons," that government is wholly necessary to enforce property rights, that the only solution to pollution is to tax the polluter or subsidize the victim, and that without the power of the state, the economy could not function. Coase cleverly demonstrates that even without legal recourse, those damaged by theft or pollution have incentives to negotiate with the offenders, as long as the benefits exceed the cost, including the transaction costs of making a deal.

When Stigler heard of Coase's theorem, he rejected it outright, wondering "how so fine an economist could make such an obvious mistake" (Stigler 1988:75). Coase, who was then at the University of Virginia, was invited to the home of Aaron Director to defend himself before the entire Chicago faculty. Stigler reports the incident: "We strongly objected to his heresy. Milton Friedman did most of the talking, as usual. He also did much of the thinking, as usual. In the course of two hours of argument the vote went from twenty against and one for Coase to twenty-one for Coase. What an exhilarating event! I lamented afterward that we had not had the clairvoyance to tape it" (Stigler 1988:76; see also Reder 1982:22). Stigler concludes, "In the field of law and/or economics, B. C. means Before Coase" (Stigler 1992:456). The Coase theorem has had a broad impact on legal matters, such as divorce, contracts, lawsuits, and environmental issues. It explains, for example, why most lawsuits are settled out of court. It also lead to a rationale for the theory of the firm, the necessity of government, the social optimality of common law and voluntary arbitration proceedings, and why money developed (Coase 1997 [1991]: 13, 16-17).[6]

Buchanan, Tullock and Public Choice

During the 1950s and 1960s, *Public Finance in Theory and Practice* (1958) by Harvard professor Richard Musgrave was the standard textbook for students studying public policy. Musgrave saw the need for a three-pronged government policy: (1) allocation: to provide public goods that the private sector cannot or does not provide adequately; (2) distribution: to redistribute wealth and institute social justice; and (3) stabilization: to tame "unbridled capitalism." Musgrave defended social insurance, progressive taxation, and the growth of the public sector as the "price we pay for civilization."

However, during the ensuing half-century, the intellectual climate has shifted from the Harvard model of public finance (Musgrave's text is no longer in print) to the Virginia School of public choice, as founded by James Buchanan, Gordon Tullock, and Richard E. Wagner, among others, who developed their ideas while teaching at the University of Virginia. Buchanan, the acknowledged leader in the public choice school, is indebted to several scholars who influenced his thinking,

---

6 This is also another area that some Austrians criticize. Murray Rothbard, for example, rejects Chicago arguments of social efficiency in favor of natural rights in legal matters (Rothbard 1997:121-26).

including Frank Knight, Knut Wicksell, and Friedrich Hayek (Buchanan 2001:23). Buchanan would never classify himself as a "disciple of Hayek," but more perhaps as a "fellow traveler" with the Austrians, having borrowed many of their ideas. He was a dedicated "libertarian socialist" when he came to the University of Chicago in the 1940s, but was converted by Frank Knight to the principles of individualism, liberty, and the market process. As Buchanan himself admits, "Virginia Political Economy was born in the foyer of the Social Sciences Building at the University of Chicago in 1948" (Buchanan 2001:51). Using Chicago price and rational choice theory, the Virginia school extends market analysis to political decision-making and government institutions. After writing books such as *The Calculus of Consent* (1962), coauthored with Gordon Tullock, and *Democracy in Deficit*, coauthored with Richard E. Wagner (1977), Buchanan and Tullock started a new journal, *Public Choice*. In 1982, the public choice school shifted to George Mason University, where the Center for the Study of Public Choice is located.

Buchanan and associates built a model based on the fact that incentives and discipline of the marketplace are often missing from government policy. Voters in a democracy have little incentive to control the excesses of legislators, who in turn are more responsive to powerful interest groups.[7] As a result, government accepts the vested interests of commerce while imposing costly, wasteful regulations and taxes on the general public. The public choice school has shifted the debate from "market failure" to "government failure." Buchanan and others have recommended a series of constitutional rules to require the misguided public sector to act more responsibly, including requiring super-majorities to raise taxes, protecting minority rights, returning power to local governments, and imposing term limits. For his work, Buchanan won the Nobel Prize in 1986. Public-choice economists, including Austrians,

---

7 "The pessimistic conclusion of public choice theory rests upon the claim that it is interests rather than ideas that are the decisive causal factors in social affairs" (Barry 1987:195). Norman Barry says that this view is contrary to those of Mises, Hayek, and Keynes, who argue that ideas, not vested interests, dominate.

have recently taken exception to arguments put forth by George Stigler and Donald Wittman that government programs can operate "efficiently" in a strong democracy. See chapter 7 for a discussion of this recent debate.

Financial Economics and the Efficient Market Theory

The burgeoning field of modern portfolio theory, with its emphasis on competition and efficient markets, has its roots in Chicago. Harry Markowitz, then a graduate economics student, wrote an article on portfolio theory in the March 1952 issue of *The Journal of Finance*. It was the first attempt to quantify the economic concept of risk in stock and portfolio selection (it was Chicago's Frank Knight who wrote the seminal work, *Risk, Uncertainty and Profit*). Out of this work emerged modern portfolio theory and the "efficient market" theory, which argues that due to ubiquitous competition in the capital markets, insiders have difficulty achieving long-term advantage over the market in general, as measured by the S&P 500 or similar broad index. Therefore, they say, it is virtually impossible to outperform the market over the long term. Market efficiency also suggests that historical patterns are practically useless for predicting future returns. These ivory-tower theories were greeted with scorn by Wall Street professional managers, but were largely (but not completely) confirmed by numerous studies, including work by Eugene Fama at University of Chicago. Index funds, the economists' favorite investment vehicle, are now the largest type of mutual fund sold on Wall Street. Harry Markowitz, along with colleagues Merton Miller and William Sharpe, won the Nobel in 1990.

A new area of research called "behavioral finance" is developing at the University of Chicago under the pioneering work of Richard Thaler. (Robert Shiller at Yale and other social scientists work in this area as well.) In many ways, this new area of research is a significant break from the standard "perfect competition" or TP model of the Chicago school. The Chicago "misfit" Thaler (his words) and other behavioral economists question the principle of human rationality, arguing that investors, consumers, and business people don't always act according to the "rational economic man" standard, but instead suffer from overconfidence, overreaction, fear, greed, herding instincts, and other "animal spirits," to use John Maynard Keynes's colorful phrase. Austrians in the field of finance find some of this material appealing in their own critique of general equilibrium and perfectly competitive modeling (Skousen 1993:255-73).

The Chicago Credo

George Stigler, surveying the laundry list of Chicago influences in the social sciences, commented on the Chicago Credo: "As far back as I can remember, the Chicago economists have nourished a credo: people act efficiently in their own interests." Self-interest is not strictly a Chicago invention, of course; Adam Smith suggested it in 1776, and Hayek gave it "an elegant and powerful formulation" in his famous essay "The Use of Knowledge in Society" (Hayek 1984 [1948]). Stigler explains, "The basis of the credo is simply the fact that an economic actor on average knows better the environment in which he is acting and the probable consequences of his actions than an outsider, no matter how clever the outsider may be. I attribute the credo to Chicago only because that is where I learned it" (Stigler 1982b:11-12). The Chicago Credo is imperialistic, a powerful and versatile theory of competition and rationality which can produce suggestive hypotheses to tackle new problems. It extends "the theory of rational behavior to all areas of man's behavior" (Stigler 1982b:14).

The Disappearance of the Chicago School?

In 1982, Melvin Reder suggested that Chicago's success was due to scientific research and rationale for political conservatism, and "Chicago still wants to be the leading center of research and graduate instruction" (Reder 1982:33-35). Today Gary Becker suggests that the Chicago school is no longer distinctive enough from the mainstream discipline to be classified as a separate school. There used to be pockets of Chicago traditions, such as UCLA Economics Department, often called "The Chicago School of the West," the University of Virginia, and the St. Louis Fed, which focused primarily on monetary policy. But now, "its influence is so widespread and its techniques of empirical testing of data so pervasive that the Chicago school is losing its notoriety" (Becker, private interview). The Austrians publish their own journals, such as *The Review of Austrian Economics*, but Chicago's *The Journal of Political Economy* tends to be non-ideological.[8] Joseph Stiglitz claims that there is no longer a single Chicago school, but "many Chicago schools." That may be a sign of a sea change. Once the mainstream incorporates the heretical, the heretical is no longer out of the mainstream.

---

8 Gary Becker writes: "*The Journal of Political Economy* does not try to be the representative of the Chicago approach. Indeed, we are reluctant to publish articles that were Ph. D. dissertations at Chicago, or those by Chicago faculty. We aim to publish the most important articles on theoretical and applied topics in economics. Clearly, though, the articles sent to the *Journal* are biased in the direction of appealing to the interests of the department's editors" (private correspondence April 9, 2004).

References

Atack, Jeremy and Peter Passell. 1994. *A New Economic View of American History*. 2nd ed. New York: W. W. Norton.

Barry, Norman P. 1987. *On Classical Liberals and Libertarianism*. New York: St. Martin's Press.

Becker, Gary S. 1957. *The Economics of Discrimination*. Chicago: University of Chicago Press.

Becker, Gary S. 1976. *The Economic Approach to Human Behavior*. Chicago: University of Chicago Press.

Becker, Gary S. 1981. *A Treatise on the Family*. Cambridge: Harvard University Press.

Becker, Gary S. 1997 [1992]. "The Economic Way of Looking at Life." In Torsten Persson, ed., *Nobel Lectures in Economic Sciences, 1991-1995*. Singapore: World Scientific, 38-58.

Becker, Gary S. and Guity Nashat Becker. 1997. *The Economics of Life*. New York: McGraw-Hill.

Boettke, Peter J. 1995. "Hayek's Road to Serfdom revisited." *Eastern Economic Journal* 21:1 (Winter).

Block, Walter. 2002. "Henry Simons is Not a Supporter of Free Enterprise," *Journal of Libertarian Studies* 16:4 (Fall), 3-36.

Breit, William and Roger W. Spencer. 1982. *Lives of the Laureates: Seven Nobel Economists*. Cambridge: MIT Press.

Buchanan, James and Gordon Tullock. 1962. *The Calculus of Consent*. Ann Arbor: University of Michigan.

Buchanan, James and Richard E. Wagner. 1977. *Democracy in Deficit*. New York: Academic Press.

Buchanan, James M. 2001. *The Collected Works of James M. Buchanan: Ideas, Persons, and Events*. Vol. 19. Indianapolis: Liberty Fund.

Chamberlin, Edward H. 1933. *The Theory of Monopolistic Competition*. Cambridge: Harvard University Press.

Coase, Ronald H. 1937. "The Nature of the Firm." *Economica* 4 (November), 386-405.

Coase, Ronald H. 1960. "The Problem of Social Cost." *Journal of Law and Economics* 3 (October):1-44.

Coase, Ronald H. 1997 [1991]. "The Institutional Structure of Production." In Torsten Persson, ed., *Nobel Lectures in Economic Sciences 1991-1995*. Singapore: World Scientific, 11-20.

Davis, J. Ronnie. 1968. "Chicago Economists, Deficit Budgets, and the Early 1930's." *American Economic Review* 58 (June): 476-82.

Fogel, Robert W. and Stanley L. Engerman. 1974. *Time on the Cross.* Boston: Little, Brown.

Friedman, Milton. 1957. *Theory of the Consumption Function.* Princeton: Princeton University Press.

Friedman, Milton and David Meiselman. 1963. "The Relative Stability of Monetary Velocity and the Investment Multiplier in the United States, 1897-1958," in Commission on Money and Credit, *Stabilization Policies.* Englewood Cliffs, NJ: Prentice-Hall, 165-268.

Friedman, Milton and Anna J. Schwartz. 1963. *A Monetary History of the United States, 1867-1960.* Princeton, NJ: Princeton University Press.

Friedman, Milton. 1968. *Dollars and Deficits.* New York: Prentice-Hall.

Friedman, Milton and Walter W. Heller. 1969. *Monetary vs. Fiscal Policy.* New York: W. W. Norton.

Friedman, Milton. 1982 [1962]. *Capitalism and Freedom.* Chicago: University of Chicago Press.

Friedman, Milton. 1991. *Monetarist Economics.* Oxford: Basil Blackwell.

Friedman, Milton and Rose. 1998. *Two Lucky People.* Chicago: University of Chicago Press.

Galbraith, John Kenneth. 1975 [1965]. "How Keynes Came to America." In Milo Keynes, ed., *Essays on John Maynard Keynes.* Cambridge: Cambridge University Press, 132-41.

Hayek, Friedrich A. 1984 [1948]. "The Use of Knowledge in Society," in Chiaki Nishiyama and Kurt R. Leube, eds., *The Essence of Hayek.* Stanford: Hoover Press, 211-24.

Hazlitt, Henry. 1959. *Failure of the New Economics.* New York: Arlington House.

Hazlitt, Henry. 1977. *The Critics of Keynesian Economics.* 2nd ed. New York: Arlington House.

Hutt, William. 1979 [1963]. *The Keynesian Episode: A Reassessment.* Indianapolis: Liberty Press.

Johnson, Harry G. 1975. *On Economics and Society.* Chicago: University of Chicago Press.

Keynes, John Maynard. 1931. *Essays in Persuasion.* New York: W. W. Norton.

Keynes, John Maynard. 1973 [1936]. *The General Theory of Employment, Interest, and Money.* New York: Macmillan.

Knight, Frank H. 1948. "Preface for the Reprint of 1948." *Risk, Uncertainty, and Profit.* New York: Harper & Row.

Leeson, Robert. 2000. *The Eclipse of Keynesianism: The Political Economy of the Chicago Counter-Revolution*. New York: Palgrave.

Levitt, Steven D. and Stephen J. Dubner. 2005. *Freakonomics*. New York: William Morrow.

Lucas, Robert E., Jr. 1997 [1995]. "Monetary Neutrality." *Nobel Lectures in Economic Sciences*. Singapore: Nobel Foundation, 246-65.

Mankiw, N. Gregory. 1994. *Macroeconomics*. 2nd. New York: Worth.

Musgrave, Richard A. 1958. *Public Finance in Theory and Practice*. New York: Macmillan.

Nelson, Robert H. 2001. *Economics as Religion: From Samuelson to Chicago and Beyond*. University Park, Penns: Pennsylvania State University Press.

Patinkin, Don. 1981. *Essays on and In the Chicago Tradition*. Durham, NC: Duke University Press.

Persson, Toresten, ed. *Nobel Lectures in Economic Sciences, 1991-1995*. Singapore: World Scientific, 1997.

Phillips, A. W. H. 1958. "The Relation Between Unemployment and the Rate of Change of Money Wage Rates in the United Kingdom, 1861-1957." *Economica* 29:1-16.

Reder, Melvin W. 1982. "Chicago Economics: Permanence and Change." *Journal of Economic Literature* (March), 1-38.

Robinson, Joan. 1933. *Economics of Imperfect Competition*. Cambridge: Cambridge University Press.

Rothbard, Murray N. 1960. "Review of Hazlitt's *Critics of Keynesian Economics*," *National Review* (3 December): 150-51.

Rothbard, Murray N. 1962. *Man, Economy and State*. Princeton: Van Nostrand.

Rothbard, Murray N. 1963. *America's Great Depression*. Princeton: Van Nostrand.

Rothbard, Murray N. 1997. *The Logic of Action II: Applications and Criticisms from the Austrian School*. Cheltenham, UK: Edward Elgar.

Samuelson, Paul A. 1955. *Economics*. 3rd ed. New York: McGraw-Hill.

Samuelson, Paul A. 1977. *The Collected Scientific Papers of Paul A. Samuelson*. Vol. 4. Cambridge: MIT Press.

Samuelson, Paul A. And William D. Nordhaus. 1998. *Economics*. 16th ed. New York: McGraw-Hill.

Shaw, G. K. 1988. *Keynesian Economics: The Permanent Revolution*. Hants, UK: Edward Elgar.

Shils, Edward, ed. 1991. *Remembering the University of Chicago: Teachers, Scientists, and Scholars.* Chicago: University of Chicago Press.

Simons, Henry. 1948. *Economic Policy for a Free Society.* Chicago: University of Chicago Press.

Skousen, Mark, ed. 1992. *Dissent on Keynes: A Critical Appraisal of Keynesian Economics.* New York: Praeger.

Skousen, Mark. 1993. *Economics on Trial: Lies, Myths and Realities.* Homewood, IL: Business One Irwin.

Skousen, Mark. 2001. *The Making of Modern Economics.* New York: M. E. Sharpe.

Stanislaw, Joseph A. 2004. "Controversies Among Free Marketeers," in Richard M. Ebeling, ed., *Economics Theories and Controversies.* Hillsdale, MI: Hillsdale College, 1-12.

Stigler, George J. 1971. "The Theory of Economic Regulation." *Bell Journal of Economics and Management Science* 2:1, 3-21.

Stigler, George J. 1982. *The Economist as Preacher, and Other Essays.* Chicago: University of Chicago Press.

Stigler, George J. 1982b. *Economists and the Public Policy.* Washington, DC: American Enterprise Institute.

Stigler, George J. 1987 [1946]. *Theory of Price.* New York: Prentice Hall.

Stigler, George J. 1988. *Memoirs of an Unregulated Economist.* New York: Basic Books.

Stigler, George J. 1992. "Law or Economics?" *Journal of Law and Economics* 35:455-468 (October).

Chapter Four

METHODENSTREIT

SHOULD A THEORY BE EMPIRICALLY TESTED?

Its particular theorems are not open to any verification or falsification on the grounds of experience.

—Ludwig von Mises, *Human Action* (1966 [1949]:862)

When you cannot express it in numbers, your knowledge is of a meager and unsatisfactory kind.

—Lord Kelvin, inscription on the front of the Chicago Social Science Building

Probably the most important reason why the Chicago school has been more influential than the Austrian school is because of their sharply differing methodologies. Misesians, those Austrians who follow religiously the works of Ludwig von Mises, adopt what Murray Rothbard calls "radical apriorism," using solely deductive reasoning without resorting to historical data or experience to corroborate their theories (Mises 1966:41, 862; Rothbard 1997:100-08). To the extent that Mises, Rothbard and other Austrians interpret history, they do so in terms of subjective motivations and understanding of the individual players and institutions involved, rather than a "laboratory [of historical data] in which economic theory is continually being tested" (Salerno 2002:8). Austrians reject mathematical formulas and econometric modeling, or any kind of empirical methods to "test" or "prove" an economic hypothesis. To them economics is qualitative, and most of the works by Austrians are largely theoretical and subjective (Rothbard 1995).

Misesians are highly critical of "scientism," attempts to imitate the physical sciences in economics (Hayek 1955).

On the other hand, Chicago economists from Milton Friedman to Robert Fogel have linked theory with history. As noted earlier, according to Gary Becker, the Chicago school under Friedman and Stigler practically invented the method of testing theories with detailed empirical evidence. Following the dictum of physicist Lord Kelvin, quantitative research is now almost universally applied by economists in major universities around the world, and it would be difficult to obtain a Ph. D. in economics without doing empirical work, or at a minimum, taking courses in econometrics and statistics.[1] Chicago economist Robert Fogel has been in the forefront of the "new economic history" (Jonathan Hughes' phrase) and "historical economics" (D. N. McCloskey's term), i.e., applying economic theory and high-powered statistical methods to quantitative economic data (Fogel 1971). Historical economics has taken the profession by storm and remains extremely popular (Atack and Passell 1994:xiv). Friedman describes the Chicago approach as follows: "In discussions of economic science, 'Chicago' stands for an approach that takes seriously the use of economic theory as a tool for analyzing a startlingly wide range of concrete problems, rather than as an abstract mathematical structure of great beauty but little power; for an approach that insists on empirical testing of theoretical generalizations and rejects alike facts without theory and theory without facts" (Friedman 1974:11). Chicago economists are convinced that much of their quantitative work has persuaded the profession to abandon unadulterated Keynesianism and adopt the benefits of market economics. Stigler even suggests that professional empirical work ("scientific training") is precisely what has led economists to become more "conservative" (Stigler 1965:61, 63, Reder 1982:35).

1 Chicago's empirical testing approach has been so universally adopted by the economics profession that Jesus Huerta de Soto (Universidad de Rey Juan Carlos) combines the Chicago school with the Keynesians into a general "neoclassical" school (Huerta de Soto 1998:75 passim).

Friedman refers to three methodological approaches to theory and history among economists, as reflected in the diagram (figure 4.1) below.

| THEORY WITHOUT HISTORY | THEORY AND HISTORY | HISTORY WITHOUT THEORY |

Figure 4.1. Three methodological views

Theory without history represents pure abstract reasoning and high theory, a technique used not only by many Austrians but also by David Ricardo and Paul Samuelson. The constant testing of theory with history is the Chicago view (the middle ground). And history without theory is the viewpoint of the institutional school, as reflected by the German historical school in the 19th century, and Wesley C. Mitchell, Columbia professor and founder of the American National Bureau of Economic Research (NBER), the foremost economics research center in the United States.

History Without Theory: A Brief Review

The first battle of methods, Methodenstreit, occurred in the late 19th century between the German historical school and Carl Menger. Classical economics had reached a standstill in Germany, where professors rejected the idea of a dependable economic theory. The German historical school, founded by Wilhelm Roscher, Bruno Hildebrand, and Karl Knies, reacted negatively to the English Enlightenment and classical economics. They disliked both the deductive methods and laissez-faire conclusions of Smith, Malthus, and Ricardo. According to the Germans, there could be no scientific economic "laws" separate from politics, custom, and the legal system; in fact, the state was paramount in establishing customs and academic politics. Only through the study of history, they maintain, could scholars come to any conclusions about political economy. Gustav Schmoller, an extreme member, went so far as to declare publicly that members of the "abstract" classical school were unfit to teach in a German university. "Under the onslaughts of the Historical School," Hayek writes, "not only were the classical doctrines completely abandoned—but any attempt at theoretical analysis came to be regarded with deep distrust" (Hayek 1976:13). Carl Menger wrote his breakthrough treatise *Grundsätze* specifically to convince the Germans that universal scientific laws of economics do exist, and that he had developed the principles to prove it. He even dedicated his book to Dr. Wilhelm Roscher of the German school. But it was all in vain. The Germans rejected Menger's "general theory of the good," time structure of production, marginal utility analysis, opportunity cost, and origin of money. Schmoller called Menger's book "useless." Menger responded in kind: Schmoller was like someone who came to a building site, dumped some materials on the ground, and declared himself an architect, he said.[2]

Germany's rejection of the Austrian vision of marginalism and neoclassical analysis was Germany's loss. Fortunately, the rest of the West picked up on Austrian breakthroughs, and within a generation most of their principles were adopted in the major textbooks, including the works of Alfred Marshall, Philip Wicksteed, and Frank Fetter. As Sherwin Rosen states, "The Austrian approach dominated American economics at the turn of the century" (1997:151). It is interesting that the Austrians under Mises would later move to the other extreme, and adopt an economic science purely theoretical without the confirmation of history, thus suffering the loss of its status among economists.

In the United States, institutionalist Wesley C. Mitchell was known as the "man without theory." Ironically, Mitchell

---

2 Bruce Caldwell offers a comprehensive review of the battle of methods between the Germans and the Austrians. See Caldwell 2004:64-99.

received his Ph. D. from the University of Chicago in the 1890s, but this occurred far before Friedman and Stigler came along. In establishing NBER, Mitchell was determined to avoid political prejudices of any kind. Considered a gentleman, scholar, and athlete, the moderate Mitchell was tolerant to a fault and hated divisiveness in academia and research. Joseph Dorfman, a colleague at Columbia, said Mitchell never spoke unkind words about another worker. At NBER, his vision was that intelligent men of all philosophies, whether socialists or anarchists, could "work harmoniously" on objective data so that reason could triumph over passion. He was friendly with socialist Thorstein Veblen and market economist Milton Friedman.

Mitchell wrote an exhaustive study entitled *Business Cycles* (1913), which formed the basis of his scrupulously conducted scientific research. Mitchell gathered around him some remarkable researchers, including Simon Kuznets, Arthur F. Burns, Geoffrey Moore, and Milton Friedman, and insisted on the highest standards of meticulous research. If Mitchell could be faulted, it was for his lack of theory. In his lifelong work on business cycles, he made every effort to hide his beliefs and warned repeatedly that NBER work was to be devoid of personal biases. By 1953, however, he admitted the advantage of testing theories. All theories needed to be tested, "checked out and corrected by inductive investigation" (Mitchell 1953:11). But the focus was always on the data, not the theory.

Abstract Model-Building, Mathematics, and the Ricardian Vice

On the other extreme are the thinkers who developed economic principles without historical evidence. Ludwig von Mises wasn't the first economist to develop an economic system based solely on abstract reasoning. The British financier and economist David Ricardo is considered the founder of technical economics, a rigorous science involving mathematical precision. He had a remarkable gift for abstract reasoning, developing a simple analytical model involving only a few variables that yielded, after a series of manipulations, powerful conclusions. Never mind that the assumptions in his "corn model" were misconceived, leading to a wrong-headed labor theory of value that gave ammunition to socialists and Marxists. It is the method that counts, he believed, and his model-building approach would be adopted by many prominent economists, including John Maynard Keynes, Paul Samuelson and Milton Friedman, leading to the development of econometrics. As Mark Blaug states, "If economics is essentially an engine of analysis, a method of thinking rather than a body of substantial results, Ricardo literally invented the technique of economics" (Blaug 1978:140).

Ricardo's *On the Principles of Political Economy and Taxation* (1817) differs significantly from Adam Smith's *Wealth of Nations* (1776). Smith's work (greatly admired by Chicago economists) is a combination of theory and history, vibrant and full of life, peppered with colorful historical examples, such as the pin factory. But Ricardo's *Principles* is tedious and abstract, full of Euclidian-like deductions with no historical case studies. Students often called it "Ricardo's book of headaches."

Ricardo's technique has been both praised and damned. Friedman considers Ricardo one of the greatest economists since Adam Smith for pioneering this method, although he would insist on the testing of a theory. Any purely theoretical work without reference to data would be in the Ricardian tradition. Paul Samuelson used this Ricardian technique in his *Foundations of Economic Analysis* (1947), which consists wholly of "abstract methodology" (his words), differential equations and assumptions far removed from reality. Samuelson, in fact, has never done much empirical work in his career, which may explain his recent decline in stature, despite the fact that he was the first American to win the Nobel Prize in Economics.

(Interestingly, it was George Stigler who influenced Samuelson to use mathematics in economics, and Henry Hazlitt who influenced Samuelson to go into economics.) Neo-Ricardian socialist Piero Sraffa's *Production of Commodities by Means of Commodities* (1960) is entirely abstract. As Mark Blaug comments, "Sraffa's book is after all a perfect example of what some economists have come to believe is wrong with economics: there is hardly a sentence in the book which refers to the real world" (Blaug 1975:28). One might say the same about Keynes's *General Theory*, another book of headaches. It is full of technical jargon and incomprehensible language. As Paul Samuelson notes, "It is a badly written book, poorly organized.....It abounds in mares' nests or confusions....Flashes of insight and intuition intersperse tedious algebra. An awkward definition suddenly gives way to an unforgettable cadenza. When finally mastered, its analysis is found to be obvious and at the same time new. In short, it is a work of genius" (Samuelson 1947:148-89).

Meanwhile, critics of Ricardo and his followers label his technique "the Ricardian vice." Blackboard economics (as Ronald Coase calls it) strips economics of its past, present, and future. Chronic divorcing of theory from history, and focusing too much on mathematical model building, can create false and unrealistic economics, which Ricardo demonstrated with his "corn model" and labor theory of value. French contemporary J.-B. Say accused Ricardo of creating a model full of "gratuitous assertions" and "systems ...formed before facts have been established." Say added, "Nothing can be more idle than the opposition of theory to practice!" Writing to Robert Malthus, he exclaimed, "It is better to stick to facts and their consequences than to syllogisms." He lauded Adam Smith for assembling "the soundest principles of political economy, supported by luminous illustrations," but added that economists like Ricardo who don't support their theories with facts are "but idle dreamers, whose theories, at best only gratifying literary curiosity, [are] wholly inapplicable in practice" (Say 1880:xvii, xxi, xxxv). "The origin of the misapprehension upon which the whole of economic theory is based must be traced to David Ricardo," writes Elton Mayo, a business professor at Harvard (1945:38). Mayo blames Ricardo's unrealistic theoretizing on his background as a stockbroker, because finance and speculating in government bonds (Ricardo's specialty) were far removed from the producing economy.

Mathematical model-building entered the economic arena with the marginalist revolution in the 1870s, when Stanley Jevons and especially Leon Walras began using formal equations (but not Carl Menger, who preferred a verbal approach). Jevons contends that "all economic writers must be mathematical so far as they are scientific at all" (Jevons 1965 [1879]:xxi). Alfred Marshall, who did more than anyone to turn economics into a scientific discipline, uses mathematics and graphics extensively, though in his textbook's appendixes only. "I think you should do all you can to prevent people from using Mathematics in cases in which the English language is as short as the Mathematical" (Groenewegen 1995:413).

Samuelson took exception to Marshall's mathematical agnosticism. He "exactly reversed" Marshall's view, and preferred mathematical formulas to the traditional literary style. Samuelson and John Hicks in England led the way by converting the geometry of the 1930s to the multivariate calculus of the 1950s and 1960s. In the 1940s, John von Neumann and Oskar Morgenstern (an Austrian) added game theory. In 1945, George Stigler was the first economist to use linear programming. By 1964, Samuelson proclaimed victory: "Economics has become mathematical and technical as never before" (Samuelson 1972:xii). Indeed, by the early 1980s, a full 96 percent of all papers published in the *American Economic Review* were primarily mathematical in nature. Nearly 38 percent made no reference to historical facts at all (McCloskey 1998 [1995]:139-40).

For a while, the mathematical victory was so complete that almost every school, including Marxists, took up analytical geometry, differential equations, and least-squares regressions. "Theorems, lemmas, and mathematics are in. English is out," reports Arjo Klamer and David Colander (1990:4). However, surveys by Klamer and Colander show that graduate students in economics are depressed by academia's Ricardian vice, the growing division between high theory and reality. "Why did we get this gut feeling that much of what went on there was a waste?" (Klamer and Colander 1990:xiv). Robert Kuttner remarks, "Departments of economics are graduating a generation of *idiots savants*, brilliant at esoteric mathematics but innocent of actual economic life" (Kuttner 1985:74). And Michio Morishima agrees: "Mathematical economic theory has recently become more and more abstract, transparent and sterile" (Morishima 1976:viii).

Mises and Extreme Apriorism

Ludwig von Mises rejected the use of mathematics in economics, but by no means abandoned abstract theorizing. In fact, Mises's methodology is quite unreal. Mises's books contain no charts, tables, or graphs. His 1912 *Theory of Money and Credit* makes frequent reference to monetary history, but his later works are largely devoid of historical analysis. They contain no mathematical formulas or econometric models, no empirical studies, no quantitative proofs of any economic theory, not even supply and demand schedules, which Mises describes as "two hypothetical curves" (Mises 1966:333). Larry Wimmer, professor at Brigham Young University and a Chicago graduate, attended a weeklong seminar at the Foundation for Economic Education in the late 1960s. At the time Mises was the resident scholar and dominated the group's thinking. During a discussion, Wimmer went to the blackboard and proceeded to draw a supply and demand curve. He was immediately reprimanded for using such a "distorted" device. It was clear his Chicago viewpoint was not acceptable at FEE.

Mark Blaug comments, "In the 1920s, Mises made important contributions to monetary economics, business cycle theory and of course socialist economics, but his later writings on the foundations of economic science are so cranky and idiosyncratic that we can only wonder that they have been taken seriously by anyone" (Blaug 1980:93). "Cranky" and "idiosyncratic" indeed. Mises claimed in *Human Action* that the only pure economic science is radical apriorism—using pure deductive reasoning without the help of experience to establish first principles. Under the influence of German philosopher Immanuel Kant, who was convinced that reason alone, contra empiricism and historicism, could give universal knowledge, Mises built his entire system on logic and self-evident assumptions, similar to geometry (Selgin 1990:13). Mises rejected all forms of inductive aposteriorism, or the use of empirical studies or history to prove or disprove a theory. "The theorems of economics are derived not from the observation of facts, but through deduction from the fundamental category of action" (Mises 1960:17). Furthermore, Mises solemnly declared, "Its particular theorems are not open to any verification or falsification on the grounds of experience" (1966:862). Further, he claimed, "History cannot teach us any general rule, principle, or law....History speaks only to those people who know how to interpret it on the grounds of correct theories" (1966:41). Jesus Huerta de Soto agrees: "In other words, statistics and empirical studies cannot provide any theoretical knowledge" (Huerta de Soto 1998:88).

Mises rejected econometrics and mathematics in economics, and apparently even the use of graphs. "The mathematical method must be rejected not only on account of its barrenness. It is an entirely vicious method, starting from false assumptions and leading to fallacious inferences.....There is no such thing as quantitative economics" (1966:350-51; cf. Huerta de Soto 1998:84-85). Peter Boettke adds, "Austrians have traditionally rejected calculus, topology, and other mathematical methods on philosophical grounds" since economics essentially involves "individuals acting under the inescapably subjective conditions of time passage, ignorance, and genuine uncertainty" (Boettle and Prychitko 1994:288). In this regard, Mises strongly differed with his younger brother, Richard von Mises (1883-1954), professor of applied mathematics at Harvard. Richard, author of a book entitled *Positivism* (1951), favored logical positivism, applying empirical evidence to test one's theories. Murray Rothbard, who studied under Ludwig von Mises in New York, once asked Ludwig what he thought of his brother's book. "Mises drew himself up into an uncharacteristically stern pose, eyes flashing: 'I disagreed with that book from the first sentence until the last.' It was not a tone that invited further inquiry" (Rothbard 1988:79).

Mises Adopts Methodological Dualism

Mises separated the social from the physical sciences, dubbing the social sciences *praxeology*, or the study of human action. Mises was a dualist who divided nature into two components:

1. Human beings, who think, adopt values, make choices, and learn from the past (the social sciences).

2. Animals and things (organic and inorganic matter), which are mechanical and predictable (biological and physical sciences).

As Mises explains, "Reason and experience show us two separate realms.....No bridge connects—as far as we can see today—these two spheres" (1966:18). Such a view suggests that Mises, who expressed support in other writings for Darwinian evolution, would reject the modern-day notion that man is nothing more than a "moral animal." Mises firmly believed in the free will of humans. Mises and Hayek were critical of attempts by economists to imitate the physical sciences with terms such as "elasticity," "velocity," and "frictional unemployment." Hayek, Rothbard and other Austrians scornfully refer to such attempts as "scientism."

Predicting the Future: Causality vs. Uncertainty

Mises points to two principles in economic behavior that often work against each other, making it difficult to make accurate forecasts. The first principle is causality—for every cause there is an effect. As Mises states, "Human action is purposeful behavior" (1966:11). Yet, at the same time, there is the principle of uncertainty. People have multiple reasons for acting and they sometimes change their minds. It is simply impossible to know what everyone is doing and why. The complexity of knowledge often makes us ignorant and incapable of knowing the future—of stock prices, new products, changing consumer demand, and government policies. An astronomer can know the exact time the sun will come up in the morning, but can anyone predict precisely when a student will get out of bed in the morning? Thus, sophisticated computer models that make forecasts about interest rates, inflation, and the movement of the financial markets are almost always off the mark. The high degree of ignorance in the economy is one reason Mises and Hayek dismissed the efficacy of socialist central planning. Hayek, in particular, wrote extensively on "the unavoidable imperfection of man's knowledge" and the "unintended consequences" of man's actions (Hayek 1984:211-80).

Mises believed that the principle of uncertainty overwhelmed causality, that individuals can seldom predict accurately, nor can patterns be discernible. Regarding his anticipation of the 1929-33 economic crisis, he wrote that, even though he had foreseen these events, he could not predict "the exact date of their occurrence" (1971 [1934]:15). Elsewhere he writes, "There are no rules according to which the duration of the boom or the following depression can be computed" (1966:870-71). Efforts to apply statistical methods over long periods of economic history to discern patterns must inevitably be in vain, since, according to Mises, "History is not repetitious" (Mises 1985:219).

Hayek Shifts Ground

Hayek's position has always been more flexible than Mises in regard to his approach to economics. In 1923, Hayek spent a year in New York and met with Wesley C. Mitchell at Columbia. Impressed by the statistical work being done at NBER, Hayek returned to Vienna and convinced Mises to set up the Austrian Institute of Business Cycle Research. Throughout the 1920s, Hayek and the Institute published statistical reports on economic conditions in Europe and America. Hayek indicated that doing such empirical work helped him pinpoint the beginning of the collapse in the world economy in 1929-30 (Machlup 1976:17). When he delivered six lectures on the Austrian theory of the business cycle at the London School of Economics in 1931, he used graphs rather extensively, known as Hayekian triangles, to elucidate the Hayek-Mises macro model of the intertemporal capital-using economy (see figure 4.2 below).

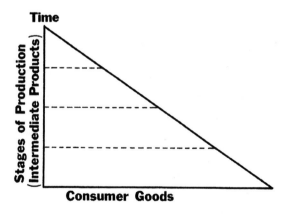

Figure 4.2. Hayek's triangles

These lectures were later published as *Prices and Production* (1931). By contrast, Mises's explanation of the business cycle in *The Theory of Money and Credit* (1971 [1934]), published originally in German in 1912, is entirely literary. Yet Hayek's triangles were highly theoretical, and Hayek made no attempt to link the theoretical stages of production to actual annual statistics for each stage that was available at the time, such as raw commodities, manufacturing, wholesale, and retail stages. This lack of empirical references in Hayek limited his influence.[3]

In a series of articles in *Economica* in 1942-44, Hayek joined Mises in criticizing economists who "slavishly imitate" the method and language of the natural sciences, labeling such behavior "scientism" (Hayek 1942-44; 1955; 1967). Friedrich Hayek's popular work *The Road to Serfdom* (1944) makes little attempt to apply his theories to historical evidence. They are general philosophical works. However, Milton Friedman notes a difference in *The Constitution of Liberty* (1960), published when Hayek was at Chicago. "*The Constitution of Liberty* is Hayek's descent into the Chicago school. It's the only one of his works that makes extensive reference to absolute experience" (Ebenstein 2003:141).[4] In short, it appears that Hayek gradually shifted away from the Misesian apriorism toward some form of positivist empiricism, but judging from his writings in later years, it was only a marginal and temporary shift.

Chicago's Arnold Harberger tells the story of Hayek's visit to Chile in 1975 after he won the Nobel Prize. A large audience attended ·his speech, where Chileans hoped to benefit from Hayek's wisdom is solving its economic crisis. According to Harberger, Hayek's policy recommendations were shockingly impractical and idealistic. He advocated abolishing immediately all trade restrictions, the income tax, and the central bank. "He was remote from the real world," Harberger reports. At the same time, the Chicago boys in Chile had developed a practical plan of gradually solving Chile's inflation, trade and other problems, most of which were adopted in the late 1970s. "But Hayek had no link to the Chicago plan. He was off in his own world."[5]

3 For an attempt to apply Hayekian triangles to a 4-stage macro model reflecting modern data, see my book *The Structure of Production* (1990). These stages are resources (raw commodities, research and development), production (manufacturing, construction), distribution (wholesale trade, shipping), and consumption (retail sales, used goods).

4 According to Peter Boettke, both Friedman and Hayek influenced each other. Friedman's *Free to Choose* (1980) contains Hayekian themes.

Murray Rothbard and Israel Kirzner

Both Israel Kirzner and Murray Rothbard considered themselves devout students of Mises. Kirzner received his Ph.D. under the guidance of Mises and taught at New York University for many years until his retirement in 2001. His books and articles are entirely theoretical in nature. He largely rejects the concept of macroeconomics and equilibrium analysis. Following the subjectivism of Friedrich Wieser, Kirzner once insisted that it is impossible to determine whether a wealthy American making a million dollars a year is "better off" than a French peasant making $200 a year, because "innercomparisons of utilities cannot be made scientifically." As Wieser wrote, "No one can take his own personal valuation of money, and of the money value of goods, outside of himself, and apply it to other people" (Wieser 1893:50). Kirzner also opposed efforts to aggregate capital, which he regarded as "unscientific."[6] Like Mises and Wieser, Kirzner seldom used graphs in his books to illustrate economic principles.

Roger Garrison (Auburn), one of the premier Austrian macroeconomists today, uses a similar approach. His major work, *Time and Money* (2001), advances Austrian macro theorizing and compares it to Keynesian models in a creative way, including the extensive use of comparative graphics, but does not engage in any significant empirical work.[7]

Murray N. Rothbard was quixotic in his pedagogical approach. When Rothbard published his treatise *Man, Economy*

5 Private interview with Arnold Harberger at the Mont Pelerin Society meetings, Salt Lake City, August 18, 2004. Harberger, now at UCLA, was chairman of the economics department at Chicago for many years and was thoroughly involved in developing close ties with Chile and the "Chicago Boys" since the 1950s.

6 According to Roger Garrison, the litmus test used to determine who was a "true Austrian" at the 1974 South Royalton conference was based upon the question, "Which country has more per capita investment capital, the United States or Mexico?" Only those who answered "It's impossible to know" were considered true Austrians. Lachmann and Kirzner fit into this category.

7 Garrison has done some empirical work recently, however. See Callahan and Garrison 2003.

and State (1962), he meticulously avoided historical examples, empirical studies, or even the naming of actual currencies (Vaughn 1994:97n). He defended the "extreme apriorism" of Mises and expressed deep suspicion of mathematics, econometrics, and cliometrics (Rothbard 1985; 1997:100-06). Yet when it came to writing his popular book, *America's Great Depression* (1963), Rothbard depended on considerable historical evidence and empirical data to prove (not just illustrate) his theories. Rothbard amassed and interpreted a wide range of historical data from 1920-33 to support an Austrian explanation of the Great Depression (see chapter 6). He meticulously measured an extremely broad definition of the money supply during the 1920s, year by year, in an attempt to prove that the money stock grew faster than the economy, creating an unsustainable inflationary boom, and eventually precipitating the 1929 Crash and Great Depression.[8] I'm convinced that the reason Rothbard's book remains so popular is because he used the Chicago empirical method, even though he applied an Austrian interpretation to the data. Rothbard was as much an historian as an economist (his Ph. D. dissertation at Columbia was *The Panic of 1819*), and he couldn't help interpreting the facts, though his approach more often involved the motivation behind historical events rather than statistical work (Salerno 2002).

Friedman Rejects Mises's Methodological Dualism

Friedman explicitly rejects the Misesian notion that the natural and social sciences are separate spheres requiring different methods of investigation. In his Nobel Memorial Lecture in 1976, Friedman claims that "there is no 'certain' substantive knowledge," only testable hypotheses. He cites the Godel theorem in mathematics and the Heisenberg uncertainty principle in the hard sciences to demonstrate uncertainty. He adopts the Popperian thesis that these theories can never be

---

8 For a discussion of Friedman's critique of Rothbard's money-supply data, see chapter 6.

proved, "but only can fail to be rejected." In both sciences, experimental testing is required, and "no experiment is ever completely controlled." The only differences are in the subject matter, the techniques of analysis, and the level of success. "Even the difficult problem of separating value-judgements from scientific judgements is not unique to the social sciences," he concludes (Friedman 1991:87-88).

At the same time, Friedman disdains studying data without any theoretical underpinnings. Speaking of Friedman's price theory class, Gary Becker comments, "Friedman emphasized that economic theory was not a game played by clever academicians, but a powerful tool to analyze the real world. His course was filled with insights both into the structure of economic theory and its implications to practical and significant problems" (Becker 1992). In short, the Chicago school distrusts studying data without theory as well as developing theory without measurement.

Friedman's Controversial Methodology

Like Mises, Friedman's methodology has led to considerable debate. In a 1953 article, "The Methodology of Positive Economics," Friedman argues that an economic model should be judged solely on its predictive power, "the only relevant test," not the realism of its assumptions. Furthermore, he declares that, "in general, the more significant a theory, the more unrealistic the assumptions." A theory with "realistic" assumptions will undoubtedly be "useless," Friedman contends. The assumptions can even be "false" if the theory "yields sufficiently accurate predictions." In fact, "to be important, therefore, a hypothesis must be descriptively false in its assumptions" (Friedman 1953:14-15). Finally, Friedman borrows Karl Popper's falsification theorem which holds that you can never demonstrate that anything is materially true; you can only disprove a theory through empirical observation.

Friedman used this approach to analyze Keynesian theories. He found beauty in Keynes's simplistic assumptions, but ultimately rejected the model "because I believe that it has been contradicted by the experience" (Friedman 1986:48). According to Friedman, Keynes's theories have failed to predict macroeconomic behavior accurately, and therefore must be discarded in favor of more accurately predictable models, such as the quantity theory of money and Say's law of markets. Friedman came to the same conclusion about the Austrian theory of the business cycle (see chapter 6). "The Hayek-Mises explanation of the business cycle is contradicted by the evidence. It is, I believe, false" (Friedman 1993:171).[9]

The Power of Empirical Studies

Clearly, the Austrians and Chicagoans differ strenuously about the way research should be conducted. Should economic science be solely a function of logic built up from basic principles, like geometry (which can be quite sophisticated), or should theories be constantly subjected to empirical evidence, discarded and added upon as necessary? Should history be interpreted by motives and ideology, or by broad statistical analysis?

First, I would take exception to Mises's view that history does not teach us important lessons, or that each event is so unique that history is never repetitive. It is clear that events, crises, and history in general sometimes play a valuable role in changing the minds of teachers, students and policy makers. Without the influence of the Scottish enlightenment, Adam Smith might not have written *The Wealth of Nations*. Without the industrial revolution, there probably would have been no *Capital* by Karl Marx. Without the Great Depression, there probably would have been no *General Theory* by Keynes, and

---

9 As we shall see in chapter 6, Friedman's empirical test of the Austrian business cycle theory was limited in scope, and did not cover all aspects of the Austrian interpretation of business cycle activity.

no Friedman counter-revolution. Without the collapse of the Soviet Union, millions would still be living under totalitarian socialism.[10]

The close study of history can be a teacher of valuable lessons. Prior to the empirical work of Friedman and Schwartz in 1963, many free-market economists attempted to explain that government mismanagement, not the free market, was responsible for the Great Depression. However, few listened until Friedman and Schwartz demonstrated forcefully, with real numbers, that the Federal Reserve, a quasi-government agency, had blundered repeatedly in making the Depression worse, causing the money supply to fall by a third. Friedman and Schwartz also questioned the belief that the international gold standard precipitated the Depression, as Barry Eichengreen and other critics contend. The gold standard didn't force the Fed to deflate; in fact, under a genuine gold standard, the money supply would have increased in the 1920s and 1930s, as gold poured into the U. S. (Friedman and Schwartz 1963:299, 360-61; Skousen 2002:143-46, 151-54). In broader terms, Friedman and Schwartz demonstrated repeatedly a systematic pattern of monetary policy on economic activity—except for wartimes, the economy expanded during times of easy money, and contracted during times of tight money.

To use another Chicago example, George J. Stigler and many other economic historians changed their minds about antitrust laws after investigating the pricing tactics of the so-called "robber barons." The conventional view was that Rockefeller's Standard Oil Company had systematically engaged in predatory price cutting to destroy the competition, when in fact Standard Oil usually found it profitable to buy out rival concerns at remunerative prices (Stigler 1988:102).

10 Oddly enough, George Stigler is agnostic toward the view that economic theory emerges out of crises or major events: "neither popular economic problems nor heroic events influence much the development of economic theory" (Stigler 1965:22).

Ohio University professors Richard K. Vedder and Lowell E. Gallaway use empirical evidence to demonstrate powerfully a close statistical relationship between real wages and unemployment, concluding that government policies cause widespread and persistent unemployment by raising wages above equilibrium levels (Vedder and Gallaway 1993). Interestingly, Vedder and Gallaway are convinced that the reason the publication of their book *Out of Work* was delayed for six years was because they offered a classical liberal/Austrian interpretation of unemployment (Vedder and Gallaway 2000:38-41).

Robert Higgs, a historian sympathetic to Austrian views, has done extensive quantitative research into the cause of the prolonged decade-long Great Depression, which he blames largely on government hampering of private investment. He also demonstrates brilliantly, using numerous statistics, that the return to prosperity did not occur until after World War II (Higgs 1992, 1997).

Supply-siders Art Laffer, a former Chicago professor, and Paul Craig Roberts have made the case that tax cuts will boost revenues, based on the Laffer Curve. But no one accepted the Laffer Curve as a real possibility until the evidence came in that a tax reduction on capital gains in 1979 increased tax revenues. Several cases have shown to demonstrate the existence of the Laffer Curve under certain conditions.

Many supporters of the second amendment to the Constitution have argued that a well-armed citizenry discourages violent crime, but they made little headway until John Lott, Jr.'s research on concealed gun permits while a fellow at the John M. Olin Law and Economics Center at the University of Chicago. He produced a variety of statistics and graphs comparing the average number of violent crimes in states before and after the concealed-handgun laws. In most states, violent crime was rising until a concealed-handgun law was passed, and then the crime rate fell. "When guns are concealed," he concluded, "criminals are unable to tell whether the victim is armed before striking, which raises the risk to criminals" (Lott 1998:5). Gary Becker pioneered the application of the incentive principle to crime. He and others working in this field have demonstrated that increasing the cost of crime through stiffer sentences, quicker trials, and higher conviction rates effectively reduces the number of criminals who rob, steal, and rape (Becker 1997:137).

The influence of the Heritage Foundation, the Cato Institute, and other free-market think tanks on public policy in Washington has undoubtedly been strengthened because of the many case studies in applied economics prepared by experts who make their case stronger with supporting data.

Discovering New Truths Through History

A second advantage of studying history is that it causes scholars to go back to the theory and discover new truths. Paul Samuelson taught for years in his textbook that lighthouses were a public good; in theory private firms could not possibly provide lighthouse services because of the free-rider problem. Then Ronald Coase (Chicago) decided to investigate the history of lighthouses, and discovered that one of the first lighthouses, Trinity House in England, has been privately run. It earned income by imposing fees on ships docking at nearby ports sufficient to make a profit (Coase 1988 [1974]:187-213). Samuelson was forced to print a partial retraction (Samuelson and Nordhaus 2001:325).

Rothbard illustrates this point. In the second edition of *America's Great Depression* (1971), he gave an astute "Austrian" explanation of stagflation, noting that consumer price inflation is "a general and universal tendency in recessions." That is, "the prices of consumer goods always tend to rise, relative to the prices of producer goods, during recessions," except this time, in the early 1970s, government inflationary policies were so strong that consumer prices rose "absolutely and visibly as well" (Rothbard 1971:xxv-xxvi). Rothbard might never have discovered this aspect of the Austrian business cycle theory had not stagflation occurred, forcing him to look into the Austrian macro model to discover the source of inflationary recession. It appears that modern Austrians approve of historical studies as a way to illuminate theory.

George Stigler summarizes the advantages of a close relationship between theory and empirical testing: "The quantitative, or better, empirical study of economic life is the only way in which one can get a real feel for the tasks and functioning of an economic system" (Stigler 1965:61). Gary Becker seconds Stigler: "Empirically oriented theories encourage the development of new sources and types of data....At the same time, puzzling empirical results force changes in theory" (Becker 1997 [1992]:52).

Empirical Evidence Gone Awry

Despite all this powerful evidence in favor of empirical work, Mises's "cranky" philosophy cannot be entirely dismissed. After all, there is a dark side to empiricism, when the data is misused, misinterpreted, and just plain wrong. Austrian economist Oskar Morgenstern wrote an entire book questioning the accuracy of economic data from price indexes to national income statistics. While rejecting Mises's "doctrinaire" position that economics is not a "non-empirical science," Morgenstern warns economists that most economic data is highly unreliable and subject to manipulation and error (Morgenstern 1963: 302-04). He labels the monthly unemployment rate nothing more than "dividing one indeterminate number by another indeterminate number" (1963:239). He questions the value of government spending (1963:247), and castigates government and private economists for placing too much reliance on "shaky" GDP data, which could have an "average margin of error....of about 10 percent" (1963:255, 298).

Bad empiricism can lead to much mischief. There are many historical examples:

1. Unrealistic data on Soviet output and deceptive propaganda by the Communists led Sidney and Beatrice Webb, Joseph Schumpeter, Paul Samuelson, Robert Heilbroner, and a host of other prestigious economists to believe in the Soviet economic miracle. As late as 1986, Samuelson's textbook listed the Soviet Union as the fastest growing country among industrial nations between 1928 and 1983, growing at a 4.9% rate, higher than the United States, the United Kingdom, Germany, and Japan (Samuelson and Nordhaus 1985:776). Conservative economist Henry C. Wallich was so impressed by the Soviet data that he wrote an entire book, *The Cost of Freedom* (1960), saying that political and economic freedom comes at a cost, i.e., lower economic growth.

2. Several studies showed that European welfare states grew slightly faster than freer economies in the 1950s and 1960s. According to Mancur Olson, "In the 1950s....there was, if anything, a faint tendency for the countries with larger welfare states to grow faster," including West Germany and Sweden (Olson 1990:10).

3. A 1994 study by David Card and Alan Krueger claimed that minimum wages benefit workers, the opposite of standard economic theory: "We find that the increase in the minimum wage increases employment" (Card and Krueger 1995). The Card-Krueger study, based on telephone interviews with fast-food restaurant managers in New Jersey and Pennsylvania, contradicted other studies that concluded that minimum wage laws increase unemployment among blacks and less skilled workers.

4. In their book *Time on the Cross* (1974), Chicago economist Robert W. Fogel and his colleague Stanley

Engerman claimed that the large-scale plantation system in the ante-bellum South was more efficient under slavery than the small farms in the free Northern states. Austrians took exception to this technique of quantitative economics known as "cliometrics" (Salerno 2002), especially the notion that slavery, or any other command economy, can be efficient or profitable.

5. Clinton supporters note that after the tax increase of 1994, the U. S. economy experienced faster economic growth, superior stock market performance, and faster tax revenue growth, contradicting the arguments of supply-side economics.

6. In a controversial book, *Growing Public* (2004), Peter Lindert, economic historian at the University of California-Davis, gives statistical evidence seeming to support the view that social spending and the welfare state have contributed to, rather than inhibited, economic growth.

How do free-market economists respond to these examples? According to Mises, the use of econometrics and statistics leads to radical political thought (Stigler 1965:61). Rothbard seconds Mises, contending that the gathering of statistics is useful primarily as "the avenues of government intervention and planning" and "the individual business firm has little or no need of statistics" (Rothbard 1997b:217, 222). Stigler sees things differently, arguing that empirical evidence makes intellectuals less radical: "it is not a coincidence that the theorists who have turned socialists or communists have usually been completely abstract theorists, and the more radical wing of the New Dealers was not distinguished for its empirical knowledge of the American economy...Consensus [of sound economics] rests in part, to be sure, on empirical research" (Stigler 1965:61, 63). Rothbard grants Stigler's argument, but goes further: "Empiricists will tend less to be full-scale socialists, but will also drift generally toward intervention" (Rothbard 1997b:225).

Gary Becker states, "If the data contradicts sound theory, I am very skeptical, and go back and look at the data again." In practically every case, investigators turn up flaws in the data (Morgenstern 1963 passim). For example, most analysts agree today that the Soviet data was simply bad. Counter-studies question the reliability of the Card-Krueger study on minimum wage laws. A similar study based on actual payroll records rather than telephone calls concludes that the higher minimum wage laws discouraged employment. And in the case of higher economic performance in Europe in the 1950s among welfare states, the added growth may be due to extraneous factors, such as the rebuilding of Europe after the war, a one-time stimulus. In the case of the Clinton tax increases in the early 1990s, growth may have been achieved because of other significant factors generating superior economic activity, such as trade, technology, and the breakdown of the Soviet socialist model in Third World countries.

Austrians complain that the empirical method is forever frustrating, that history-driven theory "is subject to constant revision on the basis of the 'new evidence' that is continually coming to light in the ongoing historical process" (Salerno 2002:38-39). Despite major advances in statistical techniques and computer technology, the results are suspect. "There has not been…a steady accumulation of well-established empirical laws," states Bruce Caldwell (Caldwell 2004:375). He cites a study by Robert Goldfarb, who documents 21 cases of empirical patterns where later "contrary results emerge that challenge or even seem to overturn that initial result" (Goldfarb 1997:221). "How is he or she to make believable inferences from such a literature, where results may have already been, or in the future be, challenged and even conceivably overturned?" (Goldfarb 1997:222) Even the statistical work of the new economic historians, known as cliometricians, have cast doubts on many traditional views of history (Atack and Passell 1994).

Yet the same complaint of unreliability can be made about the Austrians' method of identifying the self-interested motivations of the players behind historical events, which Mises calls "thymology," the evaluation of human motives. For example, Rothbard suggests a Morgan-Rockefeller conspiracy theory behind the establishment of the Federal Reserve (Rothbard 1994:116). Years later new historical documents may come to light suggesting an ulterior motives or another explanation. There are no guarantees of truth with a capital T when it comes to interpreting history or motives. Ultimately, neither method should be rejected. Both statistical analysis and thymology are useful and one does not preclude the other. There is value in examining both measurement of economic data and motives behind the actions and events. Friedman emphasizes data in *A Monetary History*, but does at times seriously discuss motives (such as the leadership of Benjamin Strong in the 1920s). Rothbard focuses on motives in *America's Great Depression*, but includes an analysis of money supply figures in the 1920s. Why not be open minded about both techniques?

Can Economists Predict the Future with Any Accuracy?

In his 1953 article on methodology, Friedman asserts that an economic theory, with or without realistic assumptions, must ultimately be judged on its ability to make accurate predictions. Mises has a point here—economists have had a difficult time making consistently accurate predictions. Often there are too many unknowns. Friedman himself has made both good and bad predictions; on the positive side, he anticipated the inflationary recession of the 1970s, but on the negative side, he debunked the power of OPEC and forecast that oil prices would fall to under $10 (inflation adjusted). In the 1980s, he underestimated disinflationary forces. False and misleading assumptions can be troublesome. For example, computer-generated econometric models have been developed to forecast stock, bond, and option trends based solely on historical patterns. These financial models, known as technical analysis, often ignore fundamentals and focus strictly on "what works," that is, what has worked in the past. Typically these models work for a while, sometimes for several years, but then collapse when the underlining fundamentals "unexpectedly" take over. This is in essence what happened to Long Term Capital Management, which lost $4 billion in 1998, despite being guided by a Nobel Prize economist. In sum, one must be suspicious of any heuristic theory that ignores fundamental economic behavior.

Austrians Make Strides in Empirical Work

Yet, despite the protests of pure Misesians, more and more Austrian economists are engaging in quantitative studies, suggesting that Chicago has won the day. We already mentioned the empirical work of Rothbard in *America's Great Depression*. Charles Wainhouse's doctoral dissertation at NYU was the first to test the Mises-Hayek business-cycle theory using time series, supporting much of the theory (Wainhouse 1984). Other quantitative efforts have been made by William A. Butos (1993); my own work in *The Structure of Production* (Skousen 1990:292-93); and George Selgin and Lawrence White whose extensive historical work on free banking in Scotland and in the United States attempts to determine the relative stability of free banking under competitive conditions (White 1984; Selgin 1988). More recently, *The Quarterly Journal of Austrian Economics* and *The Review of Austrian Economics* have published several econometric/empirical studies (Mulligan 2002; Callahan and Garrison 2003; Keller 2001).

Austrian economists have other free-market economists to produce the annual empirical study on country-by-country economic freedom indexes. *Economic Freedom of the World*, by James Gwartney, Robert A. Lawson, and in earlier studies Walter E. Block, is published simultaneously by the Fraser

Institute and several other free-market think tanks. A similar *Index of Economic Freedom* is released annually by the Heritage Foundation and the Wall Street Journal. A recent edition was written and compiled by Gerald P. O'Driscoll, Jr., who wrote his dissertation on Hayek. In both studies on economic freedom, the authors use a variety of country-by-country data to demonstrate a strong correlation both graphically and statistically between economic freedom and the rate of economic growth. Milton Friedman, in the introduction to the Fraser study, echoes Mises when he states, "It did not require the construction of an index of economic freedom for it to be widely believed that there is a close relation between economic freedom and the level and rate of economic growth." But Friedman, ever the consummate quantitative economist, contends that a picture is worth a thousand words. "No qualitative verbal description can match the power of that graph" (Friedman 1996:vii-viii).

Advantage: Chicago

Clearly, the Chicago school wins the first round in the battle over methodology. Despite some serious blunders in empirical studies from time to time, the vast majority of quantitative research done by the Chicago school and other economists has dramatically changed the way economists think, mostly for the better. To be quite frank, Misesian epistomology set back the advancement of Austrian economics and delayed the opportunity to make serious contributions to the discipline. Slowly but surely that is changing. As University of Georgia professor Peter G. Klein warns, "If Austrians focus on metaeconomics, and try to force mainstreamers to rethink abstract issues of epistemology, we'll go nowhere" (Klein 1995:7) At the same time, let us not ignore those Austrians such as Rothbard who have probed the motives of the individuals and institutions behind the events of yesteryear. They too have made an important contribution, and we need to see more of it. Peter Boettke has best summed up the complementary role of the Austrian's love of theory and the Chicago's love of history as follows: "Economics...puts parameters on people's utopias. But it also provides insights into what might be workable utopias. Economics without history, politics, culture, and morality runs the risk of becoming a barren technical enterprise. But political economy, without a firm basis in logic and evidence, runs the risk of being mere opinion and wishful thinking. The disciplines of economics and political economy can be likened to engineering science and worldly philosophy. The great minds of political economy — independent of ideological perspective — have found a way to weave together both the technical and philosophical aspects of these disciplines without becoming mutually exclusive of the other" (Boettke 2001:25).

References

Atack, Jeremy and Peter Passell. 1994. *A New Economic View of American History*. 2nd ed. New York: W. W. Norton.

Becker, Gary S. 1992. "Autobiography." http://www.nobel.se/economics/laureates/1992/becker-autobio.html.

Becker, Gary S. 1997 [1992]. "The Economic Way of Looking at Life." In Torsten Persson, ed., *Nobel Lectures in Economic Sciences, 1991-1995*. Singapore: World Scientific, 38-58.

Becker, Gary S. And Guity Nashat Becker. 1997. *The Economics of Life*. New York: McGraw-Hill.

Blaug, Mark. 1975. *The Cambridge Revolution: Success or Failure?* 2nd ed. Cambridge: Cambridge University Press.

Blaug, Mark. 1978. *Economic Theory in Retrospect*. 3rd ed. Cambridge: Cambridge University Press.

Blaug, Mark. 1980. *The Methodology of Economics*. Cambridge: Cambridge University Press.

Boettke, Peter J. and David L. Prychitko. 1994. "The Future of Austrian Economics," in Boettke and Prychitko, eds., *The Market Process: Essays in Contemporary Austrian Economics*. Brookfield, VT: Edward Elgar.

Boettke, Peter J. 2001. *Calculation and Coordination*. New York: Routledge.

Butos, William A. 1993. "The Recession and Austrian Business Cycle Theory: An Empirical Perspective." *Critical Review* 7:2-3, 277-306.

Caldwell, Bruce. 2004. *Hayek's Challenge: An Intellectual Biography of F. A. Hayek*. Chicago: University of Chicago Press.

Callahan, Gene and Roger W. Garrison. 2003. "Does Austrian Business Cycle Theory Help Explain the Dot-Com Boom and Bust?" *Quarterly Journal of Austrian Economics* 6:2 (Summer), 67-98.

Card, David and Alan Krueger. 1995. *Myth and Measurement*. Princeton: Princeton University Press.

Coase, Ronald H. 1988 [1974]. "The Lighthouse in Economics," *The Firm, the Market, and the Law*. Chicago: University of Chicago Press, 187-213.

Ebenstein, Alan. 2003. *Hayek's Journey: The Mind of Friedrich Hayek*. New York: Palgrave Macmillan.

Fogel, Robert William. 1971. "The New Economic History: Its Findings and Methods," in Robert Fogel and Stanley L. Engerman, eds., *The Reinterpretation of American History*. New York: Harper and Row.

Fogel, Robert William and Stanley L. Engerman. 1974. *Time on the Cross*. Boston: Little, Brown.

Friedman, Milton. 1953. *Essays in Positive Economics*. Chicago: University of Chicago Press.

Friedman, Milton. 1974. "Schools at Chicago," *University of Chicago Magazine* (August), 11-16.

Friedman, Milton. 1986. "Keynes's Political Legacy," in John Burton, ed. *Keynes's General Theory: Fifty Years On*. London: Institute of Economic Affairs.

Friedman, Milton. 1993. "The 'Plucking Model' of Business Fluctuations Revisited," *Economic Inquiry* (April), 171-77.

Friedman, Milton. 1991. *Monetarist Economics*. Oxford: Basil Blackwell.

Friedman, Milton. 1996. "Foreword." James Gwartney, Robert A. Lawson, and Walter E. Block. *Economic Freedom of the World, 1975-1995*. Vancouver: Fraser Institute.

Friedman, Milton and Rose. 1980. *Free to Choose*. New York: Harcourt Brace Jovanovich.

Friedman, Milton and Anna J. Schwartz. 1963. *A Monetary History of the United States, 1867-1960*. Princeton: Princeton University Press.

Garrison, Roger W. 2001. *Time and Money*. New York: Routledge.

Goldfarb, Robert. 1997. "Now You See It, Now You Don't: Emerging Contrary Results in Economics." *Journal of Economic Methodology* 4:2 (December), 221-44.

Groenewegen, Peter. 1995. *A Soaring Eagle: Alfred Marshall, 1842-1924*. Cheltenham: Edward Elgar.

Hayek, Friedrich A. 1931. *Prices and Production*. London: George Routledge & Sons.

Hayek, Friedrich A. 1942-44. "Scientism and the Study of Society," Part I: *Economica* NS 9 (1942), Part II: *Economica* 10 (1943), and Part III: *Economica* 11 (1944).

Hayek, Friedrich A. 1944. *The Road to Serfdom*. Chicago: University of Chicago Press.

Hayek, Friedrich A. 1955. *The Counter-Revolution of Science*. New York: Free Press.

Hayek, Friedrich A. 1960. *The Constitution of Liberty*. Chicago: University of Chicago Press.

Hayek, Friedrich A. 1967. *Studies in Philosophy, Politics and Economics*. Chicago: University of Chicago Press.

Hayek, Friedrich A. 1976. "Introduction: Carl Menger," in *Carl Menger, Principles of Economics*. New York: New York University Press.

Hayek, Friedrich A. 1984. *The Essence of Hayek*. Chiaki Nishihama and Kurt R. Leube, eds. Stanford: Hoover Institution.

Higgs, Robert. 1992. "Wartime Prosperity? A Reassessment of the U. S. Economy in the 1940s." *Journal of Economic History* 52 (March), 41-60.

Higgs, Robert. 1997. "Regime Uncertainty: Why the Great Depression Lasted So Long and Why Prosperity Resumed After the War." *The Independent Review* 1:4 (Spring), 561-90.

Huerta de Soto, Jesus. 1998. "The Ongoing Methodensteit of the Austrian School." *Journal des Economistes et des Etudes Humaines* 8:1 (March), 75-113.

Jevons, William Stanley. 1965 [1879]. *The Theory of Political Economy*. 5th ed. New York: Augustus M. Kelley.

Keller, James P. 2001. "Empirical Evidence on the Austrian Business Cycle Theory," *The Review of Austrian Economics* 14:4, 331-351.

Klamer, Arjo and David Colander. 1990. *The Making of an Economist*. Boulder: Westview.

Klein, Peter G., Interview, *Austrian Economics Newsletter* (winter). Auburn: Ludwig von Mises Institute.

Kuttner, Robert. 1985. "The Poverty of Economics." *Atlantic Monthly* (February): 74-84.

Lindert, Peter. 2004. *Growing Public, Vol. 1, the Story: Social Spending and Economic Growth Since the Eighteenth Century*. Cambridge: Cambridge University Press.

Lott, John R., Jr. 1998. *More Guns, Less Crime*. Chicago: University of Chicago Press.

Machlup, Fritz, ed. 1976. *Essays on Hayek*. New York: New York University Press.

Mayo, Elton. 1945. *The Social Problems of an Industrial Civilization*. Cambridge: Harvard University Press.

McCloskey, D. N. 1998 [1995]. *The Rhetoric of Economics*. 2nd ed. Madison: University of Wisconsin Press.

Mises, Ludwig von. 1960. *Epistemological Problems of Economics*. Translated by George Reisman. New York: New York University Press.

Mises, Ludwig von. 1966 [1949]. *Human Action: A Treatise on Economics*. 3rd ed. Chicago: Regnery.

Mises, Ludwig von. 1971 [1934]. *The Theory of Money and Credit*. 2nd ed. New York: Foundation for Economic Education.

Mises, Ludwig von. 1985 [1957]. *Theory and History*. Auburn, Alabama: Mises Institute.

Mises, Richard von. 1951. *Positivism*. Cambridge: Harvard College.

Mitchell, Lucy Sprague. 1953. *Two Lives: The Story of Wesley Clair Mitchell and Myself*. New York: Simon and Schuster.

Mitchell, Wesley C. 1913. *Business Cycles*. Berkeley: University of California Press.

Morgenstern, Oskar. 1963. *On The Accuracy of Economic Observations*. 2nd ed. Princeton: Princeton University Press.

Morishima, Michio. 1976. *The Economic Theory of Modern Society*. Cambridge: Cambridge University Press.

Mulligan, Robert F. 2002. "A Hayekian Analysis of the Term Structure of Production." *Quarterly Journal of Austrian Economics* 5:2 (Summer), 17-33.

Olson, Mancur. 1990. *How Bright are the Northern Lights? Some Questions About Sweden*. Lund, Sweden: Lund University.

Paqué, Karl-Heinz. 1985. "How Far is Vienna from Chicago? An Essay on the Methodology of Two Schools of Dogmatic Liberalism." *Kyklos* 38:412-434

Ricardo, David. 1951 [1817]. *On the Principles of Political Economy and Taxation*. Ed. by Piero Sraffa. Cambridge: Cambridge University Press.

Reder, Melvin W. 1982. "Chicago Economics: Permanence and Change." *Journal of Economic Literature* (March), 1-38.

Rosen, Sherwin. 1997. "Austrian and Neoclassical Economics: Any Gains from Trade?" *Journal of Economic Perspectives* 11 (fall):139-52.

Rothbard, Murray N. 1962. *Man, Economy and State*. Princeton: Van Nostrand.

Rothbard, Murray N. 1971 [1963]. *America's Great Depression*. 2nd ed. Princeton: Van Nostrand.

Rothbard, Murray N. 1988. *Ludwig von Mises: Scholar, Creator, Hero*. Auburn: Ludwig von Mises Institute.

Rothbard, Murray N. 1994. *The Case Against the Fed*. Auburn: Ludwig von Mises Institute.

Rothbard, Murray N. 1995. "Preface" to Ludwig von Mises, *Theory and History*, 2nd ed. Auburn, Alabama: Mises Institution, xi-xviii.

Rothbard, Murray N. 1997. *The Logic of Action I: Method, Money, and the Austrian School*. Cheltenham, UK: Edward Elgar.

Rothbard, Murray N. 1997b. *The Logic of Action II: Method, Money, and the Austrian School*. Cheltenham, UK: Edward Elgar.

Salerno, Joseph T. 2002. Introduction to Murray N. Rothbard, *A History of Money and Banking in the United States*. Auburn, AL: Mises Institute, 7-43.

Samuelson, Paul A. 1947. "Lord Keynes and the General Theory," in Seymour Harris, ed., *The New Economics*. New York: Alfred A. Knopf.

Samuelson, Paul A. 1972 [1947]. *Foundations of Economic Analysis*. New York: Atheneum.

Samuelson, Paul A.and William D. Nordhaus. 1985. *Economics.* 12th ed. New York: McGraw-Hill.

Samuelson, Paul A. and William D. Nordhaus. 2001. *Economics.* 17th ed. New York: McGraw-Hill Higher Education.

Say, J.-B. 1880. *A Treatise on Political Economy.* 6th ed. New York: Augustus M. Kelley.

Selgin, George A. 1988. *The Theory of Free Banking.* London: Rowman & Littlefield.

Selgin, George A. 1990. *Praxeology and Understanding: An Analysis of the Controversy in Austrian Economics.* Auburn, AL: Mises Institute.

Skousen, Mark. 1990. *The Structure of Production.* New York: New York University Press.

Skousen, Mark. 2002. *The Power of Economic Thinking.* New York: Foundation for Economic Education.

Smith, Adam. 1965 [1776]. *The Wealth of Nations.* New York: Modern Library.

Sraffa, Piero. 1960. *Production of Commodities by Means of Commodities.* Cambridge: Cambridge University Press.

Stigler, George J. 1965. *Essays in the History of Economics.* Chicago: University of Chicago Press.

Stigler, George J. 1988. *Memoirs of an Unregulated Economist.* New York: Basic Books.

Vaughn, Karen I. 1994. *Austrian Economics in America.* Cambridge: Cambridge University Press.

Vedder, Richard K.and Lowell E. Gallaway. 1993. *Out of Work.* New York: Holmes & Meier.

Vedder, Richard and Lowell Gallaway. 2000. "The Austrian Market Share in the Marketplace for Ideas, 1871-2025," *Quarterly Journal of Austrian Economics* 3:1 (Spring), 33-42.

Wainhouse, Charles E. 1994. "Hayek's Theory of the Trade Cycle: The Evidence from the Time Series." Ph. D.dissertation. New York University.

Wallich, Henry C. 1960. *The Cost of Freedom.* New York: Collier Books.

White, Lawrence H. 1984. *Free Banking in Britain.* Cambridge: Cambridge University Press.

Wieser, Friedrich von. 1893. *Natural Value.* Translated by Christian A. Malloch. London: Macmillan.

Chapter Five

GOLD VS. FIAT MONEY
WHAT IS THE IDEAL
MONETARY STANDARD?

*I therefore advocate as the soundest monetary system
and the only one fully compatible with the free market
and with the absence of force or fraud from any course:
the 100 per cent gold standard.*

—Murray N. Rothbard (1974:34-35)

*I have favored increasing the quantity of money at a steady
rate designed to keep final product prices constant,
a rate that I have estimated to be something like
4 to 5 per cent per year for the U. S. for a monetary
total defined to include currency outside the banks
and all deposits of commercial banks, demand and time.*

—Milton Friedman (1969:47)

In addition to methodology, the Austrian and Chicago
schools do battle over the ideal monetary system. Both
schools share the same goal, a stable non-inflationary
monetary framework under which a free society can flourish.
The Austrians express great faith in the ability of the market to
create and sustain a stable, non-inflationary monetary system,
while the Chicago school suggests some form of market failure
in the monetary arena. As Milton Friedman and Anna J.
Schwartz state, "It is dubious that the market can by itself
provide such a framework" (Schwartz 1987:292).

Should money consist of gold and a commodity-based system, a purely fiat money system, or some form of free banking? Austrians and supply siders favor some form of gold standard, and some even free banking, while Chicagoans support a monetarist rule, steadily increasing the money supply to approximately match the long-run growth of the economy. A monetary rule requires government control of the monetary system.[1]

Who is right, and who offers the most practical solution to monetary instability?

A Point of Agreement:
The Current Federal Reserve System Needs Reform

Let us begin with something both schools can agree on: the current central banking system is a defective monetary standard and needs reform. It has not prevented either inflation or economic instability.

In The Case Against the Fed, Murray Rothbard castigates the Federal Reserve for being "by far the most secret and least accountable operation of the federal government....The Federal Reserve System is accountable to no one; it has no budget; it is subject to no audit; and no Congressional committee knows of, or can truly supervise its operations" (1994:3). Rothbard protests too much. The Fed chairman and the other six members of the Federal Reserve Board are nominated by the President and subject to Senate approval; the chairman has to parade regularly before several House and Senate committees. And most importantly, Fed actions are graded every day in the stock, bond and foreign currency markets.

However, Rothbard makes an important point: the "independence" of the Fed is a two-edge sword. Its independence serves to resist the vested interests of a

---

1 For an in-depth comparison between the gold standard, an irredeemable fiat money system, free banking, and a flexible central banking model (current system), see my *Economics of a Pure Gold Standard* (1996).

spendthrift legislature, yet forces are at work to undermine that independence. Contrary to the argument that the Federal Reserve System is a determined foe of inflation, Rothbard and other Austrians see the Fed as the very source of bank inflation, "continually subject to a lust for inflating the money supply" (1994:8) and "deliberately designed as an engine of inflation" (Rothbard 1983:237). The long history of central banking has been to demolish, one by one, the limitations on the ability of the government to inflate, so that "virtually all natural market checks on bank inflation have been destroyed" (Rothbard 1974:iv), and to aggrandize its control over the economy's resources and solidify its power base in political circles. Rothbard points out that the creators of the Federal Reserve System were members of the Rockefeller and Morgan banking firms who met in secret with government officials at Jekyll Island in 1910 to devise a plan to monopolize the monetary system and thus gain unprecedented economic power independent of judicial and legislative restraint (1994:116). To do so required the banking system (a) to monopolize the control of money and money substitutes, and (b) to shift slowly but surely from a classical gold standard to a government paper money system that could be manipulated at will by central authorities.

The Federal Reserve Act of 1913 was a major step toward achieving these goals. It established a powerful Federal Reserve Board, composed of the Treasury secretary, comptroller of the currency and five additional members, and 12 Federal Reserve districts. Although its original mission was largely to be a lender of last resort and to avoid monetary crises such as the Panic of 1907, it gradually took on the role of a central bank (Timberlake 1993). Following the 1929-33 monetary crisis, Congress reorganized the Federal Reserve Board into a seven-member Board of Governors, with meetings in Washington, D.C., and a Federal Open Market Committee that includes the seven members of the Board of Governors and a rotating five of the twelve largely banker-selected Presidents of the regional banks. Under the

Rockefeller/Morgan houses, the powerful Federal Open Market Committee — which determines monetary aggregates through the buying and selling of government bonds, known as open-market operations — was originally run from Wall Street. But since the early 1950s, open-market operations have been controlled by the Fed in Washington, D. C. Yet, according to Rothbard, the Federal Reserve power structure has always been heavily influenced by the Rockefeller/Morgan connections, including the recent Fed chairmen (1994:133). In short, the Federal Reserve System was created "to cartelize the private commercial banks, and to help them inflate money and credit together, pumping in reserves to the banks, and bailing them out if they get into trouble" (1994:145). According to Rothbard, the Federal Deposit Insurance Corporation (FDIC) was created in the 1930s to assist in "propping up the banking system by a massive bailout guaranteed in advance" (1994:134).[2]

Though skeptical of conspiracy theories surrounding the establishment of the Federal Reserve[3], Milton Friedman agrees that today's central banking gives too much power to a small group of bankers. "Any system which gives so much power and so much discretion to a few men that mistakes — excusable or not — can have such far-reaching effects is a bad system" (1962:50). Friedman chronicles the Federal Reserve's misdeeds since its inception in 1913: "The stock of money,

---

2 Two monetary histories of the United States, from an Austrian perspective, can be found in Paul and Lehrman (1982) and Rothbard (2002). An excellent history of the Federal Reserve and central banking from a Chicago perspective can be found in Timberlake (1993) and Meltzer (2004).

3 Both Milton Friedman and Allan Meltzer omit any discussion in their histories of the Morgan/Rockefeller power circle and their private meetings at Jekyll Island in 1910. Meltzer states, "The principal source for this [conspiracy] claim is the fact that the New York bankers met with [Senator] Winthrop Aldrich at a Georgia estate and developed a plan for a central bank. Morgan had good reason to be concerned. It was his bank that organized others and took the leading role in responding to banking panics such as 1907. An important point: The New York bankers did not get the system that they wanted," Meltzer states (private correspondence, April 29, 2004). Moreover, it is worth pointing out that the Morgan/Rockefeller financial interests were severely damaged by the 1929-33 crisis. If the Federal Reserve Board were in the pockets of Wall Street interests, why didn't they respond as a lender of last resort?

prices, and output was decidedly more unstable after the establishment of the Reserve System than before" (1962:44). In particular, the Fed has a history of chronic instability, from "tight" money to "easy" money: "the severity of each of the major contractions — 1920-21, 1929-33, and 1937-38 — is directly attributable to acts of commission and omission by the Reserve authorities..." (1962:45) The Fed acted most "ineptly" in turning a garden-variety recession into the Great Depression of the 1930s by allowing the money supply to deflate by more than a third. "The contraction is in fact a tragic testimonial to the importance of monetary forces....The monetary authorities could have prevented the decline in the stock of money— indeed, could have produced almost any desired increase in the money stock" (Friedman and Schwartz 1963:300-301).

Even today the Fed and other central banks, while reducing the growth of monetary aggregates since the 1980s, has frequently shifted gears to respond to short-term problems. For example, since 1987, when Alan Greenspan became chairman, the Federal Reserve has switched the trend of interest rates seven times. The Fed Funds rate has been on a roller coaster ride in an effort to stabilize price inflation.

The Fed raised short-term rates from 1987 to 1991; then with the 1990-91 recession, it cut rates from 1991-94. In 1994, fearing inflation, the Fed raised rates; but, then, from 1995-99, generally engaged in an "easy" money policy in response to a variety of crises — the 1997 Asian currency crisis, the 1998 Russian economic crisis, and the 1999 Y2K crisis. When the Y2K crisis was resolved without serious incident, the Fed raised rates in 2000 to sop up excessive liquidity and pop the bubble on Wall Street. Yet a year later, the Fed switched policies again in January, 2001, when the manufacturing sector went into a tailspin and again when the September 11, 2001, terrorist attacks struck New York and Washington. In 2004, the Fed reversed policy again and raised short-term rates as the global economy recovered. Frequently the Federal Reserve, though well-intentioned, has been a disruptive force in the global economy, and there is a constant fear that the central banks may unexpectedly lose control of the credit markets.

However, it should be pointed out that Friedman has lately had good things to say about the Federal Reserve and other G7 central banks, and their ability to bring down price inflation to a reasonable level: "Since the mid-1980s, central banks around the world have reacted to the mounting evidence of monetary research by accepting the view that their basic responsibility is to produce price stability. More importantly they have succeeded to a remarkable extent as they discovered that, far from being a tradeoff between price stability and economic stability, they are mutually supporting....If the central banks continue to be successful in curbing price fluctuations, they will have converted the quantity of money from an unruly master to an obedient servant" (Friedman 2004:349-50).

Austrian economists would suggest that the central bank policy should go beyond price stability, and should avoid creating artificial asset bubbles and others of unsustainable imbalances in the economy.

Throughout the past century, economists and officials have hoped to devise a monetary framework consistent with liberty and prosperity. Vera C. Smith expressed the concerns in 1936: "How to discover a banking system which will not be the cause of catastrophic disturbances, which is least likely to introduce oscillations and most likely to make the correct adjustments to counteract changes from the side of the public, is the most unsettled economic problem of our day" (Smith 1936:171). It still is an unresolved issue in macroeconomics today.

The Chicago Solution: A Rigid Monetarist Rule

Milton Friedman has proposed a solution to eliminate the powerful vested interests of the bankers and the instability of the monetary authorities: replace the Fed with a computer that automatically increases the money supply (M2 or other broadly defined figure) at a steady rate equal to the long-term annual economic growth rate of the nation. Friedman has toyed with a variety of monetary growth rates, varying from 2 to 5%, with a 4% rule most common (Friedman 1969:45-48). His proposal, called the Monetarist Rule, is in sympathy with his teacher Henry Simons, who favored "rules over authorities" in monetary policy (Simons 1948:160-83). According to Friedman and Schwartz, "A rigid monetary rule is preferable to discretionary monetary management by the Federal Reserve" (Schwartz 1987:292). In the 1930s, Simons and Irving Fisher favored a "price stability" rule, but Friedman argues that price stabilization is "too loose and too imperfect" of a goal (Friedman 1960:86-87); the stabilization of monetary aggregates is a more pragmatic solution. Nor should the Fed be allowed to set interest rates by targeting the Fed Fund rates. The Discount Window should be closed. In fact, the Fed could be abolished and be replaced by a computer that executes the Monetarist Rule: "Instruct the System to use its open market powers to produce a 4% per year rate of growth in the total of currency held by the public and adjusted deposits in commercial banks," he argues (1960:100).

100% Reserve Banking and the Instability of Fractional Reserves

Friedman also supports one major banking reform measure in common with Rothbard: Impose a 100% reserves rule on bank demand deposits. Varying reserve requirements should be abolished. This policy has been a long-time favorite of Irving Fisher and Henry Simons as well as Murray Rothbard (although Rothbard's reserves would be in gold, not a fiduciary reserve). All have criticized fractional-reserve banking as inherently unstable and potentially ruinous to the banking system. In his book *100% Money* (1996: [1945]), Fisher favored a return to the old goldsmith days, when monies were entrusted to the bankers for safekeeping, and gold certificates were issued representing 100% of the gold on deposit. Simons adds, "There is likely to be extreme economic instability under any financial system where the same funds are made to serve as investment funds for industry and trade and the liquid cash reserves of individuals" (1948:55). According to Simons, the modern banking system is built largely on an "illusion" that funds can be both available on demand and invested. The danger occurs when the public loses faith in the financial system and tries to convert demand deposits into currency, leading to runs on banks, bank panics, suspensions, and drastic liquidations. Deposit insurance has severely limited this defect so far, but it is, nevertheless, an ever-present danger, because government guarantees can lead to high-risk lending and speculations. Electronic money and trading of goods on E-bay and other websites may create additional uncertainty. Moreover, the uncertainty of the currency-deposit ratio makes it impossible to target precisely the growth of the money supply. Under the 100% reserve requirement, commercial banks would divide themselves into two separate institutions: one as a purely depositary institution, a literal warehouse for money; and the other as an investment trust or brokerage firm that would acquire capital and make loans or investments (Friedman 1960:66-70).

Austrians Critical of Friedman's Monetary Rule

The Austrians agree that a 100% banking reserve for demand deposits coupled with a Monetary Rule would be far more stable than the current system, but they oppose any measure that they believe would artificially create monetary inflation, even if at a steady rate equal to real GDP growth. According to Austrians, irredeemable fiat money inflation is destablizing (see more on this point in chapter 6) and cannot be defended on ethical grounds. As E. C. Harwood, founder of the American Institute for Economic Research, writes, "Continued application of Dr. Friedman's panacea (expanding the 'money supply' continuously at the rate of 5 percent annually) might have made possible far greater distortions of the economy with even more adverse consequences" (Harwood 1970:43). Moreover, on a practical level, what is the appropriate monetary aggregate to use for the Monetarist Rule? M1, M2, or what? "The puzzle for the Friedmanites is aggravated by their having no theory of how to define the supply of money" (Rothbard 1983:254). Another problem with a rigid monetarist policy is velocity, which has been notoriously unstable since the 1980s. As a matter of practice, the Federal Reserve and other central banks have clearly opposed the adoption of a strict Monetarist Rule, although changes in the monetary aggregates have been less volatile since the early 1980s.

Gold and Silver as "Honest Money"

Most Austrians opt for gold (or commodity-money) as the numeraire in the ideal monetary standard. Why gold? There are several reasons.

First, gold, silver, and other forms of commodity-money represent what they term "honest money." Here the hard-money advocates are making a moral rather than a utilitarian argument. Taking a cue from Franz Oppenheimer, the Austrians contend that there are two paths to the acquisition of wealth, the "economic means" and the "political means." The economic means is the production of a useful good or service and the voluntary exchange of the goods and services produced by others. The other method, the political means, occurs by robbing the fruits of another person's production. Throughout history, the political means has been used to seize a person's wealth for one's own purposes. Oppenheimer defines the state as "the organization of the political means" (Oppenheimer 1997 [1926]:24-27).

Gold and silver as money originated in the private sector, and as a useful commodity, represents the economic means. As Carl Menger states, "The origin of money....is...entirely natural....Money is not an invention of the state. It is not the product of a legislative act. Certain commodities came to be money quite naturally, as the result of economic relationships that were independent of the power of the state" (Menger 1981:261-62). Banknotes and paper currency were originally warehouse receipts issued by goldsmiths and scriveners (see Skousen 1996:14-24). It was only when government monopolized the mints and printed their own banknotes that inflation and misuse of money could get out of hand. The idea of gold and silver as "honest money" or "sound money" is derived from historical experience with the dangers of paper money under the hands of the "political means." The fiat money inflation of the Assignats in 18th century France, the Continental currency during the American Revolution, the Greenbacks during the Civil War, and the hyperinflations in Germany, Latin America, and Eastern Europe during the 20th century are classic examples of government dishonesty and abuse of the nation's money system.[4] The further removed a government goes from gold or silver backing, the easier it is to defraud the public through inflation, devaluation, and bankruptcy. It is for this reason, after the experience of the Continentals, that the Founding Fathers announced a Constitutional right to "honest money," as expressed in Section 10 of Article 1 in the U. S. Constitution: "No state shall....coin money, emit bills of credit; and make any thing but gold and silver coin a tender in payment of debts."

Second, under a pure commodity standard, where every banknote is backed fully by gold or silver, it becomes very difficult for the government to defraud the public through inflation. A pure commodity standard forces the government to be honest with its citizens through a contractual relationship of property rights. In the early 20th century, the U. S. Treasury was committed under the international gold standard to issue "Gold Certificates" to the general public. The Gold Certificates

---

4 *Fiat Money Inflation in France* (1981), by historian Andrew Dickson White, traces the effects of fiat money standard gone array during the French Revolution in late 18th century France and is a favorite among gold bugs and free-market advocates.

were a legally-binding contract between the Treasury and the holder of the banknote. For example, the $20 Gold Certificate has the following language printed on the face of the currency:

> **THIS CERTIFIES THAT THERE HAVE BEEN**
> **DEPOSITED IN THE TREASURY OF**
> **THE UNITED STATES OF AMERICA**
> **TWENTY DOLLARS IN GOLD COIN**
> **PAYABLE TO THE BEARER ON DEMAND**

For every Gold Certificate minted, the Treasury was required to have a $20 gold coin on deposit in the Treasury. If an individual wanted to redeem his Gold Certificate, he could take it to the Treasury (or a Federal Reserve Bank or commercial bank) and receive a $20 gold coin in return. Historically, the Treasury actually stored more than 100% backing of its Gold Certificates. It also offered a similar Silver Certificate program. When the U. S. went off the gold standard in 1933, the contract ended and bearers of currency notes lost all property rights to gold or silver. The government no longer offered to redeem the $20 bill with gold. In short, there was no longer a contract, or a promise, to redeem money with anything of any productive value. Today there are no Gold or Silver Certificates, only Federal Reserve Notes, simply specially printed paper. The government does not promise the bearer of the dollar anything for holding its "notes," nor does it pay interest. In fact, it often forces its irredeemable currency on its citizens by passing "legal tender" laws, popularized during the Civil War when the U. S. first went off the gold standard. The exchange of money for goods is no longer voluntary.

The state is, in the view of hard-money advocates, nothing more than a legal counterfeiter. It can print money without having to use scarce resources to dig up, mint and store precious metals. Under an honest money system, "money can only be obtained by purchasing it with one's goods and services," or in the case of miners, by investing resources in producing gold and silver. But under an unbacked monetary system, the government can simply print up dollar bills at a cost of a few pennies each, and create instant value. It is inherently fraudulent. Hard-money supporters are quick to point out that "the paper dollar, with which Americans are paid today, is not real money. Almost no real work is required of the government to produce the mass-printed paper dollar bill....No longer a just and honest measure of the value of work, the dollar has ceased to be the stable standard of economic worth the world over" (Paul and Lehrman 1982:iv-v).

Third, monetary inflation beyond specie, even on a modest scale, causes an unfair redistribution of income and wealth. Ludwig von Mises makes this point. An increase in the stock of money does not increase general welfare, but does have redistribution effects: "...for it can only benefit a part of the community at the cost of a corresponding loss by the other part" (Mises 1953:208). Garrison agrees: "Actual monetary injections, whether in the presence or the absence of economic growth, are always nonneutral" (Garrison 1985:73).

According to the American Institute for Economic Research, a free-market pro-gold foundation established by E. C. Harwood in the 1930s, a gold standard offers these benefits: It inhibits unwise fiscal and banking policies; restores investors' confidence; ends fluctuations in the dollar and other currencies; lifts the veil that conceals basic economic problems; promotes maximum employment, production, and purchasing power; facilitates long-term industrial progress; and lastly, maintains the freedom of the citizens (Patterson 1964:38-48).

In sum, a pure gold standard "is the only system compatible with the fullest preservation of the rights of property. It is the only system that assures the end of inflation, and with it, of the business cycle" (Rothbard 1974:35). As Melchior Palyi states, the gold standard "was an essential instrument of economic freedom. It protected the individual against arbitrary measures of the government by offering a convenient hedge against 'confiscatory' taxation, as well as against the depreciation or devaluation of the currency. It was an instrument of 'mobility' within and beyond national borders. Above all, it raised a mighty barrier against authoritarian interferences with the economic process" (Palyi 1972:5).

Neither Inflation Nor Deflation Under Gold

One of the unique features of a full-fledged gold standard is that the world will face neither a deflationary collapse nor a serious threat of inflation. Under a pure gold standard (without fractional reserves) the money supply is unlikely to decline. As can be seen from line a in figure 5.1, the world gold stock never declined year to year from 1815-1932, when the U. K. (and the U.S. for part of that time) was on the gold standard. The reason is because gold is hardly ever consumed. It simply changes form. The amount of gold unrecovered in industry, lost at sea, or buried in some remote location is relatively small. Unlike soybeans or bricks, gold is not used up or consumed. The amount of world gold stocks increases every year 1 to 5 percent, depending on annual production (Skousen 1996:86). Even the gold rushes of California, Australia and South Africa never increased the aggregate world gold stock by more than 5% in any one year. Granted, considerable price inflation occurred near the places where gold was found, but the adjustment to new gold discoveries was fairly quick. But then how did the money supply decline by a third in the U. S. in 1929-33 when the U. S. operated under a gold standard? The answer is that we did not have a 100% gold standard, nor fully backed bank reserves, but rather fractional reserves under a gold exchange standard, a "token" gold standard, in the words of Richard Timberlake (Timberlake 2003:324; cf. 1993:254-73).

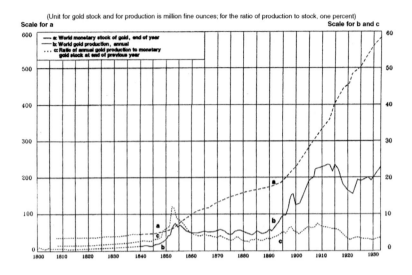

Figure 5.1. World Gold Stock and Gold Production, 1800-1932
Source: Rufus S. Tucker, "Gold and the General Price Level,"
Review of Economics and Statistics (July 1934).

Advocates make a utilitarian argument for gold: it creates a more stable monetary environment. Historically, the purchasing power of money under a classical gold standard has been more stable than under a fiat money system. As Lawrence H. White notes, "The main utilitarian arguments for adhering to a gold standard rests on the proposition that it more reliably preserves the purchasing power of money...than a fiat standard" (White 1999:40). Data by Michael D. Bordo confirm this conclusion (see figure 5.2).

As the two graphs indicate, prices were slightly deflationary under the international gold standard (except during war times); prices were significantly inflationary when nations went off the classical gold standard.

Friedman and the Case Against Gold

For a variety of reasons, Milton Friedman and the Chicago school prefer a well-administered fiat money system over an uncertain gold standard. It should first be pointed out that

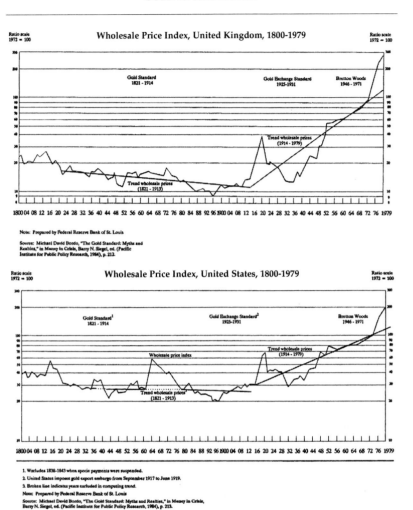

Figure 5.2. Wholesale Price Index, UK and US, 1800-1979
Source: Bordo 1984.

Friedman expressed positive comments about gold in his early writings. "A full-fledged gold standard in which all money consisted of gold or warehouse receipts for gold except perhaps for a fixed fiduciary issue would have the great merits of complete automaticity and of freedom from government control" (1960:81). Historically, Friedman praised the classic international gold standard which existed until 1914: "The blind, undesigned, and quasi-automatic workings of the gold standard turned out to produce a greater measure of predictability and regularity — perhaps because its discipline was impersonal and inescapable — than did deliberate and conscious control exercised within institutional arrangements intended to promote stability" (Friedman and Schwartz 1963:10).

Friedman defends the gold standard during the Great Depression of the 1930s. Countering Barry Eichengreen's thesis that the gold standard caused the 1929-33 crisis (Eichengreen 1995), Friedman and Schwartz maintain, "We did not permit the inflow of gold to expand the U. S. money stock. We not only sterilized it, but we went much further. Our money stock moved perversely, going down as the gold stock went up" (Friedman and Schwartz 1963:360-61). Monetary historian Richard Timberlake agrees that the Great Depression could have been avoided entirely if the U. S. had been on the classical gold standard, noting that gold reserves increased to 4,900 tons in 1933 and 18,000 tons in 1940. "Had the gold standard remained dominant, the inflows of gold that occurred, but before 1929 and throughout most of the four critical years following, would have increased the quantity of money by the 'right' amount. No recession-turned-into-a-depression could have occurred" (Timberlake 2003:325).

Nevertheless, Friedman has several complaints about gold. Because of occasional gold rushes, the money supply can vary considerably under gold. Inflation and cyclicality aren't characteristics of only fiat money systems. But Friedman's biggest complaint, echoed by economists of all types, is the "waste of resources" argument. As Paul Samuelson proclaims in his popular textbook, "How absurd to waste resources digging gold out of the bowels of the earth, only to inter it back again in the vaults of Fort Knox, Kentucky!" (Samuelson 1970:700). "The fundamental defect of a gold standard," according to Friedman, "is that it requires the use of real resources to add to the stock of money." Friedman estimates that it would cost approximately 4% of GDP each year to maintain a gold standard, while a fiduciary currency "would involve a negligible use of real resources to produce the medium of exchange" (1960:5-7).

Most economists agreed with Friedman until Auburn professor Roger W. Garrison demonstrated otherwise. In a celebrated article, Garrison demonstrates that going off the gold standard does not reduce the resource cost of a national currency. After the U. S. went completely off the gold standard in 1971, "gold continued to be mined, refined, cast or minted, stored, and guarded; the resource costs continued to be incurred. In fact, a paper standard administered by an irresponsible monetary authority may drive the monetary value of gold so high that more resource costs are incurred under the paper standard than would have incurred under a gold standard" (Garrison 1985:70). Garrison's argument is so compelling that Friedman no longer defends the "cost of resource" thesis (Schwartz 1987:310). In fact, Friedman and Schwartz seem to have changed their views, stating, "Our own conclusion—like that of Walter Bagehot and Vera Smith—is that leaving monetary and banking arrangements to the market would have produced a more satisfactory outcome than was actually achieved through government involvement" (Schwartz 1987:311). Apparently Adam Smith's concepts of the invisible hand and unintended consequences apply also to the monetary sphere.

The Austrians Debate the Nature
of a Gold Standard

If a market monetary system is going to be instituted, what kind of commodity-based standard should be adopted? Austrians differ on this question. Ludwig von Mises was highly sympathetic with the gold standard, but largely for political, not economic, reasons. "Gold is not an ideal basis for a monetary system," he declares. "Like all human creations, the gold standard is not free from shortcomings; but in the existing circumstances there is no other way of emancipating the monetary system from the changing influences of party politics and government interference....The excellence of the gold standard is to be seen in the fact that it renders the determination of the monetary unit's purchasing power independent of the policies of governments and political parties. Furthermore, it prevents rulers from eluding the financial and budgetary prerogatives of the representative assemblies" (Mises 1953:4). Mises favored a gold standard for political reasons, and was also sympathetic to a free banking system with gold as the numeraire.

Friedrich Hayek's early writings favors gold, but also strictly on political grounds: "the choice of gold with all its undeniable defects is made necessary entirely by political considerations" (Hayek 1937:74). After World World II, Hayek abandoned a pure gold standard on behalf of a composite commodity standard, where the stock of money would expand or contract according to a raw commodity index (1948:209-19). Later in the 1970s he advocated the "denationalization" of the government monopoly of money for the competitive circulation of privately issued currencies (Hayek 1976). Linking a monetary system to a commodity index, however, is likely to be highly unstable, given the volatility of commodity prices (see Rothbard's critique of Hayek's commodity currency ideas in Rothbard 1985:5-7).

As we have noted earlier, Murray Rothbard supports a genuine 100% gold standard. Fractional reserves would be prohibited for demand deposits, and Rothbard even favors replacing the dollar, the franc, and other currency names with gold weights only (Rothbard 1974, 1985). Silver would play a role, but to avoid Gresham's Law, the exchange between gold and silver should be freely-fluctuating parallel standards, not a fixed rate between the two commodities (known as bimetalism). Most importantly, gold and silver must circulate among the public in the form of coins and bank notes as gold and silver certificates.

Mises and Free Banking

Many Austrians have expressed misgivings about Rothbard's 100% gold standard policy, and now favor a more flexible "free banking" system, where government does not attempt to control the level of bank reserves for demand or time deposits. Supporters of free banking include Lawrence H. White, George Selgin, and Roger Garrison, with sympathetic support from Ludwig von Mises and Henry Hazlitt. White, in particular, has questioned Rothbard's ethical claim of fraud in fractional reserve banking. "It is difficult to see why an analyst committed to the ethic of individual sovereignty, as Rothbard elsewhere clearly is, would wish to prevent banks and their customers from making whatever sorts of contractual arrangements are mutually agreeable" (White 1985:120). According to White and other free bankers, as long as commercial banks are transparent, they should be able to offer checking accounts which "promise to pay the bearer on demand" without a reserve-holding requirement. "There is nothing to indicate that the note constitutes a warehouse receipt or establishes a bailment contract" unless the bank wishes to do so (White in Rockwell 1985:120).

What is free banking? According to Selgin and White, who have done considerable research in this area, both theoretically and historically, free banking is a form of an invisible hand or free trade in money. Government's involvement in the monetary sphere would be entirely laissez faire: "There is no government control of the quantity of exchange media. There is no state-sponsored central bank. There are no legal barriers to the entry, branching, or exit of commercial banks....There are no reserve requirements....There are no government deposit guarantees" (Selgin and White 1994:1718-19).

Wouldn't free banking without government guarantees and without reserve requirements and other forms of supervision deteriorate into chaotic "wild cat" banking? How can citizens be assured that a stable, non-inflationary monetary framework is achievable under free banking? Here White and Selgin rely primarily on historical evidence. Based on studies of free banking in Scotland and Britain in the 18th century and 19th century, "there is no evidence of a tendency toward natural monopoly in the issue of bank notes" (White 1985:118). According to White and Selgin, for over a century and a half, when Scotland had free entry and minimal government interference with the banking system, virtually all of the bank notes of different banks circulated at par, and there were few bank failures. Furthermore, they say, competition among bank note issuers assures a variety of choices in banking and minimization of insolvency risk. Advocates concur that free banking will not be destablizing: "The advantage of free banking is that a plurality of issuers minimizes the chance for large-scale errors in the money supply" (White 1985: 121). Competition would keep banks from overissuing their bank notes. "The rival banks that accept these deposits will quickly turn around and demand redemption of the first bank's liabilities through the interbank clearing system. The overexpansive bank will discover that its specie reserves are draining away, a situation it cannot let persist" (White 1985:122). Monetary inflation would be minimized. As Mises asserts, "Free banking is the only method available for the prevention of the dangers inherent in credit expansion. It would, it is true, not hinder a slow credit expansion, kept within very narrow limits, on the part of cautious banks which provide the public with all information required about their financial status....Only free banking would have rendered the market economy secure against crises and depressions" (Mises 1966:443). Although gold is not necessary as a numeraire to the free-banking system (silver may serve as a good substitute), "only with free banking is the operation of the gold standard fully self-regulating" (White 1985:122).

Friedman is not as convinced as White and Selgin about the favorable history of free banking. He points out that New England came closest to matching Scotland in its free-banking characteristics, yet regional bank notes circulated at varying discounts and did not achieve the stability Scotland had (Schwartz 1987:301-03). Rothbard is also highly critical of White and Selgin. Looking at the history of Scottish banking between 1716 and 1845, Rothbard concludes that Scottish banks were not free, and and "worked no better than central-bank-dominated English banking," pointing to a lengthy series of boom-bust cycles between 1760 and 1845 (Rothbard 1997b:311-13, 317).

As I see it, the major drawback to free banking is the high degree of faith in the market required by the public to accept this kind of laissez faire framework. Without any government regulation or reserve requirements, the degree of uncertainty in the system is far greater than a system based on 100% reserves in specie, or a Monetarist Rule. And who wants uncertainty in the money system when other secure systems are available? On a practical level, who wants to deal with potentially dozens of different kinds of privately issued bank notes? Presumably under free banking there would be no official national bank notes, and the wide variety of private notes might be intimidating (Horwitz 2000:212).

Supply Sider Alternatives

A number of supply-sider free-market economists sympathetic with the Austrian school favor less drastic measures to establish a stable, non-inflationary environment, such as a currency board, a gold exchange standard, or a central bank policy targeting the gold price. These supply siders include Art Laffer, Paul Craig Roberts, Steve Hanke, and Steve Forbes. Currency boards make sense for smaller nations that can rely on the currencies of major industrial powerhouses, such as the United States, Europe and Japan, for a stabilized banking system. Currency boards are not an option for major G7 countries, however. For them, supply siders urge a gold exchange standard. By fixing the price of gold close to the current market price in dollars or in another major currency, the government would be required to buy and sell gold at that fixed price. A country engaging in irresponsible fiscal and monetary excesses would see gold and foreign currencies leaving the country, forcing them to retrench, while a country adopting anti-inflationary measures would see their reserves increase. A third alternative offered by supply siders is to keep the current fiat money system, but use gold as a primary "monetary target." When the price of gold exceeds this price target, it would indicate excessive monetary expansion, and the central bank should tighten; if the price of gold falls below the price target, it suggests the central bank should loosen.

Critics have attacked these measures on a variety of grounds. Rothbard notes that the gold exchange standard is precisely the one that operated under the Bretton Woods Agreement in the post-war period, and it did not discourage nations from inflating. Targeting the price of gold suffers from two problems: first, the price of gold is quite volatile, so that targeting a specific price is highly improbable; and second, lags between changes in monetary policy and its effect on the price of gold and other goods and services would lead to a constant problem of overshooting the target price. Gold may not stop at the target price, but may keep going for months before turning around, creating a volatile environment.

Advantage, Chicago

Even though the Austrians have a better theoretical, historical and ethical argument in favor of the classic gold standard, the Chicago school offers better pragmatic solutions to monetary problems we currently face. Returning to a gold standard, as beneficial as it might be in the long run, would create so many distribution problems that it cannot be instituted without creating its own crisis (except in the return of gold as private money, discussed below). Even Murray Rothbard admits, "certainly a matter for genuine concern would be the enormous impetus such a change would give for several years in the mining of gold, as well as the disruption it would cause in the pattern of international trade" (Rothbard 1974:40). Stabilizing monetarist policy on the other hand is quite feasible, especially given that every nation today is already on a fiat money system. The Federal Reserve's manipulation of interest rates and reserve requirements should be minimized, and the central bank ought to be limited by monetary/constitutional rules based on a reasonable form of the quantity theory of money. Granted, monetarists have a problem deciding how to measure the money supply, but if a 100% deposit rule were adopted along with some form of monetarist rule, it could gain better control the monetary aggregates. (It should be noted, however, that the introduction of electronic money and trading on popular websites such as eBay may create new challenges to controlling money and monetary targeting.) When the world went off the gold exchange standard in 1971, inflationary pressures increased, but since the early 1980s, the monetary authorities seem to have gained better control of inflationary pressures; and so far we have avoided a worldwide banking catastrophe. Despite the defects of the banking system, it has worked so far, and the Chicago school has the upper hand. Perhaps free competitive nationwide banking, an important feature of "free banking," and currency competition, as advocated by Hayek, will make it work better.

What about the monetary role of gold? Unless the financial world faces a worldwide crisis, causing the public to lose faith in the modern monetary system, gold will play primarily a role as a hedge against inflation, crisis, and war. As such, government treasuries and central banks would be wise to hold onto their gold as an important monetary base. The unregulated market price of gold serves well as an indicator of world monetary/banking stability: a stable or slightly declining gold price suggests monetary equilibrium, a soaring gold price implies a global financial crisis (Skousen 1996:xviii-xx). But it is unlikely that the price of gold will function well as a monetary target, as the supply-siders advocate. The problem with such a policy is that, given the volatility of gold's market value and the lag time between the change in monetary policy and its effects, the Fed is likely to overshoot its target in both directions, and hence create the boom-bust cycle it is trying to prevent. General price stability has proven to be a more workable target, although the price of gold, not just the Consumer Price Index, should be a global measure of inflation.

Return to Gold as Private Money?

Recently a new electronic money — gold as measured in troy ounces — has raised the possibility of a return to private money outside the control of the Federal Reserve and the central-banking system. Although small but growing, firms such as goldmoney and e-money facilitate transactions on the internet for the purchase and sale of goods and services. Each account is adjusted following a transaction. Once dollars and other currencies are exchanged into gold, based on the current price of gold, all transactions are recorded without reference or connection to dollars, euros, yen, or other forms of government-controlled money substitutes. If this new service becomes popular enough, it could provide an alternative parallel monetary system that would eventually make the current monetary system obsolete. We could witness the opposite of Gresham's Law occurring: Good money drives out bad. The Austrians may win by choice.

References

Bordo, Michael D. 1984. "The Gold Standard" in Barry N. Siegel, ed., *Money in Crisis*. San Francisco: Pacific Research Institute.

Eichengreen, Barry. 1995. *Golden Fetters: The Gold Standard and the Great Depression, 1919-1939*. New York: Oxford University Press.

Fisher, Irving. 1996 [1945]. *100% Money*. London: Pickering & Chatto.

Friedman, Milton. 1960. *A Program for Monetary Stability*. New York: Fordham University Press.

Friedman, Milton. 1962. *Capitalism and Freedom*. Chicago: University of Chicago Press.

Friedman, Milton, and Anna J. Schwartz. 1963. *A Monetary History of the United States, 1867-1960*. Princeton: Princeton University Press.

Friedman, Milton. 1969. *The Optimum Quantity of Money and Other Essays*. London: Macmillan.

Friedman, Milton. 2004. "Reflections on A Monetary History," *Cato Journal* 23:3 (Winter), 349-51.

Friedman, Milton and Anna J. Schwartz. 1963. *A Monetary History of the United States, 1867-1960*. Princeton: Princeton University Press.

Garrison, Roger W. 1985. "The Costs of a Gold Standard," in Llewellyn H. Rockwell, Jr., ed., *The Gold Standard: An Austrian Perspective*. Lexington, Mass: Lexington Books, 61-79.

Harwood, E. C. 1970. *Reconstruction of Economics*. Great Barrington, Mass: American Institute for Economic Research.

Hayek, Friedrich. 1937. *Monetary Nationalism and International Stability*. New York: Longmans, Green).

Hayek, Friedrich. 1948. *Individualism and Economic Order*. Chicago: University of Chicago Press.

Hayek, Friedrich. 1976. *The Denationalization of Money*. London: Institute of Economic Affairs.

Horwitz, Steven. 2000. *Microfoundations and Macroeconomics: An Austrian Perspective*. London: Routledge.

Meltzer, Allan. 2004. *A History of the Federal Reserve: Volume 1, 1913-1951*. Chicago: University of Chicago Press.

Menger, Carl. 1981 [1976]. *Principles of Economics*. New York: New York University Press.

Mises, Ludwig von. 1953. *The Theory of Money and Credit*. 2nd ed. New Haven: Yale University Press.

Mises, Ludwig von. 1966. *Human Action, A Treatise on Economics*. 3rd ed. Chicago: Regnery.

Oppenheimer, Franz. 1997 [1926]. *The State.* New York: Fox and Wilkes.

Palyi, Melchior. 1972. *The Twilight of Gold 1914-1936: Myths and Realities.* Chicago: Regnery.

Patterson, Robert T. ed. 1964. *Why Gold?* Great Barrington, MA: American Institute for Economic Research.

Paul, Ron, and Lewis Lehrman. 1982. *The Case for Gold.* Washington, DC: Cato Institute.

Rockwell, Lewellyn H., Jr., ed. 1985. *The Gold Standard: An Austrian Perspective.* Lexington, MA: Lexington Books.

Rothbard, Murray N. 1974 [1962]. *The Case for a 100 Percent Gold Dollar.* Washington, DC: Libertarian Review Press.

Rothbard, Murray N. 1983. *The Mystery of Banking.* New York: Richardson and Snyder.

Rothbard, Murray N. 1985. "The Case for a Genuine Gold Dollar," in Llewellyn H. Rockwell, Jr., ed., *The Gold Standard: An Austrian Perspective.* Lexington, Mass: Lexington Books, 1-17.

Rothbard, Murray N. 1994. *The Case Against the Fed.* Auburn, AL: Mises Institute.

Rothbard, Murray N. 1997b. *The Logic of Action II: Method, Money, and the Austrian School.* Cheltenham, UK: Edward Elgar.

Rothbard, Murray N. 2002. *A History of Money and Banking in the United States.* Auburn, Alabama: Mises Institute.

Samuelson, Paul A. 1970. *Economics.* 8th ed. New York: McGraw Hill.

Schwartz, Anna J. 1987. *Money in Historical Perspective.* Chicago: University of Chicago Press.

Selgin, George and Lawrence White. 1994. "How Would the Invisible Hand Handle Money?" *Journal of Economic Literature* 22 (December), 1718-49.

Simons, Henry. 1948. *Economic Policy for a Free Society.* Chicago: University of Chicago Press.

Skousen, Mark. 1996. *Economics of a Pure Gold Standard.* 3rd ed. New York: Foundation for Economic Education.

Smith, Vera C. 1936. *The Rationale for Central Banking.* London: King.

Timberlake, Richard H. 1993. *Monetary History of the United States: An Intellectual and Institutional History.* Chicago: University of Chicago Press.

Timberlake, Richard H. 2003. "Meltzer's *History of the Federal Reserve* and the Evolution of Central Banking." *Cato Journal* 23:2 (Fall), 319-334.

White, Andrew Dickson. 1981. *Fiat Money Inflation in France*. Washington, DC: Cato Institute.

White, Lawrence H. 1985. "Free Banking and the Gold Standard," in Llewellyn H. Rockwell, Jr., ed., *The Gold Standard: An Austrian Perspective*. Lexington, Mass: Lexington Books, 113-28.

White, Lawrence H. 1999. *The Theory of Monetary Institutions*. New York: Blackwell.

Chapter Six

MACROECONOMICS, THE GREAT DEPRESSION, AND THE BUSINESS CYCLE

Fortunately, a correct theory of depression and of the business cycle does exist, even though it is universally neglected in present-day economics....[It is] known as the 'Austrian' theory of the business cycle.

—Murray N. Rothbard (in Ebeling 1996:74, 81)

The Hayek-Mises explanation of the business cycle is contradicted by the evidence. It is, I believe, false.

—Milton Friedman (1993:171)

At the September 1994 Mont Pelerin Society meetings in Cannes, France, Allan Meltzer, the highly respected monetarist from Carnegie-Mellon University, applauded Hayek's emphasis on uncertainty, the costs of information, and the concepts of coordination and spontaneous order, but rejected out of hand the macroeconomic model and business cycle theory Hayek developed in *Prices and Production* in the early 1930s. "The book is obscure and incomprehensible," he declared. His remarks are reminiscent of Keynes's brusque dismissal of *Prices and Production*: "one of the most frightful muddles I have ever read" and a "thick bank of fog" (Keynes 1931:394, 397).

When the 50th anniversary edition of Friedrich Hayek's bestseller *The Road to Serfdom* was published in 1994, Milton

Friedman gladly wrote a flattering introduction. "I am an enormous admirer of Hayek, but not for his economics. I think *Prices and Production* was a very flawed book. I think his capital theory book is unreadable. On the other hand, *The Road to Serfdom* is one of the great books of all time. His writings in [political theory] are magnificent, and I have nothing but great admiration for them" (Ebenstein 2001:81).

At another Mont Pelerin Society meeting in Vienna in 1996, several lectures were presented on Hayek, Mises and the Austrian school. At this meeting, Chicago professor Sherwin Rosen observed that Austrian capital theory failed the "market test." According to Rosen, the competitive free market of ideas tends to weed out bad economics from good economics. Good economics "passes the market test," he claimed, bad economics doesn't, and is discarded (Rosen 1997:150-51). Therefore, concludes Professor Rosen, if some Austrian concepts have not been absorbed by the "neoclassical" model, they are "useless" and should be forgotten. He cites Austrian business cycle and capital theory as an example.[1]

In 1999, on the 100th anniversary of Hayek's birth, Liberty Fund sponsored a conference on "The Legacy of Friedrich von Hayek" at the University of Chicago. Speakers included such luminaries as Gary Becker, James Buchanan, Sherwin Rosen, Richard Epstein, Kurt Leube, and Lord Ralph Harris. Topics included Hayek's contributions to the socialist calculation debate, social justice, information and the market process, but no one was invited to elucidate favorably Hayek's macroeconomic model and business cycle theory.

Frank Knight Debates Hayek

The Chicago disdain for Hayek's trade cycle and capital theories goes back, in part, to Frank Knight, who, according to

[1] It is noteworthy that Rosen's negative assessment of Austrian capital theory was omitted from his printed version in the *Journal of Economic Perspectives* (Rosen 1997).

James Buchanan, "dominated the intellectual atmosphere ....and who seemed to most of us, to epitomize the spirit of the university" (in Shils 1991:244). Knight was a firm believer in individual freedom and free markets, but rejected the Austrian theory of capital, a theory which forms the basis of the Austrians' macroeconomics and its interpretation of the cause and cure of the business cycle. Larry Wimmer reports that Austrian capital theory was one of those subjects *verboten* at Chicago.

It all goes back to a bitter debate between Knight and Hayek in the 1930s over capital theory and the business cycle. In *Prices and Production*, published originally in 1931, Hayek uses a "time structure of production" concept as the foundation of the business cycle theory that he and Ludwig von Mises employed to anticipate the Great Depression. Hayek expresses the long-standing Austrian view, held by Menger, Böhm-Bawerk, and Mises, that investment capital once invested in specific capital goods and production processes is inherently heterogeneous and specific in its use. When the government adopts an "easy money" policy by expanding the money supply and artificially lowering interest rates, the effect is felt unevenly in the economy. There are winners and losers. Monetary inflation is never neutral; it affects some industries and income earners more than others. The boom is largely in the higher-order capital goods industries and commercial building sector, where the production process lengthens. When the inflationary boom inevitably tops out and turns into a bust, it may take years for the industrial capital-goods and building markets to recover because of their specificity and heterogeneity.[2]

Hayek's dynamic malinvestment model was initially well received in England. Lionel Robbins, chairman of the London School of Economics, called it perhaps "the most fruitful scientific development of our age" in the foreword to *Prices and*

2 For an excellent summary of Hayek's theory of the business cycle, see O'Driscoll 1977:35-91.

Production (Hayek 1931:preface[3]). Joseph Schumpeter said that Hayek's little book "met with a sweeping success that has never been equaled by any strictly theoretical book," attracting young disciples John Hicks, Abba P. Lerner, Nicholas Kaldor, G. L. S. Shackle, E. F. Schumacher, and even Paul Sweezy. But within a few years, most wrote critically of Hayek's capital theory, ultimately joining the Keynesians, except for Sweezy, who became a Marxist.

Frank Knight admits that he "completely accepted it [the time-production process] for years, taught it in class lectures and expounded it in text materials," including his *Risk, Uncertainty and Profit* (1921) but then abandoned it, perhaps after reading John Bates Clark's critique of Böhm-Bawerk (see Skousen 1990, chapter 3, for a review of this debate). He became convinced that "all capital is inherently perpetual" and "homogeneous," like a "perpetual fund" of synchronized consumption and production. Clark and Knight compare capital to a reservoir, with new production flowing in, and capital flowing out when used up. Knight follows Irving Fisher, who taught that capital and interest are stock-flow concepts, where capital is a permanent asset which yields future interest income. Knight, Fisher and Clark deny that capital is heterogeneous or that the production process lengthens or shortens during the business cycle (Knight 1934). Knight further elucidates this aggregate income/expenditure concept in his "circular flow diagram" that he developed, and which Paul Samuelson popularized in his textbook as an explanation of how the macro economy works (Patinkin 1981:28, 53-72). Hayek responded by saying that Knight's "perpetual fund" view of capital is a "psuedo-concept." According to Hayek, Knight assumes "perfect foresight" when he eliminates time entirely from the capitalistic process, and

---

3 Robbins's flattering preface was removed from the 1935 second edition of *Prices and Production*. In his autobiography, Robbins called his siding with Hayek in the 1930s the "greatest mistake of my professional career...It will always be a matter of deep regret to me that, although I was acting in good faith and with a strong sense of social obligation, I should have so opposed policies which might have mitigated the economic distress of those days" (Robbins 1971:154-55).

adopted a capital concept which "leaves us with the impression that there is a sort of substance, some fluid of definite magnitude which flows from one capital good to another" (Hayek 1936).

Fritz Machlup (1902-83), a former student of Wieser and Mises, wrote a response to Knight. Calling Hayek's capital theory an "indispensable" tool of analysis, Machlup affirms, "There was and is always the choice between maintaining, increasing, or consuming capital."[4] Machlup had recently witnessed firsthand the "consumption of capital" in his homeland, Austria, between the wars, due to inflation, high taxes, and socialistic reforms. He concluded somberly, "Austria had most impressive records in five lines: she increased public expenditures, she increased wages, she increased social benefits, she increased bank credits, she increased consumption. After all these achievements she was on the verge of ruin" (Machlup 1935). Nevertheless, Knight remained unconvinced and his anti-Hayekian views prejudiced his students against the Austrian theory. Similarly, George Stigler's dissertation, written under the direction of Knight and later published as *Production and Distribution Theories* (1941), takes a dim view of Austrian capital theory.

Knight also disagrees with Hayek's and Mises's austere laissez faire solutions to the Great Depression. Hayek and Mises opposed reinflating the money supply and running deficits, while Knight, Simons, and Viner urged Washington to combat mass unemployment and deflation through vast expansionary fiscal and monetary policies (see chapter 3). Milton Friedman recalls those dark days of the Depression, where the Austrian laissez-faire prescription was considered "dismal" compared to the positive, quasi-Keynesian program of the Chicago economists (Gordon 1974:163). Given the severe

---

4 Unlike other earlier disciples of Hayek, Machlup remained a defender of Hayek and his capital theory after leaving Austrian and moving to the United States where he taught economics at Harvard, Buffalo, Johns Hopkins, and New York University. "If I had to single out the area in which Hayek's contributions were the most fundamental and pathbreaking, I would cast my vote for the theory of capital" (Machlup 1976:50).

disagreements between Hayek's and Knight's concepts of capital and the business cycle, it should not be surprising that when Hayek came to the University of Chicago in the early 1950s, he was offered a position in the Committee for Social Thought, not in the economics department.

Friedman Vs. The Austrians: What Caused the Great Depression?

In the 1950s, as Friedman was working on his massive *A Monetary History of the United States,* he took exception to the Austrian view of the cause of the Great Depression. To the Austrians and "sound money" economists, the seeds of the Great Depression were planted in the 1920s, caused by an inflationary boom that inevitably had to collapse in the 1930s. To Friedman and the Chicago school, there was no inflationary boom, only an unnecessary deflationary collapse in the early 1930s. The fault was not the Federal Reserve of the 1920s, which was run ably by Benjamin Strong, but the Federal Reserve of the 1930s, which was run "inanely" in the absence of Strong's leadership. Regarding the 1920s, Friedman writes, "I have no reason to suppose there was any over-investment boom...during the 1920s." In general, he states, "Everything going on in the 1920s was fine" (private correspondence; cf Friedman and Schwartz 1963:298).

The two schools also differ on their interpretation of events in the early 1930s, and what policies should have been pursued to end the Depression. Friedman, Meltzer, and other monetarists blame the Fed for raising interest rates in 1931, failing to bail out the commercial banks, sterilizing gold imports and squeezing credit through open-market operations (Friedman and Schwartz 1963:299-419; Meltzer 2004:277, 281-82, 727-33; Timberlake 1993:263-73). "The monetary system collapsed, but it clearly need not have done so," declare Friedman and Schwartz (1963:407). Friedman and Schwartz, in particular, argue that if Benjamin Strong had not died in late 1928, his leadership might have prevented the depression, and vigorous reinflation could have taken place to ease the crisis (1963:412-19). Certainly, as Richard Timberlake and Allan Meltzer point out, the increase in gold reserves would have justified an expansion in the money supply during the 1929-33 period, and the crisis could have been averted.

The Austrians see things quite differently. The boom of the 1920s was in part artificial, they say, and therefore required a bust. As Rothbard states, "The depression, then, far from being an evil scourge, is the necessary and beneficial return of the economy to normal after the distortions imposed by the boom" (Rothbard 1983 [1963]:20). Moreover, inflating the money supply during the Depression would only aggravate the situation and postpone the recovery. As Hayek states, "If, however, the deflation is not a cause but an effect of the unprofitableness of industry, then it is surely vain to hope that, by reversing the deflationary process, we can regain lasting prosperity" (Hayek 1933:19-20). According to Rothbard, Benjamin Strong was the wrong kind of Fed chairman in the 1920s: "Strong pursued an inflationary policy throughout his reign....It was only the end of the monetary expansion after Strong's death that brought an end to the boom and ushered in a recession — a recession that was made into chronic depression by massive intervention by Presidents Hoover and Roosevelt" (1983 [1963]:243). It appears that there is little ground for agreement regarding the great boom-bust era between the two world wars.

The Austrian View of the Great Depression

Who's right? Let's review the historical context of this debate. Recall that neither Irving Fisher, the principal monetarist of the day and an advocate of New Era prosperity, nor John Maynard Keynes, the noted Cambridge economist, anticipated the most traumatic economic collapse of the 20th century. Seeing only relatively stable prices and good times,

5 For a more complete story of who predicted the crash and who didn't, see Skousen 1991:102-06

Fisher and Keynes both rejected the idea that there were any inflationary imbalances in the economy.[5] On the other hand, although they did not pinpoint an exact date, Mises and Hayek, along with members of the sound-money movement in the United States, had forecast the 1929 crash and Depression, and had developed a theory backing their prediction.[6]

This Misesian theory drew upon the earlier works of several economists (Mises 1953:355-66):

1. Menger/Böhm-Bawerk's capital theory: According to Austrian founders Carl Menger and Eugen Böhm-Bawerk, the production process involves lengthy "roundabout" stages and capital goods specific to their use. In general, an inflationary boom sends false signals that artificially inflates this heterogeneous capital/production structure, leading to a real estate boom, high tech bubble, bull market in stocks, intensified research and development, and increased mining. When the demand for these overproduced markets falls short, the malinvested capital industries cannot easily recover and adjust to the new downsized conditions.

2. Wicksell's natural rate of interest hypothesis: The Swedish economist Knut Wicksell distinguished between the social rate of time preference, or natural saving rates of the community, which he called the "natural" rate of interest, and the actual market rate of interest for loanable funds to business. Normally, the two are the matched through the dynamics of supply

6 The sound-money economists of the 1920s and 1930s included Benjamin M. Anderson, chief economist at Chase Manhattan Bank and editor of the Chase Economic Bulletin, and H. Parker Willis, professor of banking at Columbia University. See Skousen 1993:262-64. Anderson wrote an excellent detailed economic history of the United States from World War I to the end of World War II (Anderson 1979 [1949]). I highly recommend this work for an eyewitness account of the boom-bust cycle of the first half of the 20th century global economy, in addition to a careful analysis of Keynesian economics, the gold standard, government regulation of business and finance. In the foreword, Arthur Kemp notes that of the Chicago and Austrian schools, "Anderson really belongs to neither school, but if he leans a bit, it is in the direction of the Austrians" (Anderson 1979 [1949]:11).

and demand. However, a government-controlled monetary authority can intervene and temporarily reduce the market rate below the "natural" rate through an easy-money policy. (See figure 6.1 below.) According to Wicksell, if the market rate is less than the natural rate, a "cumulative process" of price inflation occurs. Eventually the economy overheats, forcing interest rates to go back up and even rise above the natural rate. The high real interest rates choke off the boom, resulting in a depression.

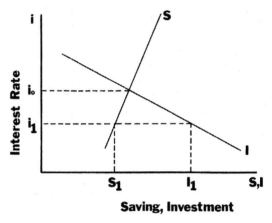

Figure 6.1 Wicksell's natural rate of interest (i_0)
Source: O'Driscoll 1977:53.

3. Hume-Ricardo specie flow mechanism: Under the international gold standard, an inflationary boom cannot last. According to the specie flow mechanism outlined by David Hume and David Ricardo, a domestic inflation raises domestic incomes, which in turn causes citizens to buy more imports than exports. The subsequent trade deficit causes gold to flow out of the country, creating a balance of payments deficit. The decline in gold causes the domestic money supply to decline, resulting in a recession. In short, under an international gold standard, an inflationary expansion must eventually cause a financial crisis and economic collapse.

Mises claims that the Federal Reserve artificially cheapened credit below the "natural" (or what Mises called the "equilibrium") rate of interest during most of the 1920s and orchestrated an unsustainable inflationary boom (i_1 in figure 6.1). Without a gold standard, this inflationary boom could have lasted years, but under the international gold standard, defective as it was, Mises and Hayek felt that the American economic expansion would inevitably end in crisis and a collapse. As Murray Rothbard states, "1929 was made inevitable by the vast bank credit expansion throughout the Western world during the 1920s: A policy deliberately adopted by the Western governments, and most importantly by the Federal Reserve System in the United States. It was made possible by the failure of the Western world to return to a genuine gold standard after World War I, and thus allowing more room for inflationary policies by government" (Rothbard 1996:88).

The Austrians emphasize that excessive credit expansion beyond gold reserves does more than increase prices; it also distorts the production process and the value of investment assets. It creates a "cluster of business errors" in the capital markets that is almost impossible to avoid (Rothbard 1983:16). By expanding the higher-order capital goods more than the lower-order consumer goods, an easy money policy creates an unsustainable boom that will inevitably collapse when the government stops expanding credit, or when interest rates rise and cut off the boom, returning the consumption/investment ratio to previous levels. Thus, when Mises and Hayek witnessed the Fed's alleged easy-credit policies in the mid-1920s, they sounded the alarm and warned that the "New Era" boom could not last, but must end in Depression. As Mises states after the crash, "From 1926 to 1929 the attention of the world was chiefly focused upon the question of American prosperity. As in all previous booms brought about by expansion of credit, it was then believed that the prosperity would last forever, and the warnings of the [Austrian] economists were disregarded. The turn of the tide in 1929 and the subsequent severe economic crisis were not a surprise for [Austrian] economists; they had foreseen them, even if they had not been able to predict the exact date of their occurrence" (Mises 1953:15).

Benjamin Anderson, chief economist at Chase Manhattan Bank, issued similar warnings. He notes that private individual saving, business capital, and taxation for capital spending are "never carried to excess," but excessive bank credit artificially stimulated by the government's central bank can create speculative imbalances in the stock market and Manhattan real estate. Anderson also points out that between 1921 and 1928, while demand deposits grew only 34%, time deposits jumped 135% (Anderson 1979 [1949]:182-204).

The Monetarist Interpretation of the 1920s

Milton Friedman sees things differently. In reviewing the monetary data of the U. S. during the 1920s, he concludes that there was no excessively liberal monetary policy nor an "overinvestment boom." The 1920s, he writes, was the "high tide" of Federal Reserve policy, where monetary inflation was modest, prices were relatively stable, and economic growth was reasonably high. "Far from being an inflationary decade, the twenties were the reverse" (Friedman and Schwartz 1963:298). The problem, according to Friedman, was not the 1920s, but the 1930s, when the Federal Reserve permitted the "Great Contraction" of the money supply that drove the economy into an economic tailspin. (See figures 6.2 and 6.3).

Allan H. Meltzer goes even further, arguing that monetary policy was not liberal enough in the 1920s, and castigates the Federal Reserve for adhering rigidly to a "real bills" doctrine[7] and raising interest rates in 1929 to curb speculation in the stock market. "If it had given attention to deflation instead of the booming stock market, the Federal Reserve could have recognized the symptoms of an excess demand for money and increased money growth" (Meltzer 2004:265). In other words, the Fed wasn't inflationary enough in the late 1920s. Timberlake adds that there had been a genuine gold standard and no Fed, the money supply would have expanded more than it did, based on the increase in U. S. gold reserves in the 1920s (Timberlake 1993:263-73).

Who's Right about the 1920s?

Was there an overinvestment boom and vast credit expansion in the 1920s? The answer depends on which statistics you examine. The "macro" data favor the monetarists' thesis, the "micro" data support the Austrians' view.

First, let's look at monetary policy. The Austrians argue that the Federal Reserve engaged in a "cheap-credit" policy in terms of expanding the money supply and keeping interest rates low during the 1920s. The money stock (M2) grew 46% between 1921-29, less than 4 percent per annum. Given annual GDP growth of 5.2% during the "Roaring Twenties" and a mild deflationary pressure on prices, the evidence seems to support the monetarists' claim that the growth in the money supply was not excessive. See figure 6.2, which measures the money supply growth (M2) during the 1920s.

---

7 Both Richard Timberlake (1993) and Allan Meltzer (2004) report that Federal Reserve officials were adherents to a "real bills" doctrine during the 1920s, the view that the Fed should only extend or restrict credit in conjunction with the growth of the real economy, meaning actual production and marketing of real goods, rather than for speculative purposes in stocks and real estate. According to Meltzer, the real-bills doctrine should have encouraged the Fed to expand credit more in the late 1920s, but the second part of the doctrine — extending credit in 1929 would only encourage excessive speculation on Wall Street — weighed more heavily.

The Stock of Money and Its Proximate Determinants, 1921–29

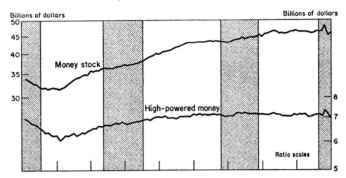

Figure 6.2. M2 growth 1920-29. *Source:* Friedman and Schwartz 1963:273

THE GREAT CONTRACTION
The Stock of Money and Its Proximate Determinants, Monthly,
1929–March 1933

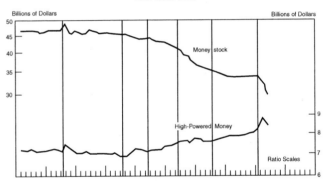

Figure 6.3. The Dramatic Decline in the Money Stock, 1929-33.
Source: Friedman and Schwartz 1963:333

Timberlake goes further: "According to all the data during the 1920s, both monetary and anecdotal, the whole tenor of Fed policymakers was to hold down on any expansion of 'credit' until the real economy began to respond" (cf Timberlake 1993:263-73).

Apparently Murray Rothbard looked at the data and admitted that it seemed far too modest to cause an "excessive" inflationary boom. He felt it necessary to prove that the monetary expansion in the 1920s was significantly higher than

Friedman's numbers by creating his own definition of the money supply. To Friedman's M2, Rothbard added shares held in savings and loans, deposits in credit unions and, surprisingly, the cash surrender values of life insurance policies—any money substitutes which conceivably could be redeemed at par. In his book *America's Great Depression*, Rothbard himself admits this broad definition of money was a "controversial suggestion" (Rothbard 1983:85). Rothbard was able to increase the money supply by 61.7% instead of Friedman's 46% figure. Most economists consider Rothbard's new definition of the money supply to be "eccentric" (Vaughn 1994:94), or in the words of Friedman, "pure chicanery." Cash surrender values of life insurance policies are not normally treated as liquid assets. Moreover, it was not necessary for Rothbard to create a contorted monetary aggregate figure to demonstrate an "easy credit" policy. The artificial boom in higher-order capital-goods industries could also be caused by lowering the rate of interest below the "natural" rate (Mises 1996:31). Austrians can point to the deliberate efforts by the Fed to lower interest rates, especially in 1924 and 1927 in an effort to help Britain maintain its gold deposits, as a means of generating an unjustifiable boom in assets and manufacturing.

Did in fact a discernible inflationary boom result from either a credit expansion or low-interest rate policy? In support of the monetarists, the broad-based price indices show little if any inflation, and a great deal of deflation. Consumer prices were relatively stable and wholesale and commodity prices fell between 1921 and 1929. However, other data support the Austrian view of an inflationary boom. The 1920s may not have been characterized by a "price" inflation, but there was, in the words of John Maynard Keynes, a "profit" inflation (Keynes 1930, vol. 2:190). After the 1920-21 depression, national output (GDP) grew at a robust 5.2% pace, substantially exceeding the national norm (3%). The Index of Manufacturing Production grew much more rapidly, virtually doubling between 1921 and 1929. So did capital investment and corporate profits.

As would happen again in the 1980s and 1990s, there appeared to be an "asset" bubble in stocks, bonds and real estate in the 1920s. A nationwide real estate boom occurred in the mid-1920s, especially a spectacular bubble in Florida that collapsed in 1927. Manhattan, the world's financial center, also experienced a boom, culminating in the decision in 1929 to build the Empire State Building, the world's largest skyscraper. The asset bubble was most pronounced on Wall Street. The Dow Jones Industrial Average began its monstrous bull market in late 1921 at a cyclical low of 66, mounting a drive that carried it to a high of 300 by mid-1929, more than quadruple its earlier value. The Standard & Poor's Index of Common Stocks was just as dramatic—Industrials, up 321%; Railroads, up 129%; and Utilities, up a remarkable 318% (Anderson 1979 [1949]:192-202). Even Allan Meltzer admits, "The rise in stock prices that ended in 1929 is extraordinary by almost any standard except 1998-2000....The increase in market capitalization relative to nominal GNP brought the ratio of the two to a level that was not surpassed until 1996" (Meltzer 2004:252).

Yet, amazingly, some monetarists deny a stock market orgy. Anna Schwartz suggests, "Had employment and economic growth continued, prices in the stock market could have been maintained" (Schwartz 1987:130). It's as if she wished to exonerate Irving Fisher's infamous blunder of declaring a week before the 1929 crash, "stock prices have reached what looks like a permanently high plateau." Fisher's leveraged position in Remington Rand and other stocks was wiped out by the crash. Schwartz's thesis depends on what appears to be reasonable price-earnings ratios for most stocks in 1929, 15.6 versus a norm of 13.6. However, P/E ratios are a notoriously misleading indicator of speculative activity. While they do tend to rise during a bull market, they severely understate the degree of speculation because both prices and earnings increase during an economic expansion. But let's look at the situation in another way. When annual national output averages 5.2% during the 1920s (a rather high figure), and the S&P Index of Common Stocks increase an average 18.6%, clearly there is a gigantic gap, and something has to give. In fact, the economy grew only 6.3% during 1927-29, while common stocks gained an unprecedented 82.2%. As the old Wall Street saying goes, "Trees don't grow to the sky." Moreover, the extremely high call rates on stock margin loans (over 15%) should have been a clue that a crash or major correction was inevitable (Skousen 1993:282).

In conclusion, was there an inflationary imbalance during the 1920s, sufficient to cause an economic crisis? The evidence is mixed, but on net balance, the Austrians have a case that the low-interest rate policies of the Fed were sufficient to create distortions in the "higher-order" sectors of the economy, and therefore a recession at minimum was necessary to correct these imbalances. But was Fed policy sufficiently easy to create a Great Depression following the 1929 stock market crash? Here the monetarists have the upper hand: only further deflationary blunders by the Federal Reserve could have turned the 1929-30 recession into the worst economic crisis of the 20th century.

Friedman's Plucking Model: A New Challenge to the Austrian Business Cycle Theory

Friedman raises additional issues with regard to the Austrian model in a 1964 article on monetary studies at the NBER and a follow-up 1993 article in *Economic Inquiry*. In both articles, Friedman questions the Mises-Hayek thesis that recessions are caused by prior inflations. He examines cyclical activity in the U. S. (as measured by GDP and other data) between 1879-1988, excluding war cycles and 1945-49. He concludes that there is no significant correlation between the length and severity of a recession and those of the preceding expansion. However, he notes, there was a fairly high correlation between the length and severity of a contraction and the succeeding expansion.

Friedman's thesis reflects a "Monetary Disequilibrium Theory" advanced over the years by Clark Warburton (1966), Don Patinkin (1965), Leland Yeager (1999), and other monetarists, where changes in economic activity are related to changes in monetary policy. Yet Friedman's business cycle theory not only questions Austrian cycle analysis, but business cycle theory in general. The traditional view is that "what goes up must come down," indicating that a bust always follows a boom. But Friedman reverses this traditional cause-and-effect relationship, suggesting "what goes down must come back up," in that busts are more related chronologically to succeeding booms. He calls it the "Plucking Model" (See figure 6.4 below).

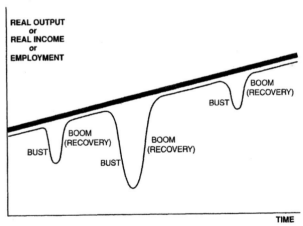

Figure 6.4. Bust and Boom Under Friedman's Plucking Model.
Source: Garrison 2001:223

Why the Plucking Model? Imagine a string with the consistency of taffy stretched across a long plane, so that the "taffy-like string is plucked down at random intervals and to various extents, so that the down-sags are identified as busts, and the up-sags as booms" (Garrison 2001:222-23). In his research, Friedman takes strong exception to the Austrian thesis that the cause of a recession is the prior inflation, and the greater the fiat inflation, the greater must be the subsequent crash, other things being equal. Friedman concludes that the evidence contradicts the view that "the higher they climb, the greater they fall." For example, there was little in the way of major inflation in the U. S. prior to the Great Depression. Similarly, the highly inflationary 1970s were followed by a relatively mild decline in GDP in the early 1980s.

However, there are several problems with Friedman's thesis and the data he relies on. First, from a theoretical and historical framework, it simply doesn't make sense to say that a recession is unrelated to prior economic trends. Clearly, monetary authorities frequently tighten money after seeing the impact of inflationary policies of the past. A correlation between boom and bust often does exist, and even Friedman's evidence in his other monetary studies supports this traditional view. Second, the data used by Friedman often masks the depth and breadth of an economic contraction. GDP statistics, which ignore intermediate production, tend to underestimate the intensity of a recession or depression, compared to corporate profits and gross business spending (Skousen 1990:290-93; 2002:175-78). Garrison observes, "The Monetarists, in the Austrians' judgment, have not disaggregated enough even to reveal the potential problems" (Garrison 2001:226). Finally, Friedman's thesis fails to take into account the fact that monetary authorities usually intervene before the recession has completely run its course and will inject massive new reserves into the banking system to reverse the economic slide and keep the malinvestments from working their way through the system. The years 1982 and 2001 are classic examples in the United States engaging in this kind of intervention to stave off a collapse.

The Austrian Case in History

Many historical examples confirm the Mises-Hayek theory of the business cycle. For example, in the U. S. monetary inflation was relatively modest throughout the 1950s and early 1960s, and so was the business cycle. But when monetary inflation picked up its pace and grew much more rapidly in the late 1960s and 1970s, the result was a much more volatile economy. The expansions were greater and the contractions were more severe, just as Mises-Hayek would predict.

A look at Japan in the 1980s and 1990s reveals some Austrian insights as well. If the Bank of Japan had adopted the Friedman monetarist rule, increasing the money supply steadily at 3-4% a year, the Austrians would have predicted only a mild inflationary build-up and subsequent recession. But the Bank of Japan engaged in an extremely liberal money policy in the 1980s, expanding the monetary base by 11 percent for four straight years and keeping interest rates artificially low. The result was (1) dramatic economic growth in the late 1980s, followed by (2) a crash and prolonged recession in the 1990s. The data supports the Mises-Hayek thesis. In fact, Japanese economist Yoshio Suzuki accepts the Austrian interpretation of his nation's boom-bust cycle: "As Hayek teaches us, easy money does not always raise the price of goods and services, but always creates an imbalance in the structure of the economy, particularly in the capital markets....This is exactly what happened in Japan [in the 1980s]" (Suzuki 1994). Suzuki also adds an important footnote, "In my 40 years' experience as a monetary economist, I have never felt as strongly as I do today the need to bring back to life the essence of Hayek's trade cycle theory."[8]

The third example is the boom-bust cycle of the late 1990s and early 2000s. What fueled the "irrational exuberance" of the high tech boom and stock bubble of the late 1990s, beyond the genuine technological advances in telecommunications and

8 For a discussion of Japan's long recession from an Austrian perspective, see Powell 2002.

computers? The Austrians point to the Federal Reserve, which deliberately cut interest rates and injected large amounts of liquidity into the banking system between 1995 and 2000, prompted by the Asian financial crisis in 1997, the Russian economic collapse in 1998, and the Y2K fears of 1999. When the Y2K disaster was averted, the Fed sopped up liquidity by squeezing the money supply and raising short-term interest rates sharply in 2000. Consequently, to use Friedman's Plucking Model terminology, the economy came "unglued" and Wall Street, especially the high-tech dominated Nasdaq, suffered its worst bear market since the Great Depression, lasting three years. *The Economist* (September 28, 2002 issue) was one of the first to acknowledge that the Austrian business cycle theory, long out of fashion, seems a plausible explanation of the 1995-2003 boom-bust cycle. Prior cycles had been explained by an exogenous oil-price shock, policy mistakes, or productivity changes, but "this cycle was different.....It was an investment-led boom that carried the seeds of its own destruction. The recent business cycles in both America and Japan displayed many 'Austrian' features" (Woodhall 2002:9; cf Callahan and Garrison 2003).

Following the *Economist*'s cover story, Barry Eichengreen (Berkeley) and Kris Mitchener (Santa Clara) collaborated in writing a working paper, "The Great Depression as a credit boom gone wrong." The authors adopt a remarkable Austrian interpretation of the 1920s and 1990s, describing both episodes as an unsustainable asset inflation in securities, property, technology, and consumer durables, caused by easy-credit policies during a period of low consumer/commodity price inflation. "The development of excesses...threaten economic stability even if there is no sign of inflationary pressure [and in case of the 1920s and the 1990s] the credit boom thus contained the seeds of the subsequent crisis" (Eichengreen and Michener 2003:1, 8). However, the authors do not go so far as to say that the credit-boom interpretation of the business cycle is superior to the standard explanations of the Great Depression—the role of the gold standard, the monetary blunders, and perverse fiscal policies. To them it is a "useful supplement to these more conventional interpretations" (2003:53). What is most surprising about this paper is that it is written by Keynesians. Discussant Michael D. Bordo, a monetarist at Rutgers, said he was "skeptical" of the Eichengreen-Mitchener paper. It appears that Keynesians may approve of the Austrian structural model before the monetarists do![9]

The Inflationary Transmission Mechanism

The debate between the Austrians and Chicagoans basically comes down to a question of whether the transmission of inflation causes structural imbalances in the economy, particularly in the "higher order" capital markets and industries. If it does, the Austrians are right. If it doesn't, or if the structural imbalances are relatively minor, then the Chicagoans are right. Friedman and the Chicago school take a cue from the Keynesians by adopting a highly aggregate "cash balance" approach. The Chicago business cycle theory bases its approach on the work of Irving Fisher and his quantity theory of money as well as on the stock-flow "perpetual fund" capital theories of John Bates Clark and Frank Knight. Under these aggregate macro conditions, there is no significant capital structure, no stages of production, and time plays no explicit role (Garrison 1981:110).

9 I asked Milton Friedman to read the Eichengreen paper. His response: "Eichengreen's paper is excellent: clear, well written, thoughtful. There is little in it that I disagree with. At the same time, I share the views expressed by his discussants, Bordo and Goodhart, that it does not contribute much to the key issue in question. That issue is whether the depth and seriousness of the depression is attributable to what took place during the twenties or to what took place during the thirties. The only item that has any bearing on that is his correlation of his measures of the credit boom with the depths of the subsequent recession (figure 6). Here he gets a positive correlation of 0.43 for the component which measures the height of the stock boom. That is pretty low. Moreover a glance at the chart shows that it is produced primarily by Canada and the United States. Neither of the other components, in particular not M2/GDP, has any correlation at all. Thus the bulk of his evidence is that what happened in the thirties explains the thirties, not what happened in the twenties" (private correspondence 3/29/2004).

According to the "cash balance" approach, the increase in the money supply, whether it takes place through the credit markets or output markets, creates no significant distortions in the economy. The new money is distributed evenly (or "as if" evenly) throughout the economy. Monetary expansion may raise interest rates, but does not alter systematically various production processes; it may raise general but not relative prices; it may stimulate general output, but not relative output.

In 1974, in the middle of an oil crisis and inflationary recession, Friedman was asked a very "Austrian" question: "What is the possibility that a process of inflation, by producing a misallocation of resources and malinvestment, will raise the natural rate of unemployment?" Friedman responds, "If the inflation is open — if there are no restrictions — there is no reason why it should produce malinvestment" (Friedman 1991:81).

Friedman uses the make-believe helicopter analogy to make his point. "Let us suppose now that one day a helicopter flies over this community and drops an additional $1,000 in bills from the sky," doubling the amount of money each individual enjoys (Friedman 1969:4; cf. Patinkin 1965:44-59). He then describes how this additional money affects the community through the "real cash balance" effect, raising prices without ultimately increasing real output. "The additional pieces of paper do not alter the basic conditions of the community," he explains (Friedman 1969:6).

In discussing the transition toward the "final position" (long run), Friedman surprisingly entertains the possibility of Austrian-type distortions. "There might be overshooting and, as a result, a cyclical adjustment pattern" (1969:6). In a seminal paper, "The Lag in Effect of Monetary Policy," Friedman identifies "first round effects" of monetary expansion through variations in interest rates, which may affect various asset classes differently. "The increased demand will spread sooner or later affecting equities, houses, durable producer goods, durable consumer goods, and so on, though not necessarily in that order" (1969:255). Following this discussion, Roger Garrison concludes tentatively, "If the misallocation of capital sets the pace, as Friedman's discussion of the lag suggests it well may, then the Monetary theory of boom and bust becomes one with the Austrian theory" (Garrison 2001:218).

But, alas, in the final analysis Friedman is unsure. "We have little confidence in our knowledge of the transmission mechanism, except in such broad and vague terms as to constitute little more than an impressionistic representation rather than an engineering blueprint" (1969:222). Axel Leijonhufvud (UCLA monetarist) adds, "The first thing to say, surely, is that we know very little about how inflations work their way through the economy. Our empirical evidence is scant, which becomes less surprising once one notices that the theoretical work needed to lend it analytical structure has been neglected, too. The neoclassical monetary general equilibrium growth model has inflation as 'near neutral' as if it made no difference. The Austrian tradition has inflation associated with systematic and serious distortions of the price system and hence of resource allocation. My own 'hunch' with regard to present-day conditions would be that the price distortions are apt to be less systematic than in the Austrian view but none the less serious. There is no good evidence for this view either" (Leijonhufvud 1977:287).

Nevertheless, evidence of Austrian-type asset bubbles and unsustainable industrial booms are clearly demonstrated in the business cycles over the years. Capital-intensive goods and industries, including real estate, manufacturing, and mining, are far more cyclical than consumer-goods and government-oriented industries. Austrian capital theory predicts that the further removed the production process is from final consumption, the more volatile are prices, employment, inventories, and output, due to the time value of money (interest rates). Indeed, the data supports this Austrian insight: earlier-stage prices, employment, inventories, and output are more volatile over the business cycle than later-stage markets. Research on a variety of U. S. prices from 1952-84 reveals that "raw industrial materials prices proved to be the most volatile, consumer prices the most stable, and producer prices somewhere in between" (Skousen 1990:293). See figure 6.5 below. Empirical work and time-series evidence by Frederick C. Mills at NBER in the 1930s and 1940s and Charles Wainhouse's doctoral dissertation at NYU confirms significant malinvestment, structural imbalances, and intertemporal volatility in the real economy throughout the business cycle. The most recent 1995-2003 experience in the high-tech economy supports the relevance of the Austrian model, and it can no longer be so easily dismissed.

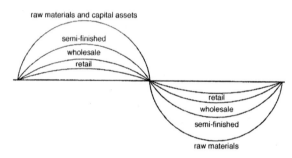

Figure 6.5 Variations in Sectors in Periods of Expansion and Contraction

Mises and the Austrians reject as unrealistic the helicopter analogy by Friedman. New money isn't distributed equally, but usually through open-market operations in the banking system. "Who gets the money first?" is the overwhelming question the Austrians want answered. Mises suggests that an increase in the quantity of money can affect either consumer goods, producer goods, or both, depending on "whether those first receiving the new quantities of money use this new wealth for consumption or production" (Mises 1978:124-25). Hayek adds, "Everything depends on the point where the additional money is injected into circulation (or where the money is withdrawn from circulation), and the effects may be quite opposite according as the additional money comes first into the hands of traders and manufacturers or directly into the hands of salaried people employed by the State" (Hayek 1931:11). Lately the answer has been the banks, the mortgage companies, and Wall Street.

Why are the Chicago economists so blind to the Austrian evidence, when they are normally willing to change their minds in the face of empirical evidence? Three reasons are suggested: First, the overwhelming influence of Knight (and to some extent Marshall and Fisher) against the Austrian capital theory; Second, the philosophical underpinnings of Friedman and other New Classical economists, the notion that "markets work" and a freely competitive environment will quickly erase distortions in the economy, so that any Austrian-style malinvestments are of secondary importance; and third, a lack of familiarity with the empirical evidence on intertemporal business cycle data. Robert Lucas, Jr. reiterates this view, dismissing Austrian capital theory, malinvestments, and behavioral economics all in one as "too small" in their effects and importance. Gary Becker, however, was more open-minded on the issue. In a private interview, Becker acknowledged that "malinvestments do occur and are important in the economy." As Fritz Machlup concluded in an interview, "I don't know why a man as intelligent as Milton Friedman doesn't see that point. It is quite true that his ideas on price level and expectations of rising price levels explain much — but not everything. There are many things that are very important but cannot be explained by that approach alone. I don't understand why he doesn't give more emphasis to relative prices, relative costs, even in an inflationary period" (Machlup 1980).

Austrian Economics and the Market Test

Given that the Austrian business cycle theory is making a comeback as an explanation of the boom-bust cycles of the recent past, what about Sherwin Rosen's "market test" of ideas? William Baumol, an economist and textbook writer at New York University, boldly asserts, "there is absolutely nothing wrong with the current state of economics," because, he claims, the mainstream economic approach "is a superb machine for grinding out theorems" (Baumol 1988:323-4). In other words, since the competitive process works in economic research and model building, it must work in the textbook world of ideas as well. Through trial and error, economists sift and test theories, acquire good ones, and discard bad ones in a never-ending upward spiral of academic success. The science of economics marches onward and upward to its current advanced stage of knowledge and wisdom. Based on this rather complacent view, Professor Baumol dismisses criticisms of mainstream economics and the top-ten textbooks (including his) in *Economics on Trial* by reiterating, "I am totally unrepentant. There is absolutely nothing wrong...." (in Skousen 1991:1).

But does the competitive process in the academic world of ideas work well enough that only good and true economics survives the market test, even over the long run? It depends on who the customer is. As Peter Boettke (George Mason University) notes, the economics discipline, like most social sciences, is a market of fashion and popularity, not necessary the free and equal exchange of ideas through a rigorous scientific method. Roger Garrison (Auburn) asks, "Is the academic market more like the market for wheat in Chicago or the market for tulips in 17th-century Holland?" (Yeager 1997:161). Leland Yeager (Auburn) notes that there is often a bandwagon effect, where "secondhanders....trade on the prevalence of that mind-set among other people. An ambitious secondhander seeks fame, prestige, admiration, envy— greatness in other people's eyes" (Yeager 1997:162).

Thomas Kuhn makes this point forcefully in his work, *The Structure of Scientific Revolutions* (1962), when he points out that the history of science works very differently. Once a central paradigm is established, very little testing or sifting is done until a series of failures or anomalies emerges. False ideas have lingered for decades and even centuries in natural science, medicine, geography, history, and economics (Yeager 1997:163). Only when a "crisis" arises does the profession seek out a new paradigm, and there is no assurance that the next paradigm will be more correct than the previous one.

It's ironic that Sherwin Rosen, a Chicago economist, would suggest that Austrian cycle theory is obsolete after what the Chicago school went through to gain recognition in the face of the Keynesian monolith. The lesson from this episode of academic suppression is chilling. After the uphill battle over several decades for Milton Friedman and other free-market economists to be heard, we must not fall into the trap of thinking that economic errors automatically are eliminated in the classroom, or that deeply flawed ideas cannot be resurrected. Murray Rothbard calls this progressive view of history the "Whig Theory" because nineteenth-century Whigs maintained that things were always getting better. He states, "the consequence [of the Whig theory of history] is the firm if implicit position that....there can be no such thing as gross systemic error that deeply flawed, or even invalidated, an entire school of economic thought, much less sent the world of economics permanently astray." Rejecting the Whig theory of history, he concludes, "there can....be no presumption whatever in economics that later thought is better than earlier" (Rothbard 1995:xi).

The market/survival test can also be objected to on the grounds that in a free market there is no tendency toward one perfect good, service, or idea, but an increase in the quantity, quality and variety of goods, services, or ideas. The market produces "goods" and "bads." There is a market for Marxist ideas as well as for Austrian theories, the popularity of which can vary depending on historical events. As Leland Yeager concludes, "Since when, anyway, was the market, even the actual business market, the arbiter of excellence in consumer goods, literature, art, music, science, or scholarship? Since when does the market decide truth and beauty?" (Yeager 1997:161). Ironically, it was only a few years after Sherwin Rosen's comments about how the market test weeds out bad economic ideas that the *Economist* and the Bank of International Settlements began applying the Austrian theory of the business cycle to the asset bubble inflation of the 1990s and early 2000s.

Advantage: Vienna

The Austrians have an advantage in business cycle analysis. Their time-structural approach to capital and the macro economy is more sophisticated and explains more than the monetary disequilibrium model of the Chicago school. There is far more to the business cycle than black-and-white monetary-induced tight money and easy money, expansions and contractions, and boom and bust. Monetary inflation creates structural imbalances in the economy that can have significant mal-effects on employment, profits, the distribution of income, the fortunes of companies, and the wealth of nations. It creates asset bubbles that can wreak havoc in the global economy when they collapse. The Austrian theory of the business cycle applies the Heinlein/Friedman maxim, "there is no such thing as a free lunch," to the monetary sphere. Inflation does more than simply raise prices or stimulate output. It is a disruptive force that produces lasting effects.

John Maynard Keynes's comment on Irving Fisher's quantity theory of money could well apply to the Chicago monetarist view of business cycles. He calls the monetary perspective a "misleading guide to current affairs," writing, "Economists set themselves too easy, too useless a task if in tempestuous seasons they can only tell us that when the storm is long past the ocean is flat again" (Keynes 1971:65). Perhaps in a sense Friedman recognizes this view when he says that monetary stimulus only has short-term effects; in the long run, the non-monetary real effects take over.

Many have found the Austrian business cycle theory useful in making investment decisions and economic forecasting. There is strong evidence that industries and companies in the early stages of production, such as natural resources, research & development, manufacturing, and construction, are far more cyclical than later stages of production, such as consumables, entertainment, and utilities (Skousen 1990:292-93, 374-77; 1994). Recognizing that an inflationary boom cannot last, investors and business leaders can be on guard to protect their investments and their businesses from a collapse that most others fail to recognize. They may not be able to predict the exact timing of the top (or the bottom) of the market, but they can be on alert and ready to act when it happens. As Bertrand de Jouvenel observes, "A forecast is never so useful as when it warns men of a crisis" (1957:126).

Fritz Machlup, friend of Hayek and Friedman alike, concludes, "A return to Austrian School tenets, both in capital theory, and in monetary theory, and also in business-cycle theory, is absolutely needed." I agree. It is time to reprint Hayek's *Prices and Production*.

References

Anderson, Benjamin M. 1979 [1949]. *Economics and the Public Welfare.* Indianapolis: Liberty Press.

Baumol, William. 1988. "Economic Education and the Critics of Mainstream Economics." *Journal of Economic Education* (fall).

Callaway, Gene and Roger W. Garrison. 2003. "Does Austrian Business Cycle Theory Help Explain the Dot-Com Boom and Bust?" *Quarterly Journal of Austrian Economics* 6:2 (Summer), 67-98.

Ebenstein, Alan. 2001. *Friedrich Hayek, A Biography.* New York: St. Martin's Press.

Ebeling, Richard, ed. 1996. *The Austrian Theory of the Trade Cycle and Other Essays.* Auburn, AL: Ludwig von Mises Institute.

Eichengreen, Barry and Kris Mitchener. 2003. "The Great Depression as a credit boom gone wrong." BIS Working Papers No. 137 (September). Basel: Bank for International Settlements.

Friedman, Milton and Anna J. Schwartz. 1963. *A Monetary History of the United States, 1867-1960.* Princeton: Princeton University Press.

Friedman, Milton. 1969. *The Optimum Quantity of Money and Other Essays.* London: Macmillan.

Friedman, Milton. 1991. *Monetarist Economics.* Oxford: Basil Blackwell.

Friedman, Milton. 1993. "The 'Plucking Model' of Business Fluctuations Revisited," *Economic Inquiry* (April), 171-77.

Garrison, Roger W. 1981. "The Austrian-Neoclassical Relation: A Study in Monetary Dynamics." Ph. D. Dissertation, University of Virginia.

Garrison, Roger W. 2001. *Time and Money: The Macroeconomics of Capital Structure.* London: Routledge.

Gordon, Robert J., ed. 1974. *Milton Friedman's Monetary Framework.* Chicago: University of Chicago Press.

Hayek, Friedrich A. 1931. *Prices and Production.* London: George Rutledge.

Hayek, Friedrich A. 1933. *Monetary Theory and the Trade Cycle.* London: Jonathan Cape.

Hayek, Friedrich A. 1936. "The Mythology of Capital," *Quarterly Journal of Economics* (February), 199-228.

Jouvenel, Bertrand de. 1957. *The Art of Conjecture.* New York: Basic Books.

Keynes, John Maynard. 1930. *A Treatise on Money*. New York: Harcourt, Brace and Co., 2 volumes.

Keynes, John Maynard. 1931. "The Pure Theory of Money: A Reply to Dr. Hayek," *Economica* 11.

Keynes, John Maynard. 1971. *Activities 1906-1914: India and Cambridge. The Collected Works of John Maynard Keynes*. Vol. 15. London: Macmillan.

Knight, Frank H. 1921. *Risk, Uncertainty and Profit*. Chicago: University of Chicago Press.

Knight, Frank H. 1934. "Capital, Time, and the Interest Rate." *Economica* New Series 3 (August), 257-86.

Kuhn, Thomas. 1962. *The Structure of Scientific Revolutions*. Chicago: University of Chicago Press.

Leijonhufvud, Axel. 1977. "Costs and Consequences of Inflation," in G. C. Harcourt, ed., *Microeconomic Foundations of Macroeconomics*. New York: Stockton Press.

Machlup, Fritz. 1935. "The Consumption of Capital in Austria." *Review of Economic Statistics* 17(1), 13-19.

Machlup, Fritz, ed. 1976. *Essays on Hayek*. New York: New York University Press.

Machlup, Fritz. 1980. "An Interview with Fritz Machlup." *Austrian Economics Newsletter* (summer), 3:1.

Meltzer, Allan. 2004. *A History of the Federal Reserve: Volume 1, 1913-1951*. Chicago: University of Chicago Press.

Mises, Ludwig von. 1953. *The Theory of Money and Credit*. 2nd ed. New Haven: Yale University Press.

Mises, Ludwig von. 1978. *On the Manipulation of Money and Credit*. Translated by Bettina B. Greaves, edited by Percy L. Greaves, Jr. New York: Free Market Books.

Mises, Ludwig von. 1996. "The 'Austrian' Theory of the Business Cycle," in Richard Ebeling, ed., *The Austrian Theory of the Trade Cycle and Other Essays*. Auburn, AL: Ludwig von Mises Institute, 25-36.

O'Driscoll, Gerald P., Jr. 1977. *Economics as a Coordination Problem: The Contributions of Friedrich A. Hayek*. Kansas City: Sheed Andrews and McMeel.

Patinkin, Don. 1965. *Money, Interest and Prices*. 2nd ed. New York: Harper & Row.

Patinkin, Don. 1981. *Essays on and In the Chicago Tradition*. Durham, NC: Duke University Press.

Powell, Benjamin. 2002. "Explaining Japan's Recession," *Quarterly Journal of Austrian Economics* 5:2 (Summer), 35-50.

Robbins, Lionel. 1971. *Autobiography of an Economist*. London: Macmillan.

Rosen, Sherwin. 1997. "Austrian and Neoclassical Economics: Any Gains From Trade?" *Journal of Economic Perspectives* 11:4 (Fall), 139-152.

Rothbard, Murray N. 1983 [1963]. *America's Great Depression*. 4th ed. New York: Richardson & Snyder.

Rothbard, Murray N. 1995. *Economic Thought Before Adam Smith*. London: Edward Elgar.

Rothbard, Murray N. 1996. "Economic Depressions: Their Cause and Cure," in Ebeling, Richard, ed. 1996. *The Austrian Theory of the Trade Cycle and Other Essays*. Auburn, AL: Ludwig von Mises Institute, 65-94.

Schwartz, Anna J. 1987. *Money in Historical Perspective*. Chicago: University of Chicago Press.

Shils, Edward, ed. 1991. *Remembering the University of Chicago: Teachers, Scientists, and Scholars*. Chicago: University of Chicago Press.

Skousen, Mark. 1990. *The Structure of Production*. New York: New York University Press.

Skousen, Mark. 1991. *Economics on Trial*. Homewood, IL: Dow Jones Irwin.

Skousen, Mark. 1993. "Who Predicted the 1929 Crash?" In Jeffrey M. Herbener, *The Meaning of Ludwig von Mises*. Auburn, AL: Ludwig von Mises Institute, 247-283.

Skousen, Mark. 1994. "Financial Economics," in Peter J. Boettke, ed., *The Elgar Companion to Austrian Economics*. Brookfield, VT: Edward Elgar.

Skousen, Mark. 2002. *The Power of Economic Thinking*. New York: Foundation for Economic Education.

Stigler, George J. 1941. *Production and Distribution Theories*. New York: Macmillan.

Suzuki, Yoshio. "Comment on Papers by Benegas Lunch and Skousen," Mont Pelerin Society Meetings, September 27, 1994, Cannes, France.

Timberlake, Richard H. 1993. *Monetary Policy in the United States, An Intellectual and Institutional History*. Chicago: University of Chicago Press.

Warburton, Clark. 1966. *Depression, Inflation, and Monetary Policy: Selected Papers, 1945-53*. Baltimore: John Hopkins University Press.

Woodhall, Pam. 2002. "The Unfinished Recession: A Survey of the World Economy." *The Economist* (September 28), 3-28.

Vaughn, Karen I. 1994. *Austrian Economics in America*. Cambridge: Cambridge University Press.

Yeager, Leland B. 1997. "Austrian Economics, Neoclassicism, and the Market Test," *Journal of Economic Perspectives* 11:4 (Fall), 153-65.

Yeager, Leland B. 1999. *The Fluttering Veil: Essays on Monetary Disequilibrium*. Indianapolis, IN: Liberty Fund.

Chapter Seven

ANTITRUST, PUBLIC CHOICE AND POLITICAL ECONOMY
WHAT IS THE PROPER ROLE OF GOVERNMENT?

[I]n 1950 I believed that monopoly posed a major problem in public policy in the United States, and that it should be dealt with boldly by breaking up dominant firms and severely punishing businesses that engaged in collusion.

—George J. Stigler (1988:99)

In this respect, perfect competition is not only impossible but inferior, and has no title to being set up as a model of ideal efficiency.....
[T]here are superior methods available to the monopolist.

—Joseph A. Schumpeter (1950:101, 106)

The critics of capitalism — from Marxists to Keynesians — see "market failure" on both the macro and micro level. Such criticism reached its zenith in the 1930s, when opponents of Adam Smith's model of free-market capitalism made a two-pronged attack. On the macro level, the critics of capitalism claimed that the market could not maintain a stable economy with full employment, and therefore government was necessary to stabilize a crisis-prone market system. On the micro level, the critics of capitalism contended that the free market inherently favored monopolistic power of a few large dominating firms, requiring state intervention to break up private monopolies through antitrust legislation to encourage a more competitive environment.

Free-market economists responded at both levels of this alleged market failure. On the macro level, the Chicago and Austrian economists countered the charges that government was essential to stabilize the economy, saying in fact that just the opposite was true. More often than not, government was the culprit which destablized the economy. But there was a second part of the Keynesian counterrevolution, the "imperfect competition" or "monopolistic competition" model of market failure. The classical model of competition was challenged independently by two economists in the 1930s. According to Adam Smith, all that is necessary to achieve "universal opulence which extends itself to the lowest ranks of the people" are freedom, competition, minimal taxation, and a "tolerable administration of justice." Smith dubbed his model the "system of natural liberty" (Smith 1965 [1776]:11, 128, 549). But in 1933, Harvard University Press released *The Theory of Monopolistic Competition* by Edward H. Chamberlin (1899-1967) and Cambridge University Press published the *Economics of Imperfect Competition* by Joan Robinson (1903-83). The "imperfect" or "monopolistic" competition model has become known as the Cambridge model, because the authors were from Cambridge, England, and Cambridge, Massachusetts. Both economists replaced the traditional Smithian view of competition as a dynamic process with the radical idea that various levels of competition exist in the marketplace, from "pure competition" at one extreme to "pure monopoly" at the other. The Cambridge model contends that most market conditions are "imperfect" and involve degrees of monopoly power, as measured by the level of concentration, takeovers, tying agreements, and other monopolistic practices by a few firms in an industry. The conventional belief of the post-war era was that "private monopoly" was ubiquitous. The Cambridge model of imperfect competition captured the imaginations of the profession and has been an integral feature of orthodox microeconomics and "industrial organization" (IO) textbooks ever since. It was viewed as complementary to the Keynesian macro model of imperfect capitalism. It has strong policy implications: Laissez faire is defective and cannot ensure competitive conditions in capitalism; the government must intervene through controls and antitrust actions to curtail the natural monopolistic tendencies of business; the "perfectly competitive" ideal consists of small firms, homogenous products, and ease of entry. The policy implications of this model were severe: Big businesses and corporate trusts should be broken up, major takeovers and mergers should be prohibited or severely limited, and industry must be highly regulated to keep output high and prices low and make the market more like the "perfectly competitive" ideal. Figure 7.1 illustrates the case for antitrust action against a big business dominating an industry.

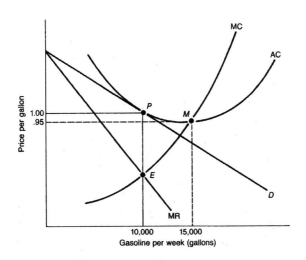

Figure 7.1. The Effect of Monopoly Power on Output and Prices.
Source: Baumol and Blinder 1988:615

As the graph shows, monopolistic power of large firms misallocates resources to below the optimal level (M) by restricting production and raising prices. Thus, by imposing regulations and antitrust measures on monopolistic firms, prices would theoretically fall and output would rise (from P to M).

Antitrust Laws: A Review

Antitrust laws and business regulations were legislated decades before the Chamberlin and Robinson "imperfect" competition models were developed. The most important antitrust laws are:

1. The Sherman Antitrust Act of 1890, which made it illegal to "conspire" to restrain trade;

2. The Clayton Antitrust Act of 1914, which made it unlawful to engage in most forms of price discrimination, tying agreements, and mergers that reduce competition;

3. The Federal Trade Commission Act of 1914, which made it unlawful for business to engage in "unfair" or "deceptive" methods of competition, and prohibited false and misleading advertising; and

4. The Robinson-Patman Act of 1936, an amendment of the Clayton Act, which prevented discriminating in price between different purchases of commodities of like grade and quality, an anti-consumer policy aimed against large chain discount stores.

Numerous cases have been filed and ruled upon since these antitrust and commercial regulations were passed. They include:

1. Standard Oil. In 1911, the Supreme Court ruled that Rockefeller's giant oil company had to be split up.

2. U. S. Steel. In 1920, the Supreme Court agreed with a local court decision that the giant steel company had not restrained trade or monopolized the steel industry.

3. Alcoa. In 1945, Alcoa had achieved a 90% market share in aluminum by anticipating growth and keeping prices low. The Supreme Court ruled that Alcoa had monopolized the industry, even though its practices

were lawful. Alcoa voluntarily sold some of its operations to competitors and thus avoided being broken up.

4. International Business Machines (IBM). In 1969, the Justice Department sued IBM for engaging in monopolistic practices. IBM vigorously denied the charge, arguing that it achieved its dominance through "superior skill, foresight, and industry." The Justice lawsuit against IBM lasted more than a decade, costing millions of dollars, but was dropped by the Reagan administration in 1982 as a case "without merit."

5. Microsoft. In 1997, the government sued Microsoft for creating a monopoly in its "Windows" operating software. Microsoft, the world's largest software company and controlling more than 80% of the world's computer operating systems, settled the case with the government in 2002, paying more than $600 million in fines, and has since faced an additional lawsuit from the European Union (EU).

The Austrian View:
Antitrust Laws Are Unnecessary,
Counterproductive, and a Violation of Liberty

The Austrian school has more consistently opposed all forms of antitrust intervention in the economy, based on economic and libertarian grounds. Beginning with Schumpeter, the Austrian economists have rejected the Cambridge model of "perfect" and "monopolistic" competition models. They oppose the idea that a market with product differentiation, price discrimination, advertising and concentration is somehow "imperfect" and requires government intervention. They see the Cambridge view of "perfect" competition as a straw man (Armentano 1972:31). Hayek observes, "'perfect competition' means indeed the absence of all competitive activities" to differentiate, discriminate, advertise, and concentrate (Hayek 1948:96). Thus the Austrians favor a dynamic "market process" model of competition, based on profit and loss, rather than static equilibrium (Kirzner 1997).

According to the Austrians, it is impossible to determine the optimal number of firms in an industry (Mises 1966:362). The best model is the "market test," a discovery process of trial and error, where each industry determines its own optimal size and pricing structure through competitive profit seeking (Hayek 1978:179-90; Kirzner 1992:149-51; Skousen 2000:188). According to this model, an open market allows any firm with sufficient capital and ability to enter an industry and create whatever products and services consumers desire. While the market test allows market barriers, such as minimum capital requirements, to restrict entry, governments should impose no artificial barriers, such as special licenses and import quotas. The end result will be that some markets produce few differentiated products, a diversity of buyers and sellers, and few barriers to entry; and other markets produce only a few players, high capital and technological requirements, and considerable economies of scale. In this natural approach, the optimal number of firms and the level of concentration will vary from industry to industry. This discovery process suggests that competition is a dynamic process that cannot be measured by conventional IO methods. Hayek rejects the idea that perfect knowledge is required for "pure" competition to operate. In fact, he notes that all markets are distinguished by decentralized and dispersed knowledge; entrepreneurs' ability to profit from the competitors comes from their unique local and thus superior information (Hayek 1948:77-91).

Schumpeter as Apologist for Big Business

Joseph Schumpeter, a student of Böhm-Bawerk and Wieser in Austria, writes eloquently about the dynamics of market capitalism and how the disruptive forces of technology undermine equilibrium conditions. A Harvard professor, Schumpeter was the first to criticize the Cambridge model. He sees the entrepreneur as the central catalyst of the "creative destruction" process of the market system; capitalism "never can be stationary," he writes. The industrial process "incessantly revolutionizes the economic structure *from within,* incessantly destroying the old one, incessantly creating a new one" (Schumpeter 1950:82-83). Schumpeter was an apologist for big business, justifying the dominance of major multinational corporations such as Ford, Standard Oil, and International Business Machines. Monopolistic firms in their embryonic growth stages are highly innovative and require enormous risk capital, he observes. They also attract strong competition, so that a generation later, new upstarts replace the old monopolies. Benjamin Rogge, a Wabash College professor who lectured regularly on the subject at the Foundation for Economic Education in Irvington, New York, calls it the "leap frogging" effect. Indeed, the long-time front runner IBM has now been replaced by Microsoft, Intel, and Dell Computers. Sears has lost its top position to WalMart. The examples are endless.

According to Schumpeter and Rogge, "concentration ratios," a favorite statistic used to measure monopoly power, are highly misleading. They don't capture the degree of dynamic competition over time. Schumpeter rejects out of hand the Cambridge "perfect competition" model of homogeneous products and price-takers. According to Schumpeter, "perfect competition is not only impossible but inferior, and has no title to being set up as a model of ideal efficiency" (1950:106). In Schumpeter's mind, competition is a process, not a state; a process constantly reinventing itself, not a point of static equilibrium. He concludes, "Now a theoretical construction which neglects this essential element of the case....is like *Hamlet* without the Danish prince" (1950:86).

Rothbard's Contribution to Monopoly Theory

Murray N. Rothbard consistently opposes all forms of antitrust law on both theoretical and practical grounds. He takes issue with the standard definition of monopoly, used even by most Austrians, as a "single seller" or a group of sellers controlling the price (cartel). For Rothbard, the conditions are the same for all buyers and sellers in the unhampered market; all sellers have some influence over prices and costs, and market information is never perfect. There is neither "monopolistic" nor "competitive" pricing in the unhampered market, there's only a "free-market price" that leads to an optimal size and output (Rothbard 1962:615). Furthermore: "The only viable definition of a monopoly is a grant of privilege from the government....The only way for the government to decrease monopoly...is to remove its own monopoly grants. The antitrust laws, therefore, do not in the least 'diminish monopoly.' What they do accomplish is to impose a continual, capricious harassment of efficient business enterprise" (Rothbard 1970:45). This definition of monopoly has historic support. Until 1850, the word *monopoly* usually referred to the exclusive trade rights conferred by Parliament (Stigler 1988:91). D. T. Armentano agrees: "Government, and not the market, is the source of monopoly power. Government licensing, certificates of public convenience, franchises, tariffs, and other legally restrictive devices can and do create monopoly, and monopoly power, for specific business organizations protected from open competition" (Armentano 1990:3).

Armentano's Immense Body of Work on Antitrust

The most comprehensive work against antitrust legislation has been done by Dominick T. Armentano, professor emeritus at the University of Hartford. Armentano uses the best of Austrian and Chicago economics to analyze and dissect the antitrust arguments and the case for a truly free society, where big business is neither subsidized nor fettered. Armentano considers himself a libertarian economist, drawing equally from the works of Joseph Schumpeter, Ludwig von Mises, Friedrich Hayek, Henry Hazlitt, Murray Rothbard, and other Austrians, as well as Yale Brozen, Harold Demsetz, George Stigler, Armen Alchian and other Chicago economists. But his conclusions run ultimately along Austrian lines: Government has absolutely no legitimate role in the antitrust arena, including any effort to forbid price-fixing or collusion.

Armentano, influenced by Ayn Rand's novel *The Fountainhead*, became a libertarian at an early age. At graduate school at the University of Connecticut, his intellectual hero was the social Darwinian economist and Yale gadfly William Graham Sumner, whom he used as the subject of his Ph. D. dissertation. Sumner was a fierce, uncompromising opponent of tariffs, military imperialism, and other forms of government interventionism.[1] As a young professor at the private University of Hartford, Armentano discovered a disturbing anti-business bias in most textbooks, and started doing his own research on the business practices that led to the Sherman Act and other antitrust laws. He soon discovered that the epithet "Robber Barons" was a misnomer. The standard "monopolistic" competition model predicts that large dominant corporations will cut output and raise prices, yet he found that Standard Oil, Ford Motor Company, U. S. Steel and other giant corporations did exactly the opposite: they drastically cut prices as they expanded output rapidly. As Isabel Paterson writes, "Standard Oil did not restrain trade; it went out to the ends of the earth to make a market" (Paterson 1943:172).

Armentano spent the next four years buried in legal decisions and trial record material for his book on the classic antitrust cases from an economic perspective. Did firms abuse customers? The evidence indicates that customers enjoyed

1 Armentano notes that sadly Sumner is now largely forgotten, including his own essay "The Forgotten Man."

lower prices and better products, especially from Rockefeller's Standard Oil. "Now the conduct-performance record of the industry indicates....that prices fell, costs fell, outputs expanded, product quality improved, and hundreds of firms at one time or another produced and sold refined petroleum products in competition with Standard Oil" (1972:83). Similar results are found in the giant steel industry and others. Did concentration in petroleum or tobacco actually occur, and did it increase over time? History fails to support this claim: "There is surprisingly little empirical evidence that there has been any tendency for average market concentration to increase over time and, therefore, for competition to decline" (1972:46). Why did firms merge and were there barriers to entry that unfairly kept new competitors out? The only way to discourage competition consistently is to keep ahead of the competition by increasing the quantity, quality and variety of goods at cheaper prices. Armentano discovers that monopoly and price fixing, even when intended, seldom works out and makes little economic sense. Business collusion turns out to be a myth since high fixed costs and legally open markets encourage price cheating and secret discounts to customers. His research even shows that the infamous electric equipment conspiracy of the early 1960s, involving General Electric and Westinghouse, didn't really work (1972:158). The sacred cow of antitrust, it turns out, is a "hoax." Most antitrust cases are brought by private firms against their rivals and Armentano boldly concludes that the entire legal framework hurts both consumers and business, and should be repealed.

Not surprisingly, Armentano's revisionist history was turned down by every major academic publisher in the country. "The prevailing view," he writes in 1972, "is that without these laws, a free, competitive economic system could not long endure, and that these laws protect the public from potentially exploitative business monopolies" (Armentano 1972:11). His book was finally published by the conservative Arlington House in New Rochelle, New York, under the title *The Myths of Antitrust: Economic Theory and Legal Cases* (1972).

Like many of the first efforts by free-market economists, Armentano's challenge of the Sherman Act and other antitrust laws has been ignored or ridiculed. While repeal of antitrust policies is a faraway dream, progress has been made on the academic front as more economists and public officials have been convinced that business regulations have been counterproductive and should be reduced or eliminated in some instances. A new edition of Armentano's book was published by a well-known academic press, John Wiley & Sons, in 1982, and a new edition was released in 1990.

Yet while critics no longer ignore Armentano, their relationship is far from cordial. In a heated 1992 exchange in *Critical Review*, F. M. Scherer, a nationally recognized expert in industrial organization and author of the most influential textbook in the subject, *Industrial Market Structure and Economic Performance* (1970), takes Armentano to task for his extreme subjectivist, laissez faire, anti-government, "single-minded zeal" toward antitrust issues. According to Scherer, economists do not need to adopt a "perfect" competition straitjacket to recognize that price-fixing, collusion, and concentration can have ill-effects on consumers and competitors, citing the OPEC oil cartel as one example (Scherer 1991:503-04). Scherer grants some concessions to Armentano's arguments, but overall is unrepentant in his call for vigorous enforcement of antitrust laws: "There is rich historical evidence that the United States Steel Corporation, Standard Oil, American Tobacco, and others did possess and exercise monopoly power," even though prices declined and output increased (Scherer 1992:43). Moreover, according to Scherer, "It is doubtful that early antitrust activism, however wrong-headed, did long-run damage to the United States economy" (1991:508). Scherer notes a paradox: Standard Oil, American Tobacco, and DuPont all flourished after they were broken up, while United States Steel, United Shoe Machinery, and International Harvester escaped divestiture and "became fat and apathetic" (Scherer 1991:508).

In response, Armentano denies that his findings were based on philosophical prejudices, but rather that his research confirms the theory that under reasonable competitive conditions, cartels and other concentrated industries — shorn of government support — are unable to damage the economy as Scherer and others of the Cambridge structuralist school claimed. Regarding OPEC, Armentano retorts, "But all of this makes my point, that government cartels based on coercion can be effective while private cartels inherently fail" (Armentano 1992:34). He reiterates that a Hayek/Kirzner model of competition is better suited to understanding how the real economy works—"to see competition as an entrepreneurial process of information discovery and supply adjustments under conditions of uncertainty;...To discover which products and services consumers desire, and at what prices, and to discover how to supply those products and services over time at the lowest cost" (Armentano 1992:38).

Armentano, now retired, has influenced a large number of economists, including members of the Chicago school, to reverse their stance on many antitrust issues. Yale Brozen of the Chicago School of Business writes a flattering foreword to Armentano's *Antitrust and Monopoly*, accusing the antitrust division of the Justice Department of engaging in a "judicial lynching" of big business, which, "unsupported by government regulation and government barriers to entry, is not a problem," and joining Armentano in calling for repeal of "wrong-headed" antitrust laws (Armentano 1990:xi).

Early Chicago School:
Henry Simons's Attack on Big Business

While the Austrian school has been a consistent defender of a competitive society and an opponent to antitrust laws, the Chicago school has experienced a major transformation in the post-war period, converting from an aggressive critic of big business to a major critic of government regulation of business.

Chapter 3 demonstrates how the early Chicago school of the 1930s had been "Keynesian before Keynes." Similarly, when it came to business regulation, the Chicago school advocated a high level of state intervention, and in many ways used a partial equilibrium model along the lines of Chamberlin-Robinson (Kirzner 1997). Frank Knight was convinced in the 1930s that major corporations are naturally monopolistic. "No error is more egregious than that of confounding freedom with free competition....As elementary theory itself shows, the members of any economic group can always make more by combining than they can by competing..." (in Patinkin 1981:37). However, Knight gradually came to the conclusion that labor unions are more a menace than big business.

In an essay entitled "A Positive Program for Laissez Faire," published as part of *Economic Policy for a Free Society* (1948), Henry Simons advocates nationalization of basic industries such as telephones and railroads, and detailed regulation of advertising, which he regards as wasteful. Simons was influenced by Adam Smith's hatred of the "wretched spirit of monopoly" and the "mean rapacity" of privileged businessmen (Smith 1965 [1776]:428). "Thus, the great enemy of democracy is monopoly, in all its forms: gigantic corporations, trade-unions—or, in general, organizations and concentrations of power...." (Simons 1948:43). He was also affected by the times. Between the wars, in the 1920s and 1930s, monopoly came as close to being labeled a sin as any economic activity. In 1932, Columbia economist Arthur R. Burns (not Arthur F. Burns, who later became chairman of the Council of Economic Advisors) wrote an influential book with an ominous title, *The Decline of Competition*. The New Deal produced 45 volumes on the evils of monopoly, which encouraged Thurman Arnold, author of *The Folklore of Capitalism* (1937), to resurrect the powers of the Antitrust Division of the Justice Department.

To "save" capitalism from being replaced by a totalitarian collectivist state or a "resurgence of mercantilism," Simons insists that the federal government take drastic measures, instituting a "complete New Deal" that would gain support "from liberals who are not naively romantic and from conservatives who are not stupidly reactionary" (Simons 1948:55-56). In addition to supporting 100% banking reserves to ensure monetary stability and sharply curtailing tariffs, he advocates that "the state should face the necessity of actually taking over, owning, and managing directly, both the railroads and the utilities, and all other industries in which it is impossible to maintain effectively competitive conditions" (Simons 1948:51). Private monopoly "in all its forms" must be abolished, he urges. In addition, Simons hopes to severely limit "the squandering of our resources in advertising and selling activities" through punitive taxation (1948:57, 73). Certainly horizontal mergers should be prohibited all together.

Most libertarians today are highly critical of Simons' policies.[2] Walter Block mockingly labels his title "A Positive Program for Laissez Faire," an instance of "fraud and false advertising" (Block 2002:4) Though he speaks favorably of Simons's support for 100% banking, free trade, and his opposition of rent and price controls, Block attacks Simons' support for progressive taxation, egalitarian redistribution schemes, perfect competition model, and corporate bashing a la Galbraith (Block 2002 passim).

George Stigler's About Face

Simons's drastic measures are almost matched by George Stigler in the early 1950s. Known as Chicago's "Mr. Micro," Stigler received his Ph. D. from the University of Chicago in 1938, but didn't return until 1958. Nevertheless, Stigler was captivated by Simons's bold new proposals, and he joined the aggressive chorus of critics of big business who were pushing

2 Exceptions are Hayek and Arthur Laffer, both of whom spent time at the University of Chicago.

to smash private monopoly power. Stigler relied upon data that showed a high degree of concentration in a variety of industries, which most economists at the time considered *prime facie* evidence of monopoly power. In 1950, Stigler, then a professor at Columbia University, appeared before a subcommittee of the House Judiciary Committee advocating the breakup of U. S. Steel Corporation as well as the steel workers' union. "So, in 1950 I believed that monopoly posed a major problem in public policy in the United States, and that it should be dealt with boldly by breaking up dominant firms and severely punishing businesses that engaged in collusion" (Stigler 1988:99).

Then doubts began to creep in. Stigler cites Joseph Schumpeter as perhaps the first to raise questions in his mind about the importance of the monopoly problem (Stigler 1988:100). But it wasn't until he moved to Chicago that Stigler changed his mind dramatically and expressed "embarrassment" about his past beliefs (1988:99). It was Aaron Director, older brother of Rose Director Friedman and founder of the Law and Economics Department at Chicago, who transformed Stigler's philosophy. In his course on antitrust law, Director questions the conventional legend that Standard Oil had achieved its dominant position in the petroleum industry by engaging in predatory price cutting, bribery, and sabotage. Studies by one of Director's students demonstrate that predatory pricing is a myth, and that the company usually found it more profitable to simply buy out its rivals at remuneratively attractive prices. Additional empirical work by Sam Peltzman and Harold Demsetz raise further doubts about the relevance of monopoly power. It wasn't long before Stigler had reversed his position, concluding that "competition is a tough weed, not a delicate flower" (Stigler 1988:104). His conversion was so complete that Edward Chamberlin once said to Stigler, during an airplane flight together, "You and Professor Knight are the two most mistaken economists I know on the subject of monopolistic competition." Stigler comments, "Thank heaven it was a short trip" (Stigler 1988:58n).

Other Chicago economists have come to the same conclusion, agreeing with Stigler that private monopolies should not be regulated. Gary Becker sees it as a tradeoff. In his view, "it may be preferable not to regulate economic monopolies and to suffer their bad effects, rather than to regulate them and suffer the effects of political imperfections" (in Reder 1982:122). Milton Friedman concurs: "When technical conditions make a monopoly the natural outcome of market forces, there are only three alternatives that seem available: private monopoly, public monopoly, or public regulation. All those are bad so we must choose among evils. Henry Simons, observing public regulation of monopoly in the United States, found the results so distasteful that he concluded that public monopoly would be a lesser evil. Walter Eucken, a noted German Liberal, observing public monopoly in German railroads, found the results so distasteful that he concluded public regulations would be a lesser evil. Having learned from both, I reluctantly conclude that, if tolerable, private monopoly may be the least of evils" (Friedman 1982 [1962]:28)

Stigler Creates His Own Counter-Revolution at Chicago

Stigler's epiphany led to a one-two punch by him and Milton Friedman at Chicago. In the early 1950s, Friedman established the Money and Banking Workshop to address macro issues, resulting in a monetary counter-revolution to Keynesianism. Then, in the late 1950s, Stigler established the Industrial Organization Workshop at Chicago to address micro issues, and that resulted in a counter-revolution TKO to the Cambridge model of imperfect competition. Together they were known as Mr. Macro and Mr. Micro.

George Stigler, Frank Knight, and Richard Posner, among others, criticize the Cambridge model of Joe Bain, Frederick Scherer, and John Kenneth Galbraith, as inaccurate and damaging. According to the Chicago school, the Cambridge model, known as the structure-conduct-performance paradigm, assumes "that consumers are irrational and manipulative" (Posner 1979:930). The Cambridge economists focus primarily on structural evidence of monopoly power, such as concentration ratios, that imply joint profit maximizing and possible collusion. It seems vital, therefore, that big business be regulated through the vigorous enforcement of antitrust laws (Eisner 1991:100). But according to the Chicago school, empirical evidence demonstrates time and again that even concentrated markets behave "as if" they are competitive, and therefore most antitrust measures are unnecessary and may even be damaging. In fact, following Schumpeter, "concentration is absolutely essential in order to achieve economic efficiency" (Schmidt and Rittaler 1989:65). As Harold Demsetz suggests, "Relatively large firms in concentrated industries produce at lower cost than their smaller rivals" (in Eisner 1991:104).

The theoretical framework for the Chicago model, developed by Stigler, Knight, and others is what we might call the "as if" perfect competition model. Stigler uses this model in his popular textbook, *Theory of Price* (1987 [1946]). It's not that they believe perfect competition (large number of buyers and sellers, perfect information, homogenous products) actually exists, but the reality is that unfettered markets act "as if" they are perfectly competitive. In other words, because of economic incentives, pressure from global competitors, and informative advertising, big business acts "as if" industries are highly competitive, consumers are rational, and companies are profit maximizers. They believe that the historical evidence supports their "as if" thesis. "When left to function freely, markets will tend toward the Pareto optimum. Departures from this state of affairs are considered 'random disturbances' which will prove insignificant in the long run" (Eisner 1991:103).

Experimental Economics Supports
Free-Market Position

The growing field of experimental economics has contributed to the antitrust debate. Vernon Smith, a Harvard graduate, began experiments in the mid-1950s with his students, allowing each to bid on a product to determine the final price. Half the students were buyers and the other half sellers, each having minimum bids. In the process of bidding, the students created a supply and demand curve similar to the standard model of competition. In doing so, Smith made an interesting observation. When he reduced the number of buyers and sellers in his experiments to only a few participants, the results were the same—the final price approached the same competitive price that was achieved with a large number of buyers and sellers. By implication, competition within an industry is not necessarily reduced when it is limited to only a few large companies. In short, experimental economics confirms the Chicago position that concentrated industries behave "as if" competition is ubiquitous (Smith 1987).

Influence in the Ivory Tower
and the Halls of Power

The Chicago school has had a major influence in both academia and government policy. In academia, Chicago economists demonstrate that when a small number of firms dominate an industry, it is probably due to efficiency over their competitors, the benefits of economies of scale, and technological superiority—all factors that benefit rather than exploit the consumer. "The Chicago school takes the position that the monopoly problem or the problem of welfare losses due to monopoly only play a minor role in the U. S.; losses of allocation would be more than compensated by profits due to productive efficiency" (Schmidt and Rittaler 1989:68).

To show the triumph of the Chicago model over the Cambridge model, Marc Allen Eisner examined the frequency of citation in the professional antitrust journals. During the 1960s, ten of the most-cited fifteen figures in the antitrust community were from the Cambridge school, including Donald Turner, Joe Bain, and John Kenneth Galbraith. But by the late 1970s, the Chicago school emerged as the dominant force, with half of the fifteen references coming from the Chicago camp, including Richard Posner, George Stigler, Harold Demsetz, Yale Brozen, and Robert Bork (Eisner 1991:107-11). Moreover, according to Eisner, many structuralists modified their position in favor of Chicago's positive view toward big business (Eisner 1991:109).

The Chicago influence came to fruition during the Reagan presidency. Starting in 1981, Chicago-style lawyers and economists were appointed to the antitrust agencies, including William Baxter as assistant attorney general for antitrust and James C. Miller III as chairman of the Federal Trade Commission. Miller, a graduate of the Chicago-style University of Virginia, was the first economist ever to sit on the commission. Under Reagan, these free-market economists reorganized the antitrust agencies to reflect principles of maximizing consumer welfare and business efficiency, not social or political agendas (Bork 1978:7). According to Posner, "the proper lens for viewing antitrust problems is price theory" (Posner 1979:925) Drawing on microeconomic theory, the new Reagan antitrust officials declined to enforce the Robinson-Patman law against price discrimination, reciprocity, monopolization, and vertical mergers. The AT&T case was settled and the IBM suit was dismissed after 12 years of litigation. In an effort to deregulate the economy, the staff of the antitrust division of the Justice Department and the FTC were cut sharply. New guidelines stressed the positive role of mergers: "Although they sometimes harm competition, mergers generally play an important role in a free enterprise economy. They can penalize ineffective management and facilitate the efficient flow of investment capital and the redeployment of existing productive assets. While we challenge competitively harmful mergers, the Department seeks to avoid unnecessary interference with the larger universe of mergers that are either competitively beneficial or neutral" (Eisner 1991:196).

Between the Austrian and Chicago schools, there is no doubt that trust-busting has lost much of its popularity, but it would be a mistake to think that antitrust is dead in today's global community. Stigler observed in 1988, "the enthusiasm for antitrust has diminished, although it has not disappeared" (1988:104). The U. S. still regulates large horizontal mergers and forbids price-fixing, foreign dumping and so-called "predatory" practices. The Justice Department also goes after major companies like Microsoft. Judging from how the issue of competition is taught in today's micro textbooks, it is apparent that most economists continue to support "vigorous" enforcement of antitrust laws.

A Partial Conversion?

However, the Chicago school has not abandoned all forms of antitrust policy. While they oppose interfering with vertical mergers, price discrimination, and monopolies per se, most Chicago economists support policies prohibiting price fixing and horizontal mergers. Vertical mergers serve usually to increase productive efficiency and not to obtain monopoly power, but collusionary horizontal mergers may cause a restriction in output and a welfare loss (Schmidt and Rittaler 1989:84-85). In short, the Chicago school has moved toward the Austrian position, but not completely, and many Austrians argue that the Chicago school still adopts an Walrasian "equilibrium always" model of perfect competition rather than a dynamic competitive non-equilibrating process (Kirzner 1997).

Chicago Political Economy:
Can Economists Make a Difference Politically?

Austrians point to the persistence of the Chicago perfect-competition model in the transformation of the Chicago school of political economy, as reflected in the later writings of George Stigler and Donald Wittman. The original Chicago position, as reflected in the works of Milton Friedman, James Buchanan, and Ronald Coase, held that government is frequently inefficient and underperforms due to the power of strong vested interests and a lack of incentives and property rights. Only through constitutional rights and restraints, dispersion of power, and the application of market principles such as choice and competition can a political society be optimized. Friedman and other Chicago economists have actively sought to reform and improve government performance by recommending laissez-faire policies.

However, George Stigler has been a long-time critic of what he terms "preaching" by economists. In this regard, Stigler advances two theses. First: "My central thesis is that economists exert a minor and scarcely detectable influence on the societies in which they live" (Stigler 1982:63). Such a startling conclusion appears to counter much evidence that Adam Smith, Ricardo and other classical economists had something to do with the international movement toward free trade and the gradual decline in tariffs; that Marx's theories of exploitation, alienation and crisis in capitalism had an impact on Lenin and the communist movement; or that Keynes and Keynesianism influenced the growth of government and the welfare state. Stigler, a well-respected economic historian, suggests otherwise, arguing for example that the Irish famine, not the theory of free trade, may have been responsible for the repeal of the Corn Laws in 1846 (Stigler 1982:64). In the case of Keynes, Stigler suggests the possibility that economists simply provided a theory to support the popular post-Depression full-employment policies, rather than the other way around

(1982:65). In any case, "the thesis should of course be tested" (1982:63).

Stigler's second thesis is even more controversial, that economists have little useful to tell society and their policy advice is pretty worthless and little more than wishful thinking. "Economists....should be reluctant to characterize a large fraction of political activity as mistaken," he declares (1982:9). He castigates Adam Smith for attacking the mercantile system. "I say, with great fear and trembling, that it is more probably that Smith, not the nobility of England, was mistaken as to the costs and benefits of the mercantile system" (1982:10). The source for this shocking conclusion[3] is Stigler's efficient utility-maximizer, that people, including political agents, know their self-interest better than most people realize, and that the political arena is a free society in a market place not unlike the financial or economic markets, where political agents maximize their goals. According to Melvin Reder, Stigler's political apathy may have had an impact on the attitudes of graduate students at Chicago, who were largely "apolitical" (Reder 1982:26).

In his last published article, Stigler claims that politics in a democracy is just another market with "buyers and sellers of legislation" and, therefore, "every durable social institution or practice is efficient, or it would not persist over time" (Stigler 1992:459). He points to the sugar price support program, which at the time was responsible for a subsidy of $3 billion annually from sugar consumers to domestic sugar producers. The program was necessarily "efficient" because it had met the "market test"—it had been around for 50 years.[4]

Under Stigler's editorial direction, *Journal of Political Economy* published a controversial paper by Donald Wittman,

---

3 In a review of Stigler's book, Israel Kirzner uses other stronger adjectives to describe Stigler's essay on preaching: "bizarre....disturbing....unfortunate....affront to common sense" (Kirzner 1999:128 passim).

4 Stigler's market test idea reminds me of Sherwin Rosen's market test of ideas discussed in chapter 6.

"Why Democracies Produce Efficient Results" (1989), which developed into a book, *The Myth of Democratic Failure* (Wittman 1995). According to critics, Wittman applied the Chicago perfection competition model to the extreme in the political arena, contending that with highly competitive elections and informed voters, democracies work just as well as the marketplace, and therefore, privatization and other market reforms in government are unnecessary.

The idea that democracy works as well as the market economy is a far cry from the views of Ludwig von Mises, James Buchanan, and even Milton Friedman, all of whom have developed a series of reasons why government will inevitably fail unless it adopts constitutional restraints and applies sound market principles. Peter Boettke devoted an entire issue of the *Review of Austrian Economics* on this debate, noting that Austrian economics challenges the assumptions of perfect knowledge, zero transaction actions, and institutionless analysis in the new Chicago political economy (Boettke and Lopez 2002, Sutter 2002). Political agents do not operate in the same marketplace as people do in business. Voting is not like buying or selling individual products in the marketplace. Legislators and presidents are not elected every day or even every year, and they are seldom elected on the basis of a specific issue. And once elected, there is no assurance that 535 legislators on Capitol Hill are going to pass legislation that truly reflects the citizenry's views. Moreover, career bureaucrats and lobbying interests are far more powerful than individual legislators or voters. Therefore, it's conceivable that fiercely competitive voting do in fact elect the most popular leaders, but such elections in no way maximize national output or necessarily fulfill the wishes of the majority of constituents (political consumers). It certainly is no guarantee of efficient government. India has enjoyed the world's largest democracy, yet few would regard Indian government as productive or Pareto optimal.

Stigler contends, "a theory that says that a large set of persistent policies are mistaken is profoundly anti-intellectual unless it is joined to a theory of mistakes" (1982: 10). Indeed, Kirzner responds that a lack of such a theory of mistakes is precisely the problem with the standard errorless equilibrium model: "the assumption that error is absent from economic analysis has carried with it a rather heavy price" (Kirzner 1999:129). What Stigler and the Chicago efficient market theorists need is, according to Kirzner, a theory of imperfect knowledge involving the entrepreneurial discovery process that the Austrians and other schools have developed (Kirzner 1999:130). Kirzner concludes, "It will be unfortunate indeed if this fascinating volume succeeds in popularizing the altogether unfounded notion that greater and more widespread economic understanding can make no contribution to the betterment of the human condition" (1999:131). "You could blame this blind spot on Chicago's excessive faith in the power of economics," adds Bryan Caplan (2005:16).

Advantage: Vienna

Austrian economists have had a tremendous influence on Chicago in viewing the economy as a market disequilibrium process, whether it comes to antitrust legislation or optimizing government activity. Chicago has largely accepted the Austrian position in the area of antitrust, with sound reasoning and strong empirical support. As Adam Smith observes in *The Wealth of Nations*, a law that interferes with private and voluntary agreements cannot be "consistent with liberty and justice" (Smith 1965 [1776]:128). Because the Chicago economists have worked directly with government in dealing with the antitrust laws, they have not completely embraced the hardline Austrian position of abolishing all antitrust laws, but they have come a long way toward the Austrian ideal.

Equally, there are some Chicago economists who hold tenaciously to the "as if" perfectly competitive equilibrium model and therefore fail to see systematic failure in government. Yet public-choice economists, including the Virginia school of political economy, draw implicitly on Austrian insights to demonstrate failure in and ways to improve government behavior.

References

Armentano, D. T. 1972. *The Myths of Antitrust: Economic Theory and Legal Cases*. New York: Arlington House.

Armentano, D. T. 1990 [1982]. *Antitrust and Monopoly: Anatomy of a Policy Failure*. 2nd ed. San Francisco: Independent Institute.

Armentano, D. T. 1992. "Anti-Antitrust: Ideology or Economics? Reply to Scherer." *Critical Review* 6:1.

Arnold, Thurman. 1937. *The Folklore of Capitalism*. New Haven: Yale University Press.

Baumol, William J. and Alan S. Blinder. 1988. *Economics: Principles and Policy*. New York: Harcourt Brace Jovanovich.

Block, Walter. 2002. "Henry Simons is Not a Supporter of Free Enterprise." *Journal of Libertarian Studies* 16:4 (fall), 3-36.

Boettke, Peter J. and Edward J. Lopez. 2002. "Austrian Economics and Public Choice." *The Review of Austrian Economics* 15:2/3, 111-119.

Bork, Robert H. 1978. *The Antitrust Paradox*. New York: Basic Books.

Burns, Arthur R. 1936. *The Decline of Competition*. New York: McGraw-Hill.

Caplan, Bryan. 2005. "From Friedman to Wittman: The Transformation of Chicago Political Economy." *Economic Journal Watch* 2:1, 1-21 (April).

Chamberlin, Edward H. 1933. *The Theory of Monopolistic Competition*. Cambridge: Harvard University Press.

Eisner, Marc Allen. 1991. *Antitrust and the Triumph of Economics*. University of North Carolina Press.

Friedman, Milton. 1982 [1962]. *Capitalism and Freedom*. Chicago: University of Chicago Press.

Hayek, Friedrich A. 1948. *Individualism and Economic Order*. Chicago: University of Chicago Press.

Hayek, Friedrich A. 1978. *New Studies in Philosophy, Politics, Economics and the History of Ideas*. London: Routledge.

Kirzner, Israel M. 1992. *The Meaning of Market Process*. London: Routledge.

Kirzner, Israel M. 1997. "Between Mises and Keynes: An Interview with Israel M. Kirzner." *Austrian Economics Newsletter* 17:1 (Spring).

Kirzner, Israel M. 1999. "Economists and the Correction of Error," in Daniel B. Klein, ed. *What Do Economists Contribute?* New York: New York University Press, 125-132.

Mises, Ludwig von. 1966. *Human Action: A Treatise on Economics*. 3rd ed. Chicago: Regnery.

Patinkin, Don. 1981. *Essays on and In the Chicago Tradition*. Durham, NC: Duke University Press.

Paterson, Isabel. 1943. *The God of the Machine*. New York: G. P. Putnam's Sons.

Posner, Richard A. 1979. "The Chicago School of Antitrust Analysis." *University of Pennsylvania Law Review* 127 (April), 925-48.

Reder, Melvin W. 1982. "Chicago Economics: Permanence and Change." *Journal of Economic Literature* 20 (March).

Robinson, Joan. 1933. *Economics of Imperfect Competition*. Cambridge: Cambridge University Press.

Rothbard, Murray N. 1962. *Man, Economy and State*. Princeton: Van Nostrand & Co.

Rothbard, Murray N. 1970. *Power and Market: Government and the Economy*. Menlo Park, California: Institute for Humane Studies.

Scherer, F. M. 1970. *Industrial Market Structure and Economic Performance*. Chicago: Rand McNally.

Scherer, F. M. 1991. "Antitrust: Ideology or Economics?" *Critical Review* 5:4, 497-511.

Scherer, F. M. 1992. "Anti-Antitrust: Ideology or Economics? Rejoinder to Armentano." *Critical Review* 6:1, 41-44.

Schumpeter, Joseph A. 1950. *Capitalism, Socialism, and Democracy*. 3rd ed. New York: Harper & Row.

Schmidt, Ingo L. O. And Jan B. Rittaler. 1989. *A Critical Evaluation of the Chicago School of Antitrust Analysis*. Dordrecht, Germany: Kluwer Academic Publishers.

Simons, Henry. 1948. *Economic Policy for a Free Society*. Chicago: University of Chicago Press.

Skousen, Mark. 2000. *Economic Logic*. Washington, DC: Capital Press.

Smith, Adam. 1965 [1776]. *The Wealth of Nations*. New York: Modern Library.

Smith, Vernon. 1987. "Experimental Methods in Economics." *The New Palgrave: A Dictionary in Economics*. Vol. 2, 241-49.

Stigler, George J. 1982. *The Economist as Preacher, and Other Essays*. University of Chicago Press.

Stigler, George J. 1987 [1946]. *Theory of Price*. 4th ed. New York: Macmillan.

Stigler, George J. 1988. *Memoirs of an Unregulated Economist*. New York: Basic Books.

Stigler, George J. 1992. "Law or Economics?" *Journal of Law and Economics* 35:455-468 (October).

Sutter, Daniel. 2002. "The Democratic Efficiency Debate and Definitions of Political Equilibrium." *The Review of Austrian Economics* 15:2/3, 199-209.

Wittman, Donald. 1989. "Why Democracies Produce Efficient Results." *The Journal of Political Economy* 97(6): 1395-1424.

Wittman, Donald. 1995. *The Myth of Democratic Failure: Why Political Institutions are Efficient.* Chicago: University of Chicago Press.

Chapter Eight

WHO ARE THE GREAT ECONOMISTS?

*Adam Smith was a radical and a revolutionary
in his time–just as those of us who
preach laissez faire are in our time.*

—Milton Friedman (in Glahe 1978:7)

*Adam Smith....shunted economics on to a false path....
Under Ricardo, this unfortunate shift in focus
was intensified and systematized.*

—Murray N. Rothbard (1995a:xi)

If members of the Austrian and Chicago schools have expressed sharp differences about methodology, the ideal monetary standard, and the business cycle, we should not be surprised to learn that they also differ frequently in their views regarding the great economists and the warring schools of economics. They agree in a few areas, such as their support of the French laissez faire school of J.-B. Say and Frederic Bastiat, and their criticism of Karl Marx and John Kenneth Galbraith (see below), but in almost every other arena, they do battle, sometimes fiercely, starting with the founder of modern economics.

Adam Smith as Hero

In recent times, Adam Smith and the classical school have met with divided loyalties. It wasn't always that way. In 1976, the Mont Pelerin Society held its general meeting in St. Andrews, Scotland, to honor the bicentennial of the publication of Adam Smith's *Wealth of Nations.* Appropriately, George Stigler was chairman of the society on the occasion, and many society members sported Adam Smith ties. Adam Smith is Stigler's favorite economist; he was so devoted to Smith that he edited a special edition, *Selections from the Wealth of Nations.* In the introduction, Stigler waxes eloquent about the "grandparent of modern economics": "his bold explorations, his resourceful detective work..., his duels and triumphs and defeats....[his] superior mind...a clear-eyed and tough-minded observer...*The Wealth of Nations* has joined the great literature of all time; it was the most powerful assault ever launched against the mercantile philosophy that dominated Western Europe from 1500 to 1800" (Stigler 1957:vii-viii).

In the December, 1976, issue of the *Journal of Political Economy,* Stigler identifies Adam Smith as the architect of the "crown jewel" of economics, "the most important substantive proposition in all of economics." Referring to the invisible hand doctrine and the first fundamental theorem of welfare economics, Stigler writes, "Smith had one overwhelmingly important triumph: he put into the center of economics the systematic analysis of the behavior of individuals pursuing their self-interests under conditions of competition" (Stigler 1976:1201). Stigler praises Adam Smith for articulating in a profound way that a "system of natural liberty" (Smith's phrase for a laissez faire economy) would be self-regulating and highly prosperous. By allowing individuals to pursue their own self-interest under conditions of competition and common law, and by eliminating restrictions on prices, labor, and trade, "universal opulence" should be achieved through lower prices, higher wages, and better products. Smith predicted that laissez faire would benefit the poor as much as the rich (Smith 1965 [1776]:11). When students at Chicago asked Stigler the source of any great principle, his most common reply was "It's all in Adam Smith."

Milton Friedman seconds Stigler's accolades of the founder of modern economics. Calling Smith's invisible hand doctrine a "highly sophisticated and subtle insight," Friedman praises Smith as "a radical and a revolutionary in his time—just as those of us who preach laissez faire are in our time" (Friedman in Glahe 1978:7). Friedman joins Hayek in citing his favorite quotation of Smith. The quotation, taken from *The Theory of Moral Sentiments* (1759), expresses eloquently the universal principles of individualism, liberty, and the dangers of government:

> "The man of system...seems to imagine that he can arrange the different members of a great society with as much ease as the hand arranges the different pieces upon a chessboard. He does not consider that the pieces upon the chessboard have no other principle of motion besides that which the hand impresses upon them; but that, in the great chessboard of human society, every single piece has a principle of motion of its own, altogether different from that which the legislature might choose to impress upon it. If those two principles coincide and act in the same direction, the game of human society will go on easily and harmoniously, and is very likely to be happy and successful. If they are opposite or different, the game will go on miserably, and the society must be at all times in the highest degree of disorder (Smith 1976 [1759]:233-34)

Mises's Defense of Adam Smith

This is one area where Ludwig von Mises and Friedrich Hayek agree with Friedman and Stigler. Labeling *The Wealth of Nations* a "great book," Mises writes a glowing introduction to a Regnery edition, saying that Smith's works are "the consummation, summarization, and perfection....of a marvelous system of ideas...presented with admirable logical clarity and in an impeccable literary form....[representing] the essence of the ideology of freedom, individualism, and prosperity" (Mises 1998:xi). Smith's work is immensely positive: "Its publication date—1776—marks the dawn of freedom both political and economic....It paved the way for the unprecedented achievements of laissez-faire capitalism," especially for the common man and the average wage-earner. Smith demolished mercantilism and other forms of government intervention. Mises warns the reader against "smear campaigns" and "still ruder insults" by the critics of capitalism. The founder of modern Austrianism urged readers to study the important chapters themselves. "There can hardly be found another book that could initiate a man better into the study of the history of modern ideas and the prosperity created by industrialization" (1998:xiii).

Hayek wrote a laudatory article about Adam Smith on the 200th anniversary of the publication date of the *Wealth of Nations*. After praising earlier economists and warning of defects in Smith's value and distribution theories, Hayek goes on to extol Smith as "the greatest of them all" because the Scottish economist, more than any of his contemporaries or ancestors, recognized that "a man's efforts will benefit more people, and on the whole satisfy greater needs, when he lets himself be guided by the abstract signals of prices rather than by perceived needs," and thus he will help to create a "great society" (Hayek 1991:119, 121).

George Reisman, a student of Mises, expresses similar positive comments about Smith as well as his British disciples Thomas Robert Malthus, David Ricardo, and John Stuart Mill. In his large work *Capitalism*, Reisman identifies four great economists: Ludwig von Mises, Adam Smith, David Ricardo, and Eugen Böhm-Bawerk. "The classical and the Austrian schools and their allies have developed virtually all of the great positive truths of economic science," he declares (Reisman 1996:2).[1]

---

1 Reisman goes on to rationalize almost every classical theory, including Ricardo's cost-of-production theory of value, in direct contradiction of the Austrian marginalist/subjectivist theory. Richard Ebeling suggests that Reisman's hagiography of the classical economists is probably due to his conversion to Randian "Objectivism" in the 1950s.

Rothbard, the Dissenter

Austrian economics took a radical turn against Adam Smith with the writings of Murray N. Rothbard. Rothbard, often the spoiler, takes exception to the celebrated Mr. Smith in his two-volume history of economic thought, published at the time of Rothbard's death in 1995. He lambasts Adam Smith, Robert Malthus, David Ricardo, and John Stuart Mill, arguing that the classical economists apostatized from the sound doctrines and theories previously developed by pre-Adamites such as Richard Cantillion, Anne Robert Turgot, and the Spanish scholastics. He asserts that Adam Smith's contributions were "dubious" at best, that "he originated nothing that was true, and that whatever he originated was wrong," and that *The Wealth of Nations* is "rife with vagueness, ambiguity and deep inner contradictions" (Rothbard 1995a:435-6).

Rothbard has little better to say of Malthus, Ricardo, and Mill, all of whom accepted a cost-of-production/labor theory of value, the iron law of subsistence wages, and an antagonistic distribution system that gives ammunition to the socialists and the Marxists' theories of class struggle, alienation, exploitation, and crisis. Rothbard's acid attacks poisoned the attitudes of many libertarians toward Adam Smith and the classical economists, so that they now honor the Spanish scholastics and the French laissez faire school of Turgot, Say and Bastiat as far better representatives of sound economics (see, for example, Huerto de Soto 1998).

Smith and the Classicists: Who's Right?

Is it possible to reconcile the differences between Friedman/Mises and Rothbard? Only if everyone gives ground and recognizes the insights of both camps. Rothbard rightly notes the defects of Smith and the classicists. Smith does advance a crude labor theory of value, attacks landlords, and refers to the work of ministers, physicians, musicians, orators, actors, and other producers of services as "unproductive, frivolous" occupations. He also makes an odd distinction between "production for profit" and "production for use." All of these Smithian concepts made their way into the perverse thinking of Marx and the socialists. Thomas Robert Malthus challenges the optimistic world of Adam Smith, who predicted "universal opulence" by adopting his "system of natural liberty" by questioning the ability of the earth and its inhabitants to keep up with the demands of an ever-growing population. Malthus's fatalistic pessimism forecasts poverty, death, misery, war, and environmental degradation due to pressure on resources. Ricardo furthers the Marxist cause by implying that profits could only increase at the expense of workers' wages, which tend toward the subsistence level. As rents earned by idle landlords increase, profits will decline, he predicts. He also invented what economists call the "Ricardian Vice," whereby theorists build models based on false and misleading assumptions that lead to their desired results. Ricardo uses this device to "prove" his labor theory of value. As a result, some commentators have identified Ricardo as the source of today's highly abstract, mathematical, and ahistorical model-building.

Despite these theoretical blunders, Smith and the classical economists consistently defend laissez-faire capitalism: free trade, unfettered markets, the gold standard, balanced budgets, the virtue of saving and investment, and limited government. Smith ably defends the right to immigrate, opposed minimum-wage laws, and favors lower taxes and a simpler tax code. War is bad for the economy, according to Smith. He pleads for balanced budgets and limited government, and speaks favorably about saving and capital investment. His "invisible hand" doctrine declares that the voluntary self-interest of millions of individuals would create a stable, prosperous society (what Smith calls "natural harmony") without the need for central direction by the state. Smith views free-enterprise capitalism as socially harmonizing and beneficial, the opposite of Marx's view of capitalism as dehumanizing and alienating. Smith eloquently promotes the principles of "natural liberty," the freedom to do what one wishes without interference from the state, which Smith labels "the most sacred rights of mankind" (Smith 1965 [1776]:549).

Smith's words literally transformed the course of politics, dismantling the old mercantilist doctrines of protectionism and human bondage. *The Wealth of Nations* was the ideal document to accompany the Industrial Revolution and Jefferson's "Declaration of Independence." The French laissez faire school of A. R. Turgot, J.-B. Say, and Frederic Bastiat advanced the positive contributions of Adam Smith, and both Austrian and Chicago economists write favorably about the French. There appears to be universal support for Say's law of markets, free trade, entrepreneurship, frugality, and a subjective theory of value (Skousen 2001:40, 45-65).

Despite the dismal pessimism of Smith's disciples, Malthus and Ricardo favored a strict 100 percent gold standard, opposed public welfare measures and corn laws, and believed firmly in free trade. According to Milton Friedman, Ricardo must rank highly as an economist for his invention of the technique of economics. As Mark Blaug notes, "If economics is essentially an engine of analysis, a method of thinking rather than a body of substantial results, Ricardo literally invented the technique of economics" (Blaug 1978:140). Friedman and Stigler also speak highly of Alfred Marshall and his deft combination of classical political economy and marginalism, advances in the graphics of supply and demand, and the development of partial equilibrium analysis, all of which formed the basis of their price theory at Chicago.

Debate Over the Enigmatic John Stuart Mill

Friedrich Hayek takes exception to John Stuart Mill as a consistent classical economist. Despite Mill's clarion defense of

Say's Law, hard money, and personal liberty in his classic libertarian tract, *On Liberty* (1859), Hayek accuses Mill of leading "intellectuals to socialism" (in Boaz 1997:50). In his popular textbook, *Principles of Political Economy*, Mill declares in a famous passage that the "laws of distribution" are separate from the "laws of production." "The Distribution of Wealth...is a matter of human institution solely. The things once there, mankind, individually or collectively, can do with them as they like" (Mill 1884 [1848]:155). According to Hayek, it is this kind of influential thinking that led intellectuals to support myriad attacks on property and wealth, and grandiose tax and confiscation schemes that supporters thought they could accomplish without hurting economic incentives or growth. Mill himself favored heavy inheritance taxes, and taxes on unused land a la Henry George (Skousen 2001:124-25).

Rothbard agrees with Hayek on this score. "Mill's most conspicuous defection from classical political economy in general, and from Ricardianism in particular, was his numerous concessions to socialism and his apostasy from laissez faire....Mill originated the unfortunate intellectual tradition of conceding that socialism and indeed communism was the 'ideal' social system, and then drawing back by lamenting that it probably could not be attained in this cruel practical world" (Rothbard 1995b:281).

Reconciling the Two Camps on Classical Economics

Ultimately, the two camps can reconcile. The classical economists have much to offer the world. Their theories aren't always on target, but they usually propose the right policy solution. It took the subjective marginalist revolution of another generation to correct the errors of classical theory and establish the "neo-classical" model of economics, but in doing so, we must not abandon the virtues of the classical model.

Look at it this way. From a distance, a beautiful woman looks perfect and without blemish. But if you get too close, you could see the blemishes of her skin. The blemishes are the parenthetical defects of the beautiful model Adam Smith and the classical economists created. Rothbard makes the mistake of focusing so closely on the blemishes and defects of Smith and his disciples that he missed the beauty of the whole work. Anyone who has taken the time to read the entire works of Smith, especially *The Theory of Moral Sentiments* and *The Wealth of Nations*, can't help but come away deeply inspired by Smith's universal "system of natural liberty."

On Marx and Marxism

With few exceptions, Austrian and Chicago economists are highly critical of Karl Marx and Marxism. Although Chicago has traditionally hired a few socialists and institutionalists (Thorstein Veblen and Oskar Lange in the early 20th century are notable examples), the free-market economists at Chicago have generally taken a dim view of Marx. Knight "had little patience with—and, indeed, had intellectual contempt for—the labor theory of value....Knight said it was 'nonsense' to say that labor created capital: 'Capital was produced by capital and labor working together. Capital is as old as labor'....Similarly fallacious was the subsistence theory of wages" (Patinkin 1981:35-36).

The Austrians have devoted more space to dissecting the Marxist menace, including books and seminars. They have had to confront the Marxists on a regular basis. Eugen Böhm-Bawerk was the first economist to take Marxist economics seriously, seeking to dismantle Marx's exploitation theory of labor and interest by demonstrating that capitalists do not earn interest and profits by exploiting workers, but by foregoing current consumption, taking risks, and engaging in entrepreneurial profit-seeking (Böhm-Bawerk 1984 [1898]). Mises dismisses Marx readily in his book *Socialism*; Marxist doctrines, he writes, are "arbitrary, unconfirmed and easily refutable dogmas....Marxism is indeed opium for those who might take to thinking and must therefore be weaned from it" (Mises 1981:7). Mises and Hayek confronted Marxists in the socialist calculation debate in the 1930s, a debate they initially lost and then won a generation later when the Soviet Union collapsed in 1991. Rothbard devotes several chapters to Marx in his history of thought. "Karl Marx created what seems to the superficial observer to be an impressive, integrated system of thought, explaining the economy, world history, and even the workings of the universe," he writes. "In reality, he created a veritable tissue of fallacies" (Rothbard 1995b:433). Although Hayek had high regard for Marx in technical economic theory and considered him a predecessor in his business cycle theory (Ebenstein 2003:157-58), Hayek considered Marx's political and economic policies wholly pernicious, leading to a "road to serfdom." "To follow socialist morality would destroy much of present mankind and impoverish much of the rest" (Hayek 1988:7). The Marxist idea that property and wealth are acquired by the wealthy stealing from the poor is "absurd" (Hayek 1988:124).

Joseph Schumpeter, *enfant terrible* of the Austrian school, is the exception to the rule, writing more favorably toward Marx. Proclaiming Marx to be "a great genius," Schumpeter frequently flirted with Marxism, and adopted many Marxist ideas over the years, including the phrase "creative destruction" to describe the capitalist system, and the Marxist prediction that capitalism would eventually destroy itself and be replaced by "centralist socialism" (Schumpeter 1950:416-18). "Can capitalism survive? No. I do not think it can....Can socialism work? Of course it can," he declares (1950:61, 167). Schumpeter was proven wrong on both counts.

Supply-Side Economics

Supply-side economics is a school of thought closely linked to both the Austrian and Chicago schools. Well-known supply-siders include Arthur B. Laffer, George Gilder, Paul Craig Roberts, Alan Reynolds, Bruce Bartlett, Jude Wanniski, Martin Anderson, Jack Kemp, Steve Forbes, and Robert Mundell, winner of the Nobel Prize in 1999. The term was coined in 1976 by Professor Herbert Stein, who received his Ph. D. in economics from Chicago (1958) and taught at the University of Virginia (1974-84) during the "stagflation" crisis of the 1970s. Stein sees "supply side" as an alternative to the Keynesian model of demand management, which was experiencing heavy criticism. A central goal of the supply-side economists is to restore the importance of the "supply side" of the economic equation—productivity, profitability, savings, and capital formation.

What incentives would encourage the supply side? Supply siders focus primarily on how government policies encourage or discourage thrift, industry, and entrepreneurship. To them, the greatest threats to a robust growing economy are burdensome commercial regulations, including price/wage controls, an unstable inflationary money policy, and high progressive tax rates.

Supply-side economics has largely been associated with the tax-cut movement, specifically with efforts to slash high marginal tax rates. Progressive taxation coupled with growing inflation in the 1960s and 1970s had created "bracket creep," a large welfare state, and a stagnating economy. "As tax rates rise one will get less saving, more consumption, less work, and more unemployment," Bruce Bartlett observes (Barlett 1987). Supply-siders advocate a sharp reduction in marginal tax rates on income, capital gains, and other forms of wealth as a way to unleash entrepreneurship, innovation, and risk-taking, and to discourage investors and business people from engaging in wasteful "tax shelter" loopholes. As Paul Craig Roberts explains, "Supply-side economics brought a new perspective to fiscal policy. Instead of stressing the effects on spending, supply-siders showed that tax rates directly affect the supply of goods and services. Lower tax rates mean better incentives to work, to save, to take risks, and to invest. As people respond to the higher after-tax returns, or greater profitability, incomes rise and the tax base grows, thus feeding back some of the lost revenues to the Treasury. The saving rate also grows, providing more financing for government and private borrowing" (Roberts 1984:25).

Supply-side economics has been closely associated with the Republican administrations of Ronald Reagan and George W. Bush, and led to the sharp reduction in marginal tax rates on personal and corporate income, capital gains, and dividends. Many other nations around the world have adopted "supply side" tax cuts to stimulate economic activity. The movement to eliminate the current complex, loophole-ridden, wasteful tax system in the United States and replace it with a simple one-rate flat tax is closely linked to the supply-side revolution. Following the publication of *Low Tax, Simple Tax, Flat Tax* by Robert E. Hall and Alvin Rabushka (1983), the movement to set one simple low income tax rate has gained support, especially in former Communist countries, such as Russia, Latvia, and Estonia.

The Laffer Curve and Deficit Spending

The most controversial part of supply-side economics is the impact of tax cuts on government revenues. Arthur Laffer, a former Chicago professor (1970-76) and considered by many as the father of supply-side economics, claims that if the tax rate is abnormally high, a tax cut will actually pay for itself by increasing revenues. At a restaurant in the late 1970s, he drew the Laffer curve on a napkin (see figure 8.1).

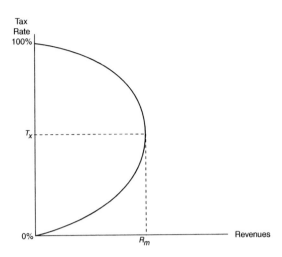

Figure 8.1. The Laffer Curve

According to Laffer, if the tax rate exceeds X percent (above T_x), a reduction in the tax rate will actually increase revenues, because the tax cut will stimulate productivity and economic growth. According to Laffer, the tax base will grow so that, even at a lower rate, more revenues will be generated. Supply-siders point to the capital gains tax cut in 1978 in the U. S. as proof that the Laffer curve exists: The reduction of the rate from 40% to 28% generated more federal revenues. The same held true when the capital gains tax was cut to 20% in 1981 under Ronald Reagan, and again in 1998 under Bill Clinton.

Experience with the income tax is more uncertain, and many economists question the inflated claims of the Laffer curve. Keynesian economists point out that deficits ballooned following the 1981 Reagan tax cut and the 2001 Bush tax reduction. Supply-siders counter that revenues actually rose during this time, but expenditures grew faster. Accordingly, the true culprit of the deficits appears to be a spendthrift Congress.

Supply-siders and Chicago economists tend to downplay the importance of the deficits. To them tax reduction is paramount, and legislators should not wait for surpluses before cutting taxes. As Milton Friedman states, "Experience... has demonstrated Parkinson's Law....[L]egislators will spend whatever the tax system will raise plus a good deal more. And therefore the only effective way to impose fiscal discipline is to reduce tax revenues. Therefore I myself have been converted to the policy of being in favor of tax reductions under any circumstances, for any excuse, for any reason, at any time" (Friedman 1991:116). But what if the tax generates more government revenues a la the Laffer curve? Friedman is clear: "If a tax cut increases government revenues, you haven't cut taxes enough."

This "deficits don't matter" thesis goes back to the Ricardian Equivalence Theorem, a principle that argues that the method of financing government spending does not matter. Harvard economist Robert Barro, a former Chicago professor, has popularized the Ricardian Equivalence Theorem, asserting that it doesn't matter whether the government borrows, taxes, or prints money; the effect is all the same in the end—higher costs and more inflation. Even then, argues Barro, a budget deficit has "no effect" on national saving, investment, or real interest rates. Supply-siders point out that interest rates declined during the 1980s and early 2000s, when the deficits skyrocketed. They maintain that people will increase their private savings in order to pay for future taxes and the deficit. Therefore, federal deficit spending is not a problem (Barro 1996:93-98).

The Austrians Critique Supply-side Economics

Austrians have been highly critical of three concepts put forward by supply-side economics and the Laffer curve—the idea that deficits don't matter, that government can maximize revenues, and that the price of gold should serve as a monetary target. Roger Garrison objects to the idea that deficits don't matter, and questions the notion that deficits are not harmful if interest rates decline. According to Garrison, the ill-effect of increased government spending depends on how the spending is financed. Garrison brilliantly explains that the government can finance its expenditures in four ways, and each has a different effect. If the government raises taxes, it hurts the productivity of the economy. If it borrows the funds domestically, interest rates will rise. If the government borrows from foreigners, a trade deficit will ensue. And if the government borrows from its own bank, the Federal Reserve, monetary inflation and a boom-bust cycle will occur (Garrison 2001:112-17). Usually a combination of all of the above will happen.

Supply-Siders and the Gold Standard

According to Rothbard, supply-siders are "old-fashioned populists" who favor promoting inflation and cheap money. They support cutting taxes over cutting spending because tax cuts are more palatable to the masses. When it comes to monetary policy, the supply-siders are, like most Austrians, gold bugs. However, they do not go so far as Rothbard and other hard-money supporters in advocating a return to a 100% gold backed currency. Instead, they favor a weaker standard, a pre-1971 gold exchange standard, where governments are willing to exchange gold at a fixed price. Nobel Prize winner Robert Mundell (a former Chicago professor) advocates the return to gold in international monetary affairs. "Gold provides a stabilizing effect in a world of entirely flexible currencies," he told a group of reporters after winning the Nobel Prize in November, 1999. According to Mundell, gold should play an essential role as a hedge against inflation. He predicts that central banks will stop selling gold. "Gold will stay at center stage in the world's central banking system" (in Skousen 2002:296). Rothbard, of course, prefers a much stricter gold standard. "The 'gold standard' they want provides only the illusion of a gold standard without the substance....what the supply-siders want is not the old hard-money gold standard, but the phony 'gold standard' of the Bretton Woods era, which collapsed under the bows of inflation and money management by the Fed" (in Rockwell 1988:340-41).

While recommending the return to a gold standard, practical-minded supply-siders such as Art Laffer and Steve Forbes urge the Federal Reserve and other central banks to target an optimal price of gold as a "monetary rule." If the price of gold falls below the target price, the Fed should ease the credit markets and expand the money supply until it returns to the key price; if the price of gold moves significantly above the target price, the Fed has been too inflationary and should tighten credit and reduce the money supply until the price of gold falls back to its target price. There are two problems with this gold target rule. First, it's impossible to tell what the appropriate "equilibrium" price of gold should be. Second, the price of gold on the free market is notoriously unstable and can easily overshoot or undershoot its target. Suppose, for example, that the target price is $500 an ounce, a hundred dollars above the current price. According to the supply-siders, the Fed could inflate until gold reaches $500 an ounce. But once the gold market starts moving upward, it's difficult to control it. It may easily hit $500 and move to $600. This would be an indication that the Fed policy has been too liberal and now must slam on the brakes, raise interest rates, and squeeze the credit markets. Once this takes effect, the gold market may plummet below $500 an ounce, requiring the Fed to reverse course again. Or, perhaps because of other factors, the price of gold may not respond as expected to this artificial stimulus. Historically, there have been times when the Fed has been extremely liberal in its monetary policy, but gold hardly budged. The years 1995-2000 are an example, when the money supply grew at double-digit rates due to a series of real and imagined crises (Asian currency crisis, Russian economic crisis, and Y2K). During this period, Forbes and other supply-siders claimed the Fed was still "too tight" because the gold price was not moving upward. But the reasons gold held steady during this time was because price and commodity inflation were relatively stable, and the gold mining industry had just gone through a major crisis of confidence due to the Bre-X mining fraud scandal. In short, gold is simply too independent and unpredictable to be a reliable monetary rule.

Rothbard Attacks the Flat Tax

Oddly enough, Rothbard and many of his disciples oppose the flat income tax, a popular policy recommendation of supply-siders. In a broad ranging series of negative articles on Reagan and Reaganomics, written in the 1980s, Rothbard lambasts the flat tax idea, which he rejects as neither simple nor fair. He lauds the current system of complex loopholes, defends special interests of homeowners and entrepreneurs, and opposes any effort to make government "more efficient" (in Rockwell 1988:342-62). But Rothbard protests too much. This is one of those areas where the iconoclast Rothbard had a tendency to overreact to any policy, theory, or history widely accepted among conservatives and libertarians. He was constantly tempted to take a critical, contrarian and pessimistic view, whether it be toward the Constitution of the United States, the Communist conspiracy, or Reaganomics. Why didn't he simply advocate cutting the tax rate down to one low rate, while leaving the loopholes intact? Surely this would fulfill everyone's dream—government would take less of everyone's income and the distortions of the tax code would be curtailed. Having lived through the era of tax shelters, where investors lost thousands of dollars on bad investments, expensive legal advice, and paperwork just to reduce their onerous tax bills, practically all investors and business people would undoubtedly welcome a simple, low, flat income tax.

Friedman on Supply-Side Economics

What do Friedman and the Chicago school think of supply-side economics? Although a staunch supporter of tax relief "everywhere and at any time," Milton Friedman surprisingly does not buy the argument that a tax cut is stimulative in the short-run. In the long run, tax cuts may well increase productivity and economic growth, but "I have never believed that fiscal policy [tax cuts or deficit spending], *given monetary policy*, is an important influence on the ups and downs of the economy" (Friedman 1982:53-54). According to Friedman, it is changes in monetary policy, and money only, that causes the business cycle (thus, the frequent criticism of Friedman that he believes that "only money matters"). Robert Mundell and other supply-siders take the opposite view. Cutting marginal tax rates can boost saving, lower interest rates, promote the stock market, and stimulate economic growth, in both the short term and the long term, they say. "Monetary policy cannot be the engine of higher noninflationary growth," declares Mundell. "Fiscal policy—both levers of it—can be.....The U. S. tax-and-spend system reduces potential growth because it penalizes success and rewards failure" (in Skousen 2002:295-96).

Friedman and the Keynes Mutiny

One might think that free-market economists would be uniform in denouncing Keynes and Keynesian economics, a system W. H. Hutt once declared to be "the most serious blow that the authority of orthodox economics has yet suffered" (Hutt 1979:12) and that Henry Hazlitt refers to as "the most subtle and mischievous assault on orthodox capitalism and free enterprise that has appeared in the English language" (Hazlitt 1977:345). Rothbard spends a considerable portion of *Man, Economy and State* (1962:679-693, 751-764, 881-882) debunking Keynesian economics, including the consumption function, the multiplier and the accelerator.

Not so Milton Friedman. Friedman has some surprisingly generous comments to make about Keynes and Keynesian economics. He reveals in his autobiography that he flirted with Keynesianism in the 1930s, defending his teachers at Chicago in advocating deficit spending and monetary inflation as the way out of the Great Depression. In the early 1940s, he recalls "how thoroughly Keynesian I then was" (Friedman and Friedman 1998:113). Even after Friedman had established himself as a famous free-market economist, *Time* magazine (December 31, 1969) quoted him as saying, "We are all Keynesians now." In an article published in 1986, Friedman glorifies Keynes as a "brilliant scholar" and "one of the great economists of all time." He once described *The General Theory* as a "great book," although he considers Keynes's *Tract on Monetary Reform* as his best work. Moreover, he declares, "I believe that Keynes's theory is the right kind of theory in its simplicity, its concentration on a few key magnitudes, its potential fruitfulness" (Friedman 1986:52). At the New Orleans Investment Conference in October, 2001, I asked Friedman in an open forum, "Who is the better economist, Keynes or Mises?" He responded, "Keynes." His answer didn't sit well with the largely conservative and libertarian audience.

Such comments have caused some Austrians to label Friedman a "Keynesian monetarist" (Gordon 1974; Garrison 1992), or worse, a "statist" wolf in sheep's clothing (Rothbard 2002). But such claims, in my judgment, are exaggerated and misplaced. The reality is that Friedman largely abandoned a Keynesian mindset soon after the war. As he explains in a letter, "I was never a Keynesian in the sense of being persuaded of the virtues of government intervention as opposed to free markets" (private correspondence). He was entirely "hostile" to the Keynesian notion that the Great Depression was a market phenomenon (Gordon 1974:48-49). Regarding the quote in *Time* magazine cited above, Friedman said that the reporter had quoted him out of context. The full quote: "In one sense, we are all Keynesians now; in another, no one is a Keynesian any longer. We all use the Keynesian language and apparatus; none of us any longer accepts the initial Keynesian conclusions" (1968:15).

Reviewing the scholarly empirical work conducted by Friedman during the 1950s and 1960s convinces one that

Friedman's mission was to dethrone Keynesianism as the established model of macroeconomics and replace it with his own monetarist model. He systematically undermines the basic theories of Keynesianism by attacking the consumption function, the alleged power of the spending multiplier, the impotence of monetary policy, the Phillips curve and the financial instability hypothesis (see Skousen 2001:398-404). In essence, Friedman, a scholar intimately familiar with the Keynesian language, apparatus and policy implications, used Keynes's own language and apparatus to prove him wrong on every count. As Friedman stated following his laudatory comments about Keynes in 1986, "I have been led to reject it [Keynesianism]...because I believe it has been contradicted by experience" (1986:48).

Nevertheless, Garrison and other critics of Friedman have a point. Friedman has never completely abandoned support for government intervention in the macro economy. He may oppose fiscal stimulus, yet he has from time to time supported the other arm of government intervention—monetary activism. In an article written in 1997, "Rx for Japan," for example, he addresses how Japan could recover from its long malaise. Rather than focusing on cutting taxes, reducing government spending, deregulating the banking industry, expanding trade, and other free-market reforms, he joins Paul Krugman and other Keynesians urging the Bank of Japan to print more yen (Friedman 1997).

Galbraith and the Institutionalists

Austrian and Chicago economists find more agreement about John Kenneth Galbraith. According to Murray Rothbard, Galbraith's popular work *The Affluent Society* is "replete with fallacies" and "grave" errors, including the "dependence effect" of advertising (Rothbard 1962:840). Galbraith may have eloquently described the glaring disparity between the public and private sectors: "public services have failed to keep abreast of private consumption" (Galbraith 1958:257), but he misunderstands the essence of this egregious "social imbalance," which Rothbard identifies as the fundamental flaw of government programs—their lack of competition, profit motive, and market incentives. The solution, writes Rothbard, is not to transfer resources via increased taxes from the affluent private sector to the starved public sector, but quite the opposite. Through privatization, the private sector could provide better and more efficient services to the public. But unfortunately, "At no time does Galbraith so much as consider the possibility of mending an ailing public sector by making that sector private" (Rothbard 1962:849).

Milton Friedman uses his standard statistical approach in "testing the evidence" to make his case against Galbraith. Are Galbraith's arguments in *The Affluent Society* or *The New Industrial State* supported by documentation? Not much. Again and again, Friedman cites evidence against Galbraith, even by economists who are sympathetic to Galbraith's political views. For example, Galbraith claims in *The New Industrial State* that managers of big business can virtually ignore stockholders because of their size and power. However, the evidence provided by numerous economists, including Galbraith's student Robert Solow (later MIT professor and Nobel Prize winner), demonstrates that stockholders of large corporations still carry a great deal of influence on current management. Yet Friedman does see some application of Galbraith's "new industrial state": "the enterprises which come closest....to conforming to Galbraith's pictures of the modern giants are some of the nationalized industries, because there indeed is no effective stock market to enforce on the managers the promotion of the interests of the enterprise" (Friedman 1991:136-37).

In a review of Galbraith's television series on the BBC in 1985, George Stigler is unforgiving in his scathing criticism: "Galbraith's treatment of [Adam] Smith's economics is simply irresponsible." According to Stigler, Galbraith places Smith's invisible hand of self-interest in a bad light, saying that it leads to self-indulgence at best and deceptive/fraudulent imperialism at worse. Stigler corrects Galbraith: "Self-interest without the checks of law and competition would lead often to fraud or monopolistic exploitation. To discuss Smith's theory without mention of competition is to discuss Napoleon without mention of war" (Stigler 1986:356). In general, Stigler faults Galbraith for engaging more in "a heavy gloss of imprecision and superficiality" than "a professional level of precision" (Stigler 1986:355).

Austrians on the Chicago School....

When it comes to opinions about each other, members of the Austrian and Chicago school are not particularly charitable. We have noted throughout this book the Austrians' characterization of the weaknesses of Milton Friedman and the Chicago school: that Chicago depends too heavily on aggregate measures of the economy, that efficiency considerations outweigh property rights, that empirical evidence is promoted over sound reasoning, that it focuses on equilibrium states rather than the dynamic market process, that it grants government too many powers in the antitrust and monetary realms, and that it is blind to the many contributions of the Austrians, particularly the Austrian business-cycle theory. There is much truth to these accusations. Unfortunately, the debate too often gets bogged down in emotional *ad hominem* debates. It doesn't help when Rothbard and his followers label Friedman a "statist" or when Mises stomps out of a meeting of the Mont Pelerin Society and declares to everyone in the room, "You're all a bunch of socialists" (Friedman 1998:161). Reading Friedman's list of 14 unjustifiable government activities in *Capitalism and Freedom* (1962:35-36), it's hard to conclude that Friedman is anywhere close to being a "socialist" or a "statist." Whatever motivated Rothbard and his followers to vastly overstate Friedman's "statist" policies, their approach reminds me of the ingenious mathematician who goes through a whole series of perfectly logical steps to show that zero to the zero power is one. It may sound logical, but the end conclusion is plainly wrongheaded.

....And Chicagoans on the Austrian School

Friedman and his followers have been equally critical of the Austrian school for its failure to engage in advanced quantitative and statistical work, inability to integrate themselves into the profession, and lack of practical advice to solve problems in government and society—in short, for its unwillingness to get their hands dirty in the practical world of politics. In general, the Chicagoans see themselves as more open-minded in attitude, and fault the Austrians for being closed-minded and authoritarian. For example, Friedman admits that Mises deserved the Nobel Prize (private correspondence), but finds his personality wanting. In an article in *Liberty* magazine, he lashes out at Mises (and novelist Ayn Rand) as intolerant and judgmental, a stubborn man who would hold grudges against his friends for years. "There is no doubt in my mind that Ludwig von Mises has done more to spread the fundamental ideas of free markets than any other individual. There is no doubt in my mind that nobody has done more than Ayn Rand to develop a popular following for many of these ideas. And yet there is also no doubt that both of them were extremely intolerant." Friedman blames Mises's methodology for the in-fighting between the Austrian and Chicago schools. "Suppose two people who share von Mises' praxeological view come to contradictory conclusions about anything. How can they reconcile their difference? The only way they can do so is by a purely logical argument. One has to say to the other, 'No, you made a mistake in reasoning.' And the other has to say, 'No, you made a mistake in reasoning.' Suppose neither believes he has made a mistake in reasoning. There's only one thing left to do: fight." Friedman feels that using empirical evidence is a better way to resolve differences.

"You tell me what facts, if they are observed, you would regard as sufficient to contradict your view....Then we go out and see which, if either, conclusion the evidence contradicts. The virtue of this modern scientific approach, as proposed by [Karl] Popper, is that it provides a way in which, at least in principle, we can resolve disagreements without a conflict" (Friedman 1991b:17-18).

In the same article, Friedman denies that his advocacy of school vouchers and the negative income tax makes him a "statist." He cites libertarian Jacob Hornberger, who advocates "no compromise" solutions, as an example of the "utopian strand in libertarianism." What is the answer to socialism in public schools? Hornberger says there is only one solution, "Freedom." Friedman responds, "Correct" and then asks, "But how do we get from here to there?....Am I a statist, as I have been labeled by a number of libertarians, because some thirty years ago I suggested the use of educational vouchers as a way of easing the transition? Is that, and I quote Hornberger again, 'simply a futile attempt to make socialism work more efficiently.' I don't believe it....It is irresponsible, immoral I would say, simply to say, 'Oh well, somehow or other we'll overnight drop the whole thing.' You have to have some mechanism of going from here to there. I believe that we lose a lot of plausibility for our ideas by not facing up to that responsibility" (Friedman 1991b:18).

How Important are Schools of Economics?

Another controversial statement by Milton Friedman is relevant to the debate between the two schools. Before a startled and disagreeable audience at a 1974 conference on Austrian economics in Vermont, Friedman fearlessly declared, "There is no Austrian economics—only good economics, and bad economics" (in Dolan 1976:4). He seems to dismiss the idea that aligning oneself with a particular school of thought is valuable. According to Edwin Dolan, who attended the meeting, Friedman's intention was not to condemn the economics of Hayek or Mises, but rather to declare that the positive contributions of Austrian economists could and should be incorporated into the whole body of mainstream economic theory. On another occasion, he was asked about supply-side economics. "I am not a supply-side economist," he stated emphatically. "I am not a monetarist economist. I am an economist" (Friedman 1982:53-54). I believe Friedman was warning economists of the dangers of schisms and bifurcation of the discipline, and how destructive it can be to label people and compartmentalize them into well-demarcated schools of thought. It is better to think of one great truth in economic theory, not of a warring chaos of ideas.

Nevertheless, students would be remiss if they failed to study the contributions of individual schools. There is great benefit in focusing on and sometimes even becoming a "follower" of a special school of thought. By specializing in one school, a scholar may uncover areas that have been ignored by the mainstream profession. For example, Austrian economics emphasizes the importance of time, the structure of production, and the vital role of saving. Richard Ebeling calls the Austrian model a "general equilibrium process model." Monetarism, notes Ebeling, examines the relationships among money, interest rates, income and the economy using a "partial equilibrium model" a la Marshall. Supply-side economics pays particular attention to tax policy and the gold standard. Marxism looks at the social interrelationships between capital and labor, and the nexus between money, goods, and financial capitalism. Studying each school brings new insights and discoveries into the marketplace of ideas. It would be a mistake to study only one school at the expense of all others, becoming a true believer with blind faith, just as it would be unfortunate not to study alternative schools just because you don't agree with their theories.

References

Barro, Robert. 1996. *Getting It Right*. Cambridge: MIT Press.

Bartlett, Bruce. 1987. "Supply-Side Economics and Austrian Economics." *The Freeman* (April).

Blaug, Mark. 1978. *Economic Theory in Retrospect*. 3rd ed. Cambridge: Cambridge University Press.

Boaz, David. 1997. *Libertarianism: A Primer*. New York: Free Press.

Böhm-Bawerk, Eugen. 1984 [1898]. *Karl Marx and the Close of His System*. Philadelphia: Orion Editions.

Dolan, Edwin G., ed. 1976. *The Foundations of Modern Austrian Economics*. Kansas City: Sheed & Ward.

Ebenstein, Alan. 2003. *Hayek's Journey: The Mind of Friedrich Hayek*. New York: Palgrave.

Friedman, Milton. 1962. *Capitalism and Freedom*. Chicago: University of Chicago Press.

Friedman, Milton. 1968. *Dollars and Deficits*. New York: Prentice-Hall.

Friedman, Milton. 1982. "Supply-Side Policies: Where Do We Go From Here?" *Supply-Side Economics in the 1980s*. Atlanta: Federal Reserve Bank of Atlanta, 53-63.

Friedman, Milton. 1986. "Keynes's Political Legacy," in *Keynes's General Theory: Fifty On*, ed., John Burton. London: Institute of Economic Affairs.

Friedman, Milton. 1991. *Monetarist Economics*. Oxford: Basil Blackwell.

Friedman, Milton. 1991b. "Friedman on Mises and Rand." *Liberty* magazine. July, 17-18.

Friedman, Milton. 1997. "Rx for Japan," *Wall Street Journal*, December 17.

Friedman, Milton and Rose. 1998. *Two Lucky People*. Chicago: University of Chicago Press.

Galbraith, John Kenneth. 1958. *The Affluent Society*. New York: Houghton Mifflin.

Garrison, Roger W. 1992. "Is Milton Friedman a Keynesian?" in *Dissent on Keynes*, ed. Mark Skousen. New York: Praeger Publishing.

Garrison, Roger W. 2001. *Time and Money*. New Yoirk: Routledge.

Glahe, Fred R., ed. 1978. *Adam Smith and the Wealth of Nations: 1776-1976 Bicentennial Essays*. Boulder, CO: Colorado Associated University Press.

Gordon, Robert J. 1974. *Milton Friedman's Monetary Framework.* Chicago: University of Chicago Press.

Hall, Robert E. and Alvin Rabuska. 1983. *Low Tax, Simple Tax, Flat Tax.* New York: McGraw-Hill.

Hayek, Friedrich A. 1991. *The Trend of Economic Thinking: Essays on Political Economists and Economic History, The Collected Works of F. A. Hayek,* ed. By W. W. Bartley III and Stephen Kresge. Chicago: University of Chicago Press.

Hazlitt, Henry. 1977 [1960]. *The Critics of Keynesian Economics.* 2nd ed. New York: Arlington House.

Huerto de Soto, Jesus. 1998. "The Ongoing Methodenstreit of the Austrian School." *Journal des Economistes et des Etudes Humaines* 8:1 (March), 75-113.

Hutt, W. H. 1979. *The Keynesian Episode: A Reassessment.* Indianapolis: Liberty Press.

Mill, John Stuart. 1884 [1848]. *Principles of Political Economy,* ed. By J. Laurence Laughlin. New York: D. Appleton.

Mises, Ludwig von. 1981 [1936]. *Socialism.* Indianapolis: Liberty Press.

Mises, Ludwig von. 1998. "Why Read Adam Smith Today?" In Adam Smith, *The Wealth of Nations.* Washington, DC: Regnery Publishing.

Patinkin, Don. 1981. *Essays on and In the Chicago Tradition.* Durham, NC: Duke University Press.

Reisman, George. 1996. *Capitalism.* Ottawa, IL: Jameson Books.

Roberts, Paul Craig. 1984. *The Supply Side Revolution.* Cambridge: Harvard University Press.

Rockwell, Llewellyn H., Jr., ed. 1988. *The Free Market Reader.* Auburn: The Mises Institute.

Rothbard, Murray N. 1962. *Man, Economy and State.* Princeton: Van Nostrand & Co.

Rothbard, Murray N. 1995a. *Economic Thought Before Adam Smith.* Hants, England: Edward Elgar.

Rothbard, Murray N. 1995b. *Classical Economics.* Hants, England: Edward Elgar.

Rothbard, Murray N. 2002. "Milton Friedman Unraveled." *Journal of Libertarian Studies* 16:4 (Fall), 37-54. Reprinted from *The Individualist* (1971).

Skousen, Mark. 2001. *The Making of Modern Economics.* New York: M. E. Sharpe.

Skousen, Mark. 2002. *The Power of Economic Thinking*. New York: Foundation for Economic Education.

Smith, Adam. 1965 [1776]. *The Wealth of Nations*. New York: Modern Library.

Smith, Adam. 1976 [1759]. *The Theory of Moral Sentiments*. Oxford: Clarendon Press, Vol. 1, *The Glasgow Edition of the Works and Correspondence of Adam Smith*.

Stigler, George. 1957. Introduction in Adam Smith, *Selections from the Wealth of Nations*. New York: Appleton-Century-Crofts.

Stigler, George. 1976. "The Successes and Failures of Professor Smith." *Journal of Political Economy* 84:6 (December), 1199-1213.

Stigler, George. 1986. *The Essence of Stigler*. Edited by Kurt R. Leube and Thomas Gale Moore. Stanford: Hoover Institution Press.

Chapter Nine

FAITH AND REASON
IN CAPITALISM

The lesson I have to teach is this:
Leave all creative energies uninhibited....
Have faith that free men and women will respond
to the Invisible Hand. This faith will be confirmed.

—Leonard Read, "I, Pencil" (Read 1958)

The ascendancy of the Chicago school also shaped the
prevailing understanding of policy by virtue of its faith in the
self-sufficiency of markets and its distinct antistatism.

—Marc Allen Eisner (1991:116)

Both the Austrian and Chicago camps are viewed as devoted followers of laissez faire and free-market economics, yet their vision and philosophy vary markedly at times. In this chapter, we use a metaphor taken from Adam Smith's writings to explore these fundamental differences, and discover why both schools have legitimate differences which may not disappear, even after resolving conflicts of misunderstanding and personal attacks.

This chapter's theory is based on a singular symbol created by Adam Smith, that of the invisible hand. Adam Smith's invisible hand doctrine — the idea that a self-interested individual who "intends only his own gain" is "led by an invisible hand to promote an end [the good of society] which was no part of his intention" — has become a popular metaphor for unfettered market capitalism (Smith 1981 [1776]:456). Although Smith uses the term only once in *The Wealth of Nations*, and sparingly elsewhere, the phrase "invisible hand" has come to symbolize the workings of the market economy as well as the workings of natural science (Ylikoski 1995). Defenders of market economics use it in a positive way, characterizing the market hand as "gentle" (Harris 1998), "wise" and "far reaching" (Joyce 2002), and one that "improves the lives of people" (Bush 2002), while contrasting it with the "visible hand," "the hidden hand," "the grabbing hand," "the dead hand," and "iron fist" of government whose "invisible foot tramples on people's hopes and destroys their dreams" (Shleifer and Vishny 1998:3-4; Lindsey 2002; Bush 2002). Critics use contrasting comparisons to characterize their hostility toward capitalism. The invisible hand of the market may be a "backhand" (Brennan and Pettit 1993), "trembling" and "getting stuck" and "amputated" (Hahn 1982), "bloody" (Rothschild 2001:119) and an "iron fist of competition" (Roemer 1988:2-3).

Universal Acclaim

The invisible-hand concept has received surprising praise from economists across the political spectrum. One would expect high praise from free-market advocates, of course. Milton Friedman refers to Adam Smith's symbol as a "key insight" into the cooperative, self-regulating "power of the market [to] produce our food, our clothing, our housing" (Friedman 1980:1). "His vision of the way in which the voluntary actions of millions of individuals can be coordinated through a price system without central direction...is a highly sophisticated and subtle insight" (Friedman 1978:17; cf. Friedman 1981). George Stigler calls it the "crown jewel" of *The Wealth of Nations* and "the most important substantive proposition in all of economics." He adds, "Smith had one overwhelmingly important triumph: he put into the center of economics the systematic analysis of the behavior of individuals pursuing their self-interests under conditions of competition" (Stigler 1976:1201).

Not to be outdone are Keynesian economists. Despite its imperfections, "the invisible hand has an astonishing capacity to handle a coordination problem of truly enormous proportions," declare William Baumol and Alan Blinder (1994:251; 2001:214). Frank Hahn honors the invisible hand theory as "astonishing" and an "exactly apposite" metaphor. "Whatever criticisms I shall level at the theory later, I should like to record that it is a major intellectual achievement....The invisible hand works in harmony [that] leads to the growth in the output of goods which people desire" (Hahn 1982:1, 4, 8).

The invisible-hand theory of the marketplace has become known as the "first fundamental theorem of welfare economics." Building on the general equilibrium (GE) modeling of Walras, Pareto, Edgeworth, and many other pioneers, Kenneth J. Arrow and Frank Hahn have written an entire book analyzing "an idealized, decentralized economy," and refer to Smith's "poetic expression of the most fundamental of economic balance relations, the equalization of rates of return...." Hahn expects anarchic chaos, but the market creates a "different answer"—spontaneous order. In a broader perspective, Arrow and Hahn declare that Smith's vision "is surely the most important intellectual contribution that economic thought has made to the general understanding of social processes" (Arrow and Hahn 1971:v, vii, 1). Not only does welfare economics (Walras's Law, Pareto Optimality, Edgeworth Box) confirm mathematically and graphically the validity of Adam Smith's principal thesis, but it shows how, in most cases, government-induced monopolies, subsidies, and other forms of non-competitive behavior lead inevitably to inefficiency and waste (Ingrao and Israel 1990).

Smith's References to the Invisible Hand

Surprisingly, Adam Smith uses the expression "invisible hand" only three times in his writings. The references are so sparse that economists and political commentators seldom mentioned the "invisible hand" idea by name in the 19th century. No references were made to it during the celebrations of the centenary of *The Wealth of Nations* in 1876. In the famed edited volume by Edwin Cannan, published in 1904, the index does not include a separate entry for "invisible hand." It has only become a popular symbol in the 20th century (Rothschild 2001:117-18). But this historical fact should not imply that Smith's metaphor is marginal to his philosophy. As we shall it, it is a central element to his world view.

The first mention of the invisible hand is found in Smith's "History of Astronomy," where he discusses superstitious natives who ascribed unusual events to handiwork of unseen gods.

"Among savages, as well as in the early ages of Heathen antiquity, it is the irregular events of nature only that are ascribed to the agency and power of their gods. Fire burns, and water refreshes; heavy bodies descend and lighter substances fly upwards, by the necessity of their own nature; nor was the invisible hand of Jupiter ever apprehended to be employed in those matters" (Smith 1982:49).

The full statement of the invisible hand's power occurs in *The Theory of Moral Sentiments*, when Smith describes some unpleasant rich landlords who in "their natural selfishness and rapacity" pursue "their own vain and insatiable desires." And yet they employ several thousand poor workers to produce luxury products:

"The rest he [the proprietor] is obliged to distribute...among those...which are employed in the economy of greatness; all of whom thus derive from his luxury and caprice, that share of the necessaries of life, which they would in vain have expected from his humanity or his justice....they divide with the poor the produce of all their improvements. They are led by an invisible hand to,...without intending it, without knowing it, advance the interests of the society" (Smith 1982 [1759]:183-85).

The third case occurs in a chapter on international trade in *The Wealth of Nations*, where Smith argues against restrictions on imports, and against the merchants and manufacturers who support their mercantilist views. Smith states:

"As every individual, therefore, endeavours as much as he can both to employ his capital in the support of domestick industry, and so to direct that industry that its produce may be of the greatest value; every individual necessarily labours to render the annual revenue of the society as great as he can. He generally, indeed, neither intends to promote the publick interest, nor knows how much he is promoting it....and by directing that industry in such a manner as its produce may be of the greatest value, he intends only his own gain, and he is in this, as in many other cases, led by an invisible hand to promote an end which was no part of his intention. Nor is it always the worse for the society that it was no part of it. By pursuing his own interest he frequently promotes that of the society more effectually than when he really intends to promote it. I have never known much good done by those who affected to trade for the publick good" (Smith 1981:[1776] 456).

A Positive or Negative Interpretation?

Most observers believe that Adam Smith uses the invisible hand in a positive way, but in her recent book, *Economic Sentiments*, Cambridge professor Emma Rothschild dissents.

Using "indirect" evidence, she concludes, "What I will suggest is that Smith did not especially esteem the invisible hand." According to Rothschild, Smith views the invisible hand imagery as a "mildly ironic joke." She goes so far to claim that it is "un-Smithian, and unimportant to his theory" (Rothschild 2001:116, 137). She even suggests that Smith may have borrowed the expression not from a Christian tradition, but from Shakespeare. Rothschild notes that Smith was thoroughly familiar with Act III of Macbeth. In the scene immediately before the banquet and Banquo's murder, Macbeth asks his dark providence to cover up the crimes he is about to commit:

> *Come, seeing night,*
> *Scarf up the tender eye of pitiful day,*
> *And with thy bloody and invisible hand*
> *Cancel and tear to pieces that great bond*
> *Which keeps me pale.*

Thus we see an invisible hand that is no longer a gentle hand, but a bloody, forceful hand. But Rothschild protests too much. Although Smith uses the "invisible hand" phrase only a few times, the idea of a beneficial invisible hand is ubiquitous in his works. Over and over again, he reiterates his claim that individuals acting in their own self interest unwittingly benefit the public weal. Jacob Viner interprets Smith's doctrine: "Providence favors trade among peoples in order to promote universal brotherhood" (Viner 1972: foreword). Smith repeatedly advocates removal of trade barriers, state-granted privileges, and employment regulations so that individuals can have the opportunity to "better their own condition" and thus make everyone better off (Smith 1981:341). The idea of the invisible-hand doctrine is cited more than Rothschild realizes. Very early in *The Theory of Moral Sentiments*, Smith makes his first statement of this doctrine:

> "The ancient stoics were of the opinion, that as the world was governed by the all-ruling providence of a wise, powerful, and good God, every single event ought to be

regarded, as making a necessary part of the plan of the universe, and as tending to promote the general order and happiness of the whole: that the vices and follies of mankind, therefore, made as necessary part of this plan as their wisdom and their virtue; and by that eternal art which educes good from ill, were made to tend equally to the prosperity and perfection of the great system of nature" (Smith 1982 [1759]:36).

How Religious Was Adam Smith?

Smith does not mention the invisible hand by name in this passage, but the theme is vividly portrayed. The author cites Deity throughout *The Theory of Moral Sentiments*, using such names as the Author of Nature, Engineer, Great Architect, Creator, the great Judge of hearts, and the all-seeing Judge of the world. As Robert Heilbroner concludes, the theme of "the Invisible Hand...runs through all of the *Moral Sentiments*....The Invisible Hand refers to the means by which 'the Author of nature' has assured that humankind will achieve His purposes despite the frailty of its reasoning powers" (Heilbroner 1986:60). That God is not mentioned in *The Wealth of Nations* has caused some observers to conclude that Adam Smith, like his closest friend of the Scottish Enlightenment, David Hume, was a non-believer. Smith did in fact share many values with Hume. Neither were church-goers or traditional believers in the Christian faith. Both Scottish philosophers oppose the Grego-Christian doctrine of anti-materialism and anti-commercialism, and the Christian philosophy that carnal desires are inherently evil. Smith, like Hume, believes that a moral prosperous society was possible in this life, and not just in the life to come, and that this civil society should be based on science and reason, not religious superstition and authoritarianism. Both advocate free trade, oppose the mercantilistic system of government subsidies and regulations, and warn of the dangers of big government (Fitzgibbons 1995:14-18).

Yet Smith explicitly opposes important aspects of Hume's philosophy. Smith rejects Hume's amoral philosophy and his nihilistic attitude toward informed judgment and extreme skepticism toward traditional virtue found in *A Treatise on Human Nature*. Unlike Hume, Smith is a believer in a final reconciler. His faith is more in keeping with the Deist belief in a Stoic god and Stoic Nature, than to a personal Christian God of revelation, or rewards and punishments in a future life. His *Theory of Moral Sentiments* endured six editions during his lifetime, and the final one, written after *The Wealth of Nations*, makes frequent references to Deity. Smith follows Hume in rejecting creeds and institutionalized churches, but there is little doubt that Adam Smith did believe in a Creator. As A. L. Macfie concludes, "the whole tone of his work will convince most that he was an essentially pious man" (Macfie 1967:111).

Adam Smith's overwhelming theme throughout his works is to provide a liberal society, a "system of natural liberty," where freedom is maximized economically, politically, and religiously, within a workable moral foundation of laws, customs, and values. Contrary to popular belief, Smith does not condone greed, egotism and Western-style decadence, nor does he want economic efficiency to replace morals. Self-interest does not mean ignoring the needs of others; in fact, it means just the opposite, that both buyer and seller benefit from every voluntary transaction. Most readers have misjudged Smith's famous quote, "It is not from the benevolence of the butcher, the brewer, or the baker, that we expect our dinner, but from their regard to their own interest." Here is the context of this statement:

> "But man has almost constant occasion for the help of his brethren, and it is in vain for him to expect it from their benevolence only. He will be more likely to prevail if he can interest their self-love in his favour, and shew them that it is for their own advantage to do for him what he requires of them....Give me that which I want, and you shall have this which you want, is the meaning of every such offer. It

is not from the benevolence of the butcher, the brewer, or the baker, that we expect our dinner, but from their regard to their own interest. We address ourselves, not to their humanity but to their self-love, and never talk to them of our own necessities but of their advantages" (Smith 1981:26-27).

What Adam Smith is saying is that you can only help yourself by helping others—the Golden Rule. Businesses that focus on fulfilling the needs and desires of their customers will be the most profitable. Smith firmly contends that freedom can only function within a system of moral justice, "the obvious and simple system of natural liberty." At the end of Book IV in *The Wealth of Nations*, which deals with "systems of political economy," Smith describes this "obvious and simple system of natural liberty" as follows: "Every man, *as long as he does not violate the laws of justice,* is left perfectly free to pursue his own interest his own way, and to bring both his industry and capital into competition with those of any other man, or order of men." In this same paragraph, Smith lists only three duties of the state: first, domestic police and national defense; second, a justice system; and third, certain public works and institutions (Smith 1981:687-88; italics added). Smith does not condone unbridled greed, but favors self-restraint. Indeed, he firmly asserts that a free commercial society functioning within the legal restraints he outlined would moderate the passions and prevent a dissent into a Hobbesian jungle, a theme he inherits from Montesquieu (Skousen 2001:24, 38). He teaches that commerce encourages people to become educated, industrious, and self-disciplined, and to defer gratification. It is the fear of losing customers "which restrains his frauds and corrects his negligence" (Smith 1981:146)

Faith in an Invisible God

Historian Antol Fitzgibbons has aptly called his new economic blueprint "Adam Smith's System of Liberty, Wealth, and Virtue." If this "new account of Smith" is true, the invisible hand metaphor is an entirely appropriate way to describe his system of natural liberty, since establishing a virtuous society requires a systematic understanding of right and wrong.

As indicated earlier, the invisible hand is another name Smith used to describe Deity. Though not a traditional Christian, Smith was familiar with the Bible and the Christian beliefs. In the Bible, providence is sometimes called the "Invisible God." St. Paul wrote to Timothy, "Now unto the King eternal, immortal, invisible, the only wise God, be honour and glory for ever. Amen" (1 Timothy 1:17; see also Colossians 1:15-16).

It is curious how frequently modern-day economists have invoked religious terminology in describing the invisible hand. In his famous essay, "I, Pencil," Leonard Read (a devotee of the Austrian school) characterizes the invisible hand's work in the creation of the pencil as a "mystery" and a "miracle" (Read 1999:10-11). Milton Friedman uses similar language (Friedman 1980:3, 11-13). Frank Hahn notes that the invisible-hand concept assumes "a lively sense of original sin [inherent in] a society of greedy and selfseeking people" (Hahn 1982:1, 5). James Tobin talks of "true believers in the invisible hand" (Tobin 1992:119). And this religious symbolism brings us to the four degrees of faith and how to apply it to the warring schools of economics.

Four Varying Degrees of Faith

The Bible discusses a hierarchy of individual faith in God and his works: those who have no faith, little faith, great faith, and complete faith in the existence of a higher being. God is "invisible." Consequently, people differ widely in their religious beliefs. In today's world, a few true believers have absolute faith in God, that he lives and works miracles in their lives, and never doubt. Others have great faith in miraculous powers, though they may occasionally doubt. At the same time there are many who have little faith in God; they occasionally see his "invisible" handiwork, but seldom attend church. Finally, there are agnostics and atheists who have no faith in God, who reject the idea of revelation or the supernatural, and who rely solely on the five senses, the natural world, and reason.

Four Schools of Faith in Capitalism

This rather long introduction to the history, concept and symbolism of the invisible hand suggests a thesis, that just as people have varying levels of faith in an "Invisible God," so do people have differing degrees of belief in the beneficial "invisible hand" of capitalism and freedom. By faith, I mean a certain degree of confidence that, left to their own devices, individuals acting in their own self-interest will generate a positive outcome for society. Faith represents a level of predictability in the future: Will an unfettered economy recover on its own from a recession? Will eliminating tariffs between two countries increase trade and jobs between them? Will decontrolling oil prices eliminate the energy crisis? Will technological unemployment in one industry lead to new employment in another? Will a competitive environment eventually break down monopolistic power in a particular market? Individuals have differing levels of confidence in the marketplace to respond positively to change or crisis. Some have full faith that all will work out for the better. Others have great faith that in most cases private actions will benefit society. Still others have little faith in the free market and worry that most of the time, private enterprise does what is best for themselves but not for society. Finally, there are a few who deny that any good thing can come from the dog-eat-dog chaotic world of Mammon, that the multi-national corporate world is so corrupt and crisis-prone that nothing can improve the matter save major institutional reform or outright revolution.

One might identify four schools of economics that fit these varying levels of belief in capitalism and free markets.

Marxists and the Iron Fist of Competition

First are the Marxists and the socialists, the secular atheists who profess no faith in the invisible hand of the capitalist system. While Adam Smith views the commercial world as harmonious, progressive, and socially stabilizing, Karl Marx sees capitalism as brutally exploitative, alienating, poverty-stricken, and crisis-prone. Marxist John E. Roemer summarizes the difference eloquently: "Smith argued that the individual's pursuit of self-interest would lead to an outcome beneficial to all, whereas Marx argued that the pursuit of self-interest would lead to anarchy, crisis, and the dissolution of the private property-based system itself....Smith spoke of the invisible hand guiding individual, self-interested agents to perform those actions that would be, despite their lack of concern for an outcome, socially optimal; for Marxism the simile is the iron fist of competition, pulverizing the workers and making them worse off than they would be in another feasible system, namely, one based on the social or public ownership of property" (Roemer 1988:2-3). To the Marxists, capitalism is so vulnerable to crisis and inequity that the only solution is its complete dissolution. The capitalist system is broken and cannot be repaired.

Keynes and the Visible Hand of Government

Second are the Keynesians. They are the agnostics and Doubting Thomases who express irregular faith in the market economy. John Maynard Keynes questions the Smithian thesis. In a talk entitled "The End of Laissez Faire" in 1926, Keynes declares: "It is *not* true that individuals possess a prescriptive 'natural liberty' in their economic activities....Nor is it true that self-interest generally *is* enlightened....Experience does *not* show that individuals, when they make up a social unit, are always less clear-sighted than when they act separately" (Keynes 1963:312). In the early 1930s, Keynes became increasingly disillusioned with the capitalist system. He attacked it in Freudian terms. Money making is a neurosis, he states, "a somewhat disgusting morbidity, one of the semi-criminal, semi-pathological propensities which one hands over with a shudder to specialists in mental disease" (Keynes 1963:369). Keynes's principal thesis is that financial capitalism is inherently unstable and therefore inescapably flawed. Paul Samuelson, Keynes's devoted disciple, correctly understands the message of his mentor: "With respect to the level of total purchasing power and employment, Keynes denies that there is an *invisible hand* channeling the self-centered action of each individual to the social optimum" (Samuelson 1947:151). In his famous textbook, Samuelson declares, "A laissez-faire economy cannot guarantee that there will be exactly the required amount of investment to insure full employment" (Samuelson 1967:197-98). And Joseph Stiglitz, the heir to Keynes and Samuelson, makes a point that although the market works most of the time, "there is market failure everywhere" (private interview).

Keynes's solution is not to adopt Marxist socialism, but to empower the federal government to stabilize an unstable capitalist system with the tools of fiscal and monetary policy. According to Keynes, when the private sector plunges into a downturn, the government should spend more; when the private sector overheats, the government should spend less. Once a counter-cyclical management policy is in place, the invisible hand of the private sector can achieve its social optimality. Thus, Keynes's model involves heavy intervention and big government (a welfare state) at the macro level, but relatively personal freedom and economic laissez faire at the micro level. It is not totalitarianism, but neither is it anarchy.

The Chicago School: Great Faith in Capitalism

Now we come to the Chicago and Austrian schools. No doubt many members of both school might object to the idea that they support free markets as a declaration of faith. The

Chicagoans might put the argument on the basis of reasoned evidence rather than unsupported faith, while the Austrians might see their rationale on the basis of pure reason (what Ayn Rand called objective reason) rather than "irrational" faith. Yet I submit that faith of varying degrees plays a vital role in the thinking of both free-market schools. To the extent that evidence or reason supports market solutions, their faith in the free market increases. But it is faith nontheless—belief that voluntary actions of self-interested individuals will solve current or future problems.

The Chicago school, led by Milton Friedman, has much stronger faith in the capitalism model than the Keynesians, and thus qualifies for the third category of "great faith" in capitalism and free markets. Speaking of Adam Smith's invisible hand doctrine, Friedman writes, "Adam Smith's flash of genius was his recognition that the prices that emerged from voluntary transactions between buyers and sellers—for short, in a free market—could coordinate the activity of millions of people, each seeking his own interest, in such a way as to make everyone better off." In his PBS television series, "Free to Choose," Friedman used the example of a pencil to illustrate the invisible hand doctrine, based upon Leonard E. Read's famous little essay, "I, Pencil" (Read 1958). A pencil—made of graphite, rubber, tin, and wood—is produced by thousands of individuals around the world without central direction, yet the end result is cheap and beneficial to everyone. "It was a startling idea then, and it remains one today, that economic order can emerge as the unintended consequence of the actions of many people, each seeking his own interest." Friedman continues, "The price system works so well, so efficiently, that we are not aware of it most of the time" (Friedman 1980:13-14).

Yet Friedman and the other members of the Chicago school, as faithful as they are to the virtues of the market, do favor intervention from time to time. As noted in earlier chapters, Henry Simons and George Stigler supported strong antitrust measures against big business, and even today, Chicago economists make some exceptions to their laissez faire policies with regard to antitrust laws (see chapter 7). In tax policy, Stigler has advocated heavy taxes on inherited wealth (Stigler 1986:98). In the macroeconomic arena, Chicago economists, like the Keynesians, encourage an activist federal government to run deficits and expand the money supply during the Great Depression of the 1930s. In the late 1990s, Milton Friedman recommended that Japan expand the money supply aggressively to get its economy going again (Friedman 1997). And in a recent *Business Week* column entitled, "Let's Make Gasoline Prices Even Higher," Gary Becker advocates a 50 cent per gallon increase in the federal gasoline tax in an effort to "cut consumption and expand oil reserves" beyond what higher market prices were already achieving in response to global terrorist threats to oil output (Becker 2004).

Faith in the Markets or Central Banking?

Does Alan Greenspan, chairman of the Federal Reserve, have confidence in the capitalist system? A devout follower of Ayn Rand earlier in his career, Greenspan has generally supported market-oriented policies. But when the economy turns south, does his faith waver? For central bankers, there is always the fear that the market economy may not recover on its own, that it may plunge further into the depths of a full-scale depression. They think that the market must not be allowed to take its natural course; it must be propped up by artificial means, through deficit spending and easy-money policies.

The Austrian School: Full Faith in Free Markets

The fourth and final category is the school that adopts "full faith" in free markets, without exception. That category belongs to the Austrian school. If there is any school of economics that has portrayed an unwavering, unfettered, complete, and perfect faith (critics might call it blind faith) in the free market, it is the school of Ludwig von Mises and Murray Rothbard, and its modern-day followers.[1] Not only do they agree with everything the Chicago school says about the virtues of the price system, but they go further and deny any need for antitrust policy against big business or macro intervention by the federal government to artificially stimulate the economy through deficit spending or easy-money policies, even during a severe recession or depression. Murray Rothbard, the American free-market economist, best describes the neo-Austrian viewpoint in the early 1980s: "The only way out of the current mess is to 'slam on the brakes,' to stop the monetary inflation in it tracks. Then, the inevitable recession will be sharp but short and swift, and the free market, allowed its head, will return to a sound recovery in a remarkably brief time." Rothbard calls for "radical surgery" in monetary policy: "denationalize the fiat dollar by returning it to be worth a unit of weight of gold....The Federal Reserve System should be abolished, and the government at last totally separated from the supply of money" (Rothbard 1983:xi-xii).

Other Austrians have urged a free and deregulated banking system as a solution to an unstable monetary policy. According to advocates Lawrence White, George Selgin, Steve Horwitz, and Roger Garrison, among others, this laissez-faire banking system involves the following recommendations: "There is no government control of the quantity of exchange media. There is no state-sponsored central bank. There are no legal barriers to the entry, branching, or exit of commercial banks....There are no reserve requirements....There are no government deposit guarantees" (Selgin and White 1994:1718-19). Clearly this demonstrates consummate faith in the invisible hand of the market.

But what about the rumor that Ludwig von Mises supported a state-sponsored opera? There is nothing in Mises's

---

1 There are a few exceptions. Hayek supports a minimal welfare state and building codes in *The Constitution of Liberty* (1960), and Hans Hermann-Hoppe favors immigration conrols (1998).

writings advocating this form of subsidy. According to Bettina Greaves, Mises's friend and biographer, the rumor came about during a discussion at FEE headquarters in Irvington-on-Hudson, New York, in the 1950s. A staff member asked Mises, "Would you favor government subsidizing anything at all?" Mises answered something along the lines, "Well, the voters should be free to vote for anything they want. And if the pros and cons of subsidies are fully explained to them, and if they still want to subsidize something, I would suggest they subsidize the opera, because I like to go to the opera" (private correspondence with Bettina Greaves, January 23, 2004).

The Pragmatist Vs. The Idealist

The Chicago and Austrian schools differ markedly in their strategy and influence. They are like two fighting brothers who really have the same goals in mind, but who often don't get along because of major differences in personality and approach. The typical Austrian brother is an uncompromising idealist and a recluse, and the Chicago brother a pragmatic activist and extrovert. We can see this comparison when it comes to both theory and policy. The Chicago school builds models involving simplified assumptions to achieve certain predictable, powerful, pragmatic conclusions, while the Austrian school, led by Mises, Kirzner, and Rothbard, criticizes any effort to engage in aggregation or inaccurate assumptions.[2] The Chicago tradition adheres to Marshallian partial equilibrium analysis, while the Austrian method is a general process analysis. Chicago uses mathematics when appropriate; Austria prefers a verbal, written economics not subject to abuse or miscalculation.

In monetary policy, many Austrians are idealistic, demanding a return to a pure 100% precious metals standard, whereby all coins, currencies and demand deposits represent

---

2 Yet, to be fair, Austrians have built heuristic models, such as the Hayekian triangles, or Mises's evenly-rotating economy, which involve simplifying assumptions, not unlike the Chicago school.

warehouse receipts of gold and silver. They talk about a return to "honest money" or an "honest to goodness" sound money system. The Chicago school is more pragmatic, advocating what is doable given the fiat money system and avoiding major blunders. Instead of an activist monetary authority, the Chicago economists favor a more stable policy, such as a monetary rule. Friedman argues pragmatically that a pure gold standard, even if justifiable on a theoretical level, could not be achieved without considerable disruption. "My conclusion is that an automatic commodity standard is neither feasible nor a desirable solution of establishing monetary arrangements for a free society....It is not feasible because the mythology and beliefs required to make it effective do not exist" (Friedman 1962:69-70).

Chicagoans often call for second-best solutions. While the Austrians oppose any form of public education and welfare, Friedman has proposed school vouchers as a practical way to improve the educational system and give underprivileged children the opportunity to get ahead. He also recommends a "negative income tax" as a more efficient, incentive-oriented way to reduce (but not eliminate) the welfare system. Most Austrians favor the outright abolition of the income tax, while Chicago economists support a "low, simple, flat" income tax. The Austrian purists offer no compromises, no partial steps in the right direction.

Modern-day Austrians often express outright disdain for government at any level. When it comes to tax collecting, Rothbard and his followers prefer bloated waste and inefficiency, rejecting any effort to run government agencies in an efficient manner through cost-benefit analysis, outsourcing, or competitive bidding. They criticize Milton Friedman for being a "technician advising the state on how to be more efficient in going about its evil work" through income tax withholding and the negative income tax (Rothbard 2002:40, 53).

Who has the most influence? The uncompromising idealist is often pessimistic, seldom sees victory, and is sometimes labeled by the establishment as nutty extremists. The pragmatic activist witnesses occasional victories and sometimes spectacular ones, and tends to be more optimistic. The Chicago school has chosen a more activist approach, reaching out through the top universities and the establishment media to make their case for practical solutions to real problems. The Nobel Prize winnings in recent years reflect that growing influence: Eight Chicago economists won Nobels during the 1990s. And Milton Friedman was presented the Presidential Freedom Award in 2002. There may be a feeling of jealousy from the older idealistic brother.

Optimists or Pessimists?

One of the apparent differences between the Austrian and Chicago schools concerns their outlook on the economy and the markets. In general, Chicago economists, especially Milton Friedman and Gary Becker, seem more upbeat than the Austrians.

Austrian Joseph Schumpeter was deeply worried about the future of capitalism and entrepreneurship. He writes, "Can capitalism survive? No. I do not think it can....Can socialism work? Of course it can" (Schumpeter 1950:61, 67) Ludwig von Mises was incurably gloomy about the future. Peter Drucker, the management expert who grew up in Vienna and had contact with Mises at New York University, expressed dismay about Mises. "He was the most depressing person I ever met," he told me. Mises's despair is clearly noticeable in his searing intellectual memoir, *Notes and Recollections* (1978).

Even Friedrich Hayek, who seems more upbeat than Schumpeter or Mises, expressed pessimism about the future of the West. For example, chapter 10 of his bestseller *The Road to Serfdom*, is entitled "Why the Worst Get on Top." Such a depressing title is understandable given that the book was written in 1943-44, during the heyday of Hitler, Mussolini, and Stalin. After World War II, would Hayek anticipate a road to freedom and prosperity? Apparently not. In both his 1956 and 1976 prefaces to the book, Hayek casts a pessimistic tone about the future of liberty, not because the West is headed toward totalitarianism but because it is endorsing a welfare state. "And both the influence of socialist ideas and the naive trust in the good intentions of the holders of totalitarian power have markedly increased since I wrote this book" (Hayek 1994:xxiv).

Many followers of Mises and Hayek, including gold bugs and hard-money financial advisors, have tended to be bearish about the stock market and, like Marxists, are constantly predicting disaster (see Skousen 1998). For instance, Murray Rothbard regularly expressed pessimism about the economy and the markets throughout the Reagan presidency.

What is the root of this pessimism? Part of it may be personal. Mises and Hayek experienced the ravages of two world wars, the Great Depression, and hyperinflation in the first half of the twentieth century. Each were treated shabbily throughout most of their profession after World War II. The Chicago school of Friedman and Stigler, on the other hand, reached its zenith after these tragic events and enjoyed a booming post-war era. And both American economists overcame personal odds and were gradually accepted by the economics profession.

Pessimism may also be inherent in the Austrian theory of the business cycle, which raises suspicion about the stability of the monetary system under a paper money standard. Austrians regard the fractional-reserve fiat-money system as inherently unstable and prone to crisis, creating unsustainable booms in the economy and the markets which must eventually go bust (Skousen 1998). Meanwhile, Chicagoans such as Milton Friedman predict that with government deposit nsurance and a seasoned central bank, the economy is largely "depression proof" (Friedman 1968:72-96). In response to economic doomsayers, Friedman and Becker frequently cite a famous statement of Adam Smith to reflect their optimism: "There is much ruin in a nation" (in Rae 1895:343). It suggests that when a nation has built up tremendous wealth, institutions, and good will over the centuries, it would take more than a major war or natural disaster to destroy a country.

Until recently, Keynesians have traditionally been positive about the "mixed" economy. In 1930, in the midst of the Great Depression, Keynes wrote an optimistic essay, "Economic Possibilities for our Grandchildren." After lambasting his disciples who predicted never-ending depression and permanent stagnation, Keynes foresaw a bright future. Through technological improvements and capital accumulation, mankind could virtually solve its economic problem within the next hundred years and achieve a "far greater progress still" (Keynes 1963 [1931]:365). Paul Samuelson, America's foremost Keynesian, wisely rejected Alvin Hansen's permanent stagnation thesis, doomsayers' predictions of another great depression, and imminent bankruptcy due to excessive national debt. "Our mixed economy — wars aside — has a great future before it" (Samuelson 1964:809).

However, Keynesians have expressed a sour note lately about the U. S. economy. In the "valediction" of his 50th anniversary edition of *Economics*, Samuelson turns pessimistic, lambasting the American economy as "ruthless" and "harsh" that might not provide "good jobs, adequate income, and a safe environment" (Samuelson and Nordhaus 1998:735). And John Kenneth Galbraith joins Paul Krugman, Robert Shiller, and Joseph Stiglitz, among others, in protesting America's penchant for massive deficits, corporate corruption, tax cuts for the rich, and military imperialism (Parker 2005:650-55).

Supply siders such as Arthur Laffer, Stephen Moore, and Julian Simon may well be the most optimistic of schools. Ignoring largely the effects of the widening trade and spending deficits in the United States, they see better times ahead.[3]

The Freedom Movement and the True Believer

Today's Austrian school tends to reject the mass popularity approach. Leonard Read built his Foundation for Economic Education on three grand principles: (1) never compromise (2) never support political parties, candidates, or specific legislation, and (3) never promote to the masses. Not surprisingly, FEE has always been more aligned with the Austrians than with the Chicago school. Mises was one of their resident scholars. Read used the candlelight as a symbol of his approach. At the end of the small individualized seminars that he would run in Irvington-on-Hudson, New York, he would turn out the lights and light a candle that all could see. His favorite scripture is "Let your light so shine" (Matthew 5:16). His view is that if you light a candle of truth, truth seekers will find you. You don't need to seek them out through heavy promotions, or advertising to the masses. Through word of mouth from individual to individual, they will seek you out. Read follows the lines of libertarian Albert Jay Nock who wrote an influential essay, "Isaiah's Job," in March 1936, a time of deep pessimism in the freedom movement. In it Nock argues that preaching to the masses is counter-productive and hopeless: "The official class and their intelligentsia will turn up their noses at you and the masses will not even listen." Better, he says, to preach to the "remnant," that small band of "obscure, unorganized, inarticulate" true believers who need reassurance, education and support. "They need to be encouraged and braced up because when everything has gone completely to the dogs, they are the ones who will come back and build up a new society; and meanwhile, your preaching

3 Stephen Moore has even written a book reflecting this eternal optimism: *It's Getting Better All the Time* (2000). See also Julian Simon, *State of Humanity* (1996), and W. Michael Cox and Richard Alm, *Myths of Rich and Poor: Why We're Better Off Than We Think* (2000).

will reassure them and keep them hanging on" (Nock 1937). Nock compares the dire situation to Old Testament prophet Isaiah, who was told by the Lord to preach only to the remnant because the world in general would never listen. Read would not allow debates to take place at FEE. Does this approach lend itself to preaching to the choir? Yes, it does, but according to Read, that is preferable to preaching to the masses.

The Mises Institute, established by Lew Rockwell and Murray Rothbard, adopts a similar "true believer" approach. While providing a much needed avenue for growing scholarship in Austrian economics, they take solace in coming under attack by the establishment media for their "nutty, crazy, extreme" views. They relish their extremism.[4] They often express intolerance for those who compromise their free-market principles. Such intolerance is nothing new. Mises himself was highly judgmental and intolerant of friends and foes alike. He frequently engaged in polemics when it came to challenging the Keynesian apologists. When the Keynesians dismissed free-market critics as "reactionary," "narrow-minded fanatics," and "old-fashioned," Mises responded by calling the interventionists "anti-economists," "pseudo-progressives," and "ignorant zealots." He was kind to his admirers, but often imparted little patience toward his critics. Sometimes he would hold a grudge for years. Even his wife Margit Mises disagreed with the adjective "gentle" when applied to her husband: "He was gentle with me because he loved me. But actually he was not gentle. He had a will of iron and a mind like a steel blade. He could be unbelievably stubborn" (Mises 1984:144). When one of his students, Fritz

---

4 For example, Rothbard frequently claimed that the United States, not the Soviet Union, was the aggressor during the Cold War: "Empirically, the most warlike, most interventionist, most imperial government throughout the twentieth century has been the United States" (Rothbard 1973:284, 294). Rockwell viciously attacks the U.S. Constitution. Referring to the U. S. presidency as "this vile office," he states, "The presidency—by which I mean the executive State—is the sum total of American tyranny....I'll go further. US Presidency is the world's leading evil...Each president has tended to be worse than the last, especially in this century...Carter was worse than Nixon, and Reagan—who doubled the national budget and permanently entrenched the warfare State—was worse than Carter. The same is true of Bush and Clinton" (Rockwell 2004:175)

Machlup, spoke out in favor of flexible exchange rates at a Mont Pelerin Society meeting, Mises, who held to a rigid gold standard with fixed exchange rates, refused to talk to Machlup until a colleague reconciled them three years later. Another incident occurred in the early years of the society's meetings. Milton Friedman, who chaired a Mont Pelerin session on income distribution, writes, "I particularly recall a discussion of this issue, in the middle of which Ludwig von Mises stood up, announced to the assembly, 'You're all a bunch of socialists,' and stomped out of the room." Friedman adds that the group "contained not a single person who, by even the loosest standards, could be called a socialist" (Friedman 1998:161). Such behavior has contributed to a lot of bad blood between the two schools over the years.

It should be noted that Mises does not own an exclusive monopoly when it comes to flashes of anger and hostility toward his critics. Other free-market economists have engaged in shouting matches, to the point that R. M. Hartwell, president of the Mont Pelerin Society in 1994, warned the audience, "The liberal should be a master of the art of civilized discourse, eschewing rudeness and what Adam Smith calls 'the insolence and brutality of anger.'"

The Mises Institute also takes an unusual position when it comes to promoting free market ideals. In a talk about "the path to victory," Lew Rockwell warns supporters not to "hide our light under a bushel." Like Read, however, Rockwell disparages the value of landing an academic chair in an ivy league school, influencing legislators, writing for *The New York Times* or *The Wall Street Journal*, or appearing on television. Rather, he says, the true believer should light a candle and seek out "Nock's remnant," the uncompromising few, and educate each other through books, journals, and the internet. Given this limited world view, it's surprising how successful the Mises Institute has become under Rockwell's leadership. It has grown rapidly, with a beautiful new building for conferences and staff, and its websites are "the most popular liberty-minded site on the net" (Rockwell 2004:386).

A Fortress or a Town?

Richard Wagner, a public-choice economist at George Mason University, accuses the Mises Institute strand of the Austrian school of adopting a "fortress mentality" of us versus them. "A fort is a closed society that involves a disjunction between who is inside and who is outside, which in turn requires rules and processes for distinguishing between insiders and outsiders. A town is an open society. People may enter or leave as they choose, depending on how attractive they find the town. Robust towns would be modeled as being strong attractors, whereas forts would not." (Oprea and Wagner 2003:107)

Clearly the missionary zeal of Milton Friedman and the Chicago school has the advantage here. Chicago is a town, Vienna is a fortress. How influential would Friedman's ideas be if he hadn't aggressively pursued writing a column for *Newsweek*, and produced the "Free to Choose" television series? The same can be argued for Gary Becker's column in *Business Week*, or John Stossel's 1-hour specials on ABC News. Have not legislators in Washington and other political centers been influenced for the better because of the outstanding work of the Cato Institute, the Heritage Foundation, and other free-market think tanks?

Today's Austrians should recall the first generation of Austrians if they want to foresee the long-term fate of a reclusive "remnant" policy. To the great detriment of Austrian economics, both founders Carl Menger and Eugen Böhm-Bawerk rigidly adhered to the view that erroneous theories should "run a free and full course" without opposition, and therefore, they should make no effort to aggressively promote their own truths in the academic world. Menger adamantly refused to grant permission to reprint his path-breaking *Principles of Economics*. Neither did Menger nor Böhm-Bawerk make any attempt to obtain appointments for their followers when they retired from the University of Vienna. As Mises comments, "while it is the duty of a pioneering mind to do all that his faculties enable him to perform, it is not incumbent upon him to propagandize for his ideas....They never tried to win the support of anybody by other means than by the convincing power developed in their books and articles" (Mises 1984:39). As a result of their miscalculation, Austrian economics is still a tiny minority among professional economists, even though they have much to offer. As Peter Boettke notes, "The Austrians have been underachievers."

In researching the sometimes tumultuous relationship between members of the Austrian and Chicago schools, we can learn a great deal from leaders who tried to build bridges between the two, such as Benjamin Rogge and Fred Glahe. Rogge was long-time professor of economics at Wabash College who arranged for Milton Friedman to deliver a series of lectures in the late 1950s which eventually became a bestselling book, *Capitalism and Freedom* (1962). At the same time, Rogge was part of the inner circle of professors who taught regularly at the Austrian-oriented Foundation for Economic Education in Irvington-on-the-Hudson, New York. Rogge had the ability to draw from the best of both schools without disparaging either.

References

Arrow, Kenneth J. and F. H. Hahn.1971. *General Competitive Analysis.* San Francisco: Holden-Day, Inc.

Baumol, William J. and Alan S. Blinder. 1994 (6th ed.), 2001 (8th ed.) Economics: *Principles and Policies.* Ft. Worth, Texas: Harcourt College Publishers.

Becker, Gary S. 2004. "Let's Make Gasoline Prices Even Higher." *Business Week* (May 31), 24.

Brennan, Geoffrey and Philip Pettit. 1993. "Hands Invisible and Intangible," *Synthese* 94:191-225.

Bush, George W. 2002. "President Honors Milton Friedman for Lifetime Achievements Remarks." www.whitehouse.gov/news/releases/2002/05/20020509.1.html

Cox, W. Michael and Richard Alm. 2000. *Myths of Rich and Poor: Why We're Better Off Than We Think.* New York: Basic Books.

Eisner, Marc Allen. 1991. *Antitrust and the Triumph of Economics.* University of North Carolina Press.

Fitzgibbons, Athol. 1995. *Adam Smith's System of Liberty, Wealth, and Virtue.* Oxford: Clarendon Press.

Friedman, Milton. 1962. "How 100% Reserves Would Work," in Leland B. Yeager, ed., *In Search of a Monetary Constitution.* Cambridge: Harvard University Press.

Friedman, Milton. 1968. *Dollars and Deficits.* Englewood Cliffs, NJ: Prentice-Hall.

Friedman, Milton. 1978. "Adam Smith's Relevance for 1976," in Fred R. Glahe, ed., *Adam Smith and the Wealth of Nations: 1776-1976 Bicentennial Essays.* Boulder, Colorado: Colorado Associated University Press, 7-20.

Friedman, Milton. 1981. *The Invisible Hand in Economics and Politics.* Singapore: Institute of Southeast Asian Studies.

Friedman, Milton. 1986. "Keynes's Political Legacy," in John Burton, ed., *Keynes's General Theory: Fifty Years On.* London: Institute of Economic Affairs.

Friedman, Milton. 1997. "Rx for Japan," *Wall Street Journal,* December 17.

Friedman, Milton and Rose. 1980. *Free to Choose: A Personal Statement.* New York: Harcourt Brace Jovanovich.

Galbraith, John Kenneth. 1958. *The Affluent Society.* Boston: Houghton Mifflin.

Hahn, Frank. 1982. "Reflections on the Invisible Hand." *Lloyds Bank Review.* April, 1-21.

Harris, Sharon. 1998. "The Invisible Hand is a Gentle Hand," HarryBrowne.org/ articles/InvisibleHand.htm (September 14).

Hayek, Friedrich A. 1960. *The Constitution of Liberty.* Chicago: University of Chicago Press.

Hayek, Friedrich A. 1994 [1944]. *The Road to Serfdom.* Chicago: University of Chicago Press.

Heilbroner, Robert, ed. 1986. *The Essential Adam Smith.* New York: W. W. Norton & Co.

Hoppe, Hans-Hermann. 1998. "The Case for Free Trade and Restricted Immigration." *Journal of Libertarian Studies* 13:2 (summer), 221-33.

Ingrao, Bruna and Giorgio Israel. 1990. *The Invisible Hand: Economic Equilibrium in the History of Science.* Cambridge: MIT Press.

Joyce 2001. "Adam Smith and the Invisible Hand," Plus Magazine, March. http://plus.maths.org/issue14/features/smith/

Keynes, John Maynard. 1963 (1931). *Essays in Persuasion.* New York: Norton.

Lindsey, Brink. 2002. *Against the Dead Hand: The Uncertain Struggle for Global Capitalism.* New York: John Wiley.

Macfie, A. L. 1967. *The Individual in Society: Papers on Adam Smith.* London: George Allen & Unwin.

Mises, Ludwig von. 1978. *Notes and Recollections.* Spring Hill, PA: Libertarian Press.

Mises, Ludwig von. 1984. *The Historical Setting of the Austrian School of Economics.* Auburn: The Mises Institute.

Mises, Margit. 1984. *My Years with Ludwig von Mises,* 2nd ed. Cedar Falls, IA: Center for Futures Education.

Moore, Stephen. 2000. *It's Getting Better All the Time.* Washington, DC: Cato Institute.

Nock, Albert Jay. 1937. *Free Speech and Plain Language.* New York: William Morrow.

Oprea, Ryan D. and Richard E. Wagner. 2003. "Institutions, Emergence, and Macro Theorizing: A Review Essay on Roger Garrison's *Time and Money.*" *Review of Austrian Economics* 16:1, 97-112.

Parker, Richard. 2005. *John Kenneth Galbraith: His Life, His Politics, His Economics.* New York: Farrar, Straus and Giroux.

Rae, John. 1895. *Life of Adam Smith.* London: Macmillan.

Read, Leonard E. 1999 [1958]. "I, Pencil: My Family Tree as Told to Leonard E. Read" *Freeman* (December).

Rockwell, Llewellyn H., Jr. 2004. *Speaking of Liberty*. Auburn: The Mises Institute.

Roemer, John E. 1988. *Free to Lose*. Cambridge: Harvard University Press.

Rothbard, Murray N. 1973. *For a New Liberty*. New York: Macmillan.

Rothbard, Murray N. 1983 (1963). "Introduction," *America's Great Depression*, 4th ed. New York: Richardson & Snyder.

Rothbard, Murray N. 2002 [1971]. "Milton Friedman Unraveled." *Journal of Libertarian Studies* 16:4 (Fall), 37-54.

Rothschild, Emma. 2001. *Economic Sentiments: Adam Smith, Condorcet, and the Enlightenment*. Cambridge: Harvard University Press.

Samuelson, Paul A. 1947. "Lord Keynes and the General Theory," in Seymour Harris, ed., *The New Economics*, ed. New York: Alfred A. Knoft.

Samuelson, Paul A. 1964. *Economics*. 6th ed. New York: McGraw Hill.

Samuelson, Paul A. 1967. *Economics*. 7th ed. New York: McGraw-Hill.

Samuelson, Paul A. and William D. Nordhaus. 1998. *Economics*. 16th ed. New York: McGraw Hill.

Schumpeter, Joseph A. 1950. *Capitalism, Socialism, and Democracy*. New York: Harper and Row.

Selgin, George and Lawrence White. 1994. "How Would the Invisible Hand Handle Money?" *Journal of Economic Literature* 22 (December).

Shleifer, Andrei and Robert W. Vishny. 1998. *The Grabbing Hand: Government Pathologies and Their Cures*. Cambridge: Harvard University Press.

Simon, Julian. 1996. *The State of Humanity*. New York: Blackwell Publishers.

Skousen, Mark. 1998. "Why Are Austrians Unusually Bearish?" *The Freeman* (January), 54-55.

Skousen, Mark. 2001. *The Making of Modern Economics*. New York: M. E. Sharpe.

Smith, Adam. 1981 [1776]. *An Inquiry into the Nature and Causes of the Wealth of Nations*. Indianapolis, Indiana: Liberty Fund.

Smith, Adam. 1982 [1759]. *The Theory of Moral Sentiments*, edited by D. D. Raphael and A. L. Macfie. Indianapolis, Indiana: Liberty Fund.

Smith, Adam. 1982. *Essays on Philosophical Subjects*, ed. W. P. D. Wightman. Indianapolis, Indiana: Liberty Fund.

Stigler, George J. 1976. "The Successes and Failures of Professor Smith." *Journal of Political Economy* 84:6 (December), 1199-213.

Stigler, George J. 1986. *The Essence of Stigler*, ed. By Kurt R. Leube and Thomas Gale Moore. Stanford: Hoover Institution Press.

Tobin, James. 1992. "The Invisible Hand in Modern Macroeconomics," in Michael Fry, ed., *Adam Smith's Legacy*. London: Routledge. 117-29.

Viner, Jacob. 1972. *The Role of Providence in the Social Order*. Princeton: Princeton University Press.

Ylikoski, Petri. 1995. "The Invisible Hand and Science," *Science Studies* 8: 32-43.

Chapter Ten

THE FUTURE OF FREE-MARKET ECONOMICS

HOW FAR IS VIENNA FROM CHICAGO?[1]

Without significant changes in its traditional research topics and strategies, Austrian economics will become increasingly irrelevant to the major intellectual currents in the next century and will ultimately fail to survive.

—Mario Rizzo (1992:245)

The Next Economics will have to be again micro-economic and centered on supply. Both productivity and capital formation are events of the micro-economy. Both also deal with the factors of production rather than being functions of demand.

—Peter F. Drucker (1981:13)

If we have learned one thing from this study, it is how a school of economics can overcome heavy odds and achieve spectacular success. The Chicago school, under the direction of Milton Friedman and George Stigler, among others, did just that. It was the Age of Keynes in the generation after World War II, a time when free-market economists had difficulty in gaining recognition and acceptance. By staying within the profession, rigorously developing market theories, and backing up those models with powerful evidence, Friedman and the Chicago school were able to convince a growing number of economists and policy leaders of the correctness of their position. Their persistence paid off. By the turn of the 21st century, the Chicago school had achieved

1 To borrow a phrase from Karl-Heinz Paqué (1985).

success in the profession not unlike the rapid recovery of Germany and Japan after World War II. Today, based on citations in the leading journals and the granting of the highest awards, the Chicago school and its graduates dominate the thinking and agenda of the discipline.

The Austrian school has the ability and the tools to emulate Chicago's success, although it will require a change in research topics and strategies, as NYU professor Mario Rizzo warns at the beginning of this chapter. The fact that the Austrians gained prominence twice in their history, in the late 19th century with the marginalist revolution, and between the great world wars (1920-40), with the great debates over socialist central planning and the Great Depression, offers reason to be optimistic.

Looking Outward

What would it take for the Austrians to duplicate Chicago's success? First, the Austrians need to look outward instead of inward, to be more of a town welcoming outsiders rather than a fortress closing out the rest of the world, to use Richard Wagner's metaphor. This means making a deliberate effort to submit papers to the top academic journals, such as the *American Economic Review* and the *Quarterly Journal of Economics*, <u>before</u> they submit them to the *Quarterly Journal of Austrian Economics* or the *Review of Austrian Economics*. It means their first priority should be participating in the annual meetings of the American Economic Association and other mainstream professional conferences, before presenting papers at their own meetings, or organizing their own separate sessions. The Marxists are known for organizing their own sessions at the annual AEA meetings, but attendance is small and their influence is waning, primarily because the Marxists are viewed as ideologues, not scientific in their approach and not to be taken seriously. Austrians have suffered from the same criticism, and need to focus on their contributions to economic science more than policy or methodology.

This new strategy would suggest that the Austrians should seek research grants from the National Bureau of Economic Research (NBER) and other established organizations pursuing scientific analysis. Austrian leaders should encourage their students to attend top ivy league universities and graduate schools, and then with Ph. D. in hand, apply for positions at major institutions. Just as Chicago graduates now teach at Harvard, Yale and Stanford, so Austrians need to follow suit. Austrians are already linked with New York University and George Mason University, creating a stimulating environment with other schools of thought. GMU, for example, offers students of Austrian economics an opportunity to associate with centers of public choice and laboratories in experimental economics, and is rapidly moving up in the ranks of top economics departments in the United States.

Building an Austrian Model

Second, Austrians need to develop and advance their micro and macro models of the economy. The fact is that the economics profession has opened the door for the Austrians in this regard. Many teachers are hungry for new micro and macro models of the economy, and the Austrians are in a good position to fill this need. Economists across the spectrum have expressed dissatisfaction with the aggregate supply and demand (AS/AD) found in most textbooks, and the failure to link micro with macro. David Colander, a prominent "neo-Keynesian," recently repudiated the standard AS/AD textbook model in an article in the *Journal of Economic Perspectives*, the most read economics journal in the world. "The AS/AD model...is seriously flawed," he writes, "a model of the worst type—a model that obscures, rather than clarifies" (Colander 1995:1969). He shows how AS-AD analysis is internally inconsistent because it relies on contradictory assumptions. The supply relationships packed into AD are at war with the supply assumptions underlying AS. Moreover, he states, the textbook model implies that supply and demand are totally independent of each other in the aggregate economy, a theory that contradicts all common sense. So what to do? Many of Colander's colleagues favor complete banishment of the AS/AD model. Reuven Brenner, an economist at McGill University, not only dismisses textbook macro as "pseudo-science" but seriously suggests astrology as its closest allied field (Colander and Brenner 1992:123-151). Mark Blaug, considered the premier historian of economics, lambasts modern economics for the "noxious influence" of Swiss economist Leon Walras in creating the "perfectly competitive general equilibrium model," or GE for short. Most textbook writers, including Paul Samuelson, are enamored with GE, because of its mathematical precision. So is the Chicago school. Blaug, however, joins Austrians in labeling perfect competition a "grossly misleading concept" that ignores the role of the entrepreneur. He urges economists to "rewrite the textbooks" and replace the current Walrasian GE model with a dynamic Austrian view of the competitive process (Blaug 1997:78-81). Austrians should jump at this opportunity.[2]

The Austrians have developed useful, rigorous macro and micro models to replace those taught in the textbooks. The intertemporal capital-using model, known as Hayekian triangles, offers a powerful way to illustrate graphically the dynamics of the whole economy, one that students can relate to. In his book *Time and Money* (2001), Roger Garrison creatively combines Hayekian triangles, the loanable funds market, and the production-possibility curve to demonstrate a variety of dynamic changes in the economy, such as how the saving rate can lead to higher economic growth, or how monetary inflation by the Federal Reserve can cause a business cycle (see figure 10.1).

---

2 N. Gregory Mankiw's popular textbook, *Principles of Economics* (2004) has taken a step in the right direction by placing the classical model of long-term growth up front in his textbook and the short-term AS/AD model in the final chapters.

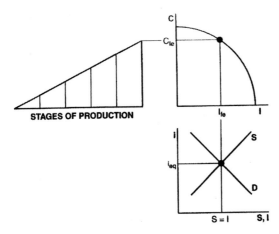

Figure 10.1. Garrison's graphics in macroeconomics

Moreover, Wicksell's natural rate of interest hypothesis is an excellent graphic tool for analyzing saving/investment trends, interest rate changes, and monetary policy (see figure 5.1). Since monetary policy dominates the textbooks when it comes to discussing recessions and inflation, Wicksell's model is another ideal pedagogical device.

My own college textbook, *Economic Logic* (2006[2000]), creates a four-stage macro model of the economy as an updated version of Hayekian triangles (see figure 10.2), and applies Garrison's graphics and Wicksell's natural rate of interest model to discuss macro issues. Similarly, in chapter 8 of *The Structure of Production* (1990), I introduce a new tool, the aggregate supply vector (ASV) and the aggregate demand vector (ADV), as a theoretical way to illustrate macroeconomic instability and an Austrian-style business cycle. Peter Boettke and David Prychitko, new co-authors of the late Paul Heyne's popular textbook, *The Economic Way of Thinking* (2003), have introduced a variety of Austrian concepts, including entrepreneurship, spontaneous order, the Austrian theory of the business cycle, and a price-making market process model as an alternative to the price-taking perfect competition model.

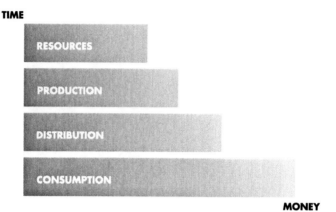

TIME

RESOURCES

PRODUCTION

DISTRIBUTION

CONSUMPTION

MONEY

Figure 10.2. Skousen's 4 stage model of the economy

Advancing Empirical Work

Third, the Austrians need to include more empirical work to support their economic theories. In the debate over methodology in chapter 4, we conclude that one reason the Chicago school has succeeded is because of the quantitative work of Friedman, Stigler, Fogel, Coase, Becker, and others. Austrians and Austrian fellow-travelers who have engaged in statistical and historical work include Murray Rothbard, Richard Vedder, Lowell Galloway, Robert Higgs, George Selgin, Lawrence White, Robert A. Lawson, and Gerald P. O'Driscoll, Jr. We need to see more of it. The Austrian theory of the business cycle, in particular, is conducive toward more empirical work to demonstrate its efficacy. Economists need to examine the extent to which easy-money policies lead to structural imbalances in various sectors of the economy, and to determine if sectors with high capital requirements or industries further removed from final consumption are subject to great volatility, as the Austrian model implies. The few studies done in this area seem to support the Austrian theory of the business cycle (Wainhouse 1984; Skousen 1990; Mulligan 2002; Callahan and Garrison 2003; Keeler 2001). More journals may be receptive to this business-cycle research given the growing interest in the Austrian view on asset inflation. And no doubt the Chicago school might be more accepting of the Austrian view of inflation if more empirical work were done in this vital area.

One potentially fruitful exercise has been to develop a new national income statistic that measures total spending in the economy, what Rothbard called the Aggregate Production Structure. The purpose of this new national statistic, which I have dubbed Gross Domestic Expenditures (GDE), is to measure spending at all stages of production, not just the final stage (see figure 10.2). Gross Domestic Product (GDP) is a Keynesian-inspired statistic that measures final output only. The widespread use of GDP as the primary measure of the economy's performance has led to much mischief, including the idea that an increase in government spending automatically increases economic growth, and the myth that consumer spending drives the economy, since personal consumption expenditures represents the largest part of GDP. By measuring total spending in the economy, including the intermediate as well as final stages, we find that consumer spending actually represents less than 40% of the economy (GDE), while total business investment, which includes intermediate production, equals over 50% of total spending in the economy (Skousen 1990:185-92). Using GDE would do much to shift the emphasis away from the consumer-driven economy toward a more business-oriented growth model.

Austrian economics can also be useful in disaggregating the economy and determining the sources of instability, structural imbalances, the business cycle, and identifying the best leading and lagging economic indicators. Studies would concentrate on disaggregating the economy into various sectors of the economy in terms of their distance from final consumption, and then determining how volatile these intertemporal sectors of the economy are. Researchers could look at the resource, manufacturing, construction, wholesale distribution, and retail markets, and to see how much change takes place in employment, prices, inventories, revenues, and profits historically over the business cycle, and how changes in monetary/fiscal policies affect these intertemporal markets. This could be an exciting new area of empirical research for Austrians.

Another promising research area is in the search for an ideal monetary system. Leland Yeager, emeritus Ludwig von Mises Professor of Economics at Auburn, edited a volume on this subject in the early 1960s, and the search continues (Yeager 1962). Lawrence White (1996), George Selgin (1988), and Steve Horwitz (2000) have led the way in developing a sophisticated theory of free banking and examining historical evidence of free-banking regimes.

Finally, Peter Boettke has focused on the unique contributions of Austrian economics in the realm of public policy and the benefits of decentralized decision making in government, based on his exhaustive works on Soviet economics and socialist central planning (Boettke 1993, 2001).

All in all, advances in high theory and empirical studies will help dispel the notion that Austrian economics is nothing more than ideology, and does in fact have a major role to play in developing economics as science, and can indeed develop a *wertfrei* (value free) science, the cherished belief of Weber, Mises and most Austrians (Boettke 2001:9-18).

The Next Economics

In the early 1980s, Daniel Bell and Irving Kristol invited a group of policy makers and economists to consider the growing crisis in economic theory. Representatives of each major school (Keynesian, Chicago, Austrian, etc.) were invited to present papers, which were later published (Bell and Kristol 1981). The most penetrating paper was presented by managerial guru Peter F. Drucker entitled "Toward the Next economics." Drucker criticizes Keynesianism for its inability to tackle the central policy problems of the developing economies—productivity and capital formation." He claims that none of the alternatives, including monetarism, rational expectations, or Marxism, could respond to the most severe problem in today's world, namely, the decline in capital formation. In sum, Drucker concludes, it is time for a new economic theory: "That there is both a productivity crisis and a capital-formation crisis makes certain that the Next Economics will have to be again micro-economic and centered on supply. Both productivity and capital formation are events of the micro-economy. Both also deal with the factors of production rather than being functions of demand" (Drucker 1981:13).

In the summer of 1988, I had the opportunity to meet 84-year-old Sir John Hicks, the Nobel laureate who transformed Keynesian economics into the grand neoclassical synthesis with his 1937 article in *Econometrica*, "Mr Keynes and the 'Classics.'" Despite his age and physical ailments, Hicks's mind was alert and, during our meeting, he recounted how he had gradually become disenchanted with many aspects of the modern economic theory he helped to develop. In particular, he seemed greatly displeased by the failure of orthodox economists to teach the importance of time and the stages-of-production concept in macroeconomics, a subject he learned from the Austrians and one he emphasizes in his own textbook, *The Social Framework*, and more recently in his treatise, *Capital and Time* (1973). He called it a great mistake that most economists had abandoned this essential doctrine.

The Austrian school is ideally suited to fulfill Drucker's dream of the next economics, and Hicks's desire that time and capital be taught once again in the classroom. The Austrian school is indeed the only school founded on microeconomic principles, and can therefore solve the "missing link" between micro and macro that economists have long sought (Skousen

1990:207-08; Horwitz 2000:40-61). It treats genuine saving as a virtue and as one of the key elements, along with productivity, of sustainable economic growth. It is the only school that focuses on the time structure of production — the production process from the resource stage to the retail stage — as a focal point in economic performance. It is the only school that preaches Say's law, that saving and investment are the most important ingredients to future economic growth, and that an increase in consumer spending is the effect, not the cause, of prosperity. If there is one word to describe Austrian economics, it is "capital." And if there is anything lacking in today's global economy, it is capital formation.

Austrian economics is the only school that applies the general rule, "There is no such thing as a free lunch," to the monetary sphere. Government cannot create genuine long-run prosperity with the printing press. The results of monetary mischief are in fact the opposite, a boom-bust cycle that has lasting ill-effects on the economy. It is the first school to recognize the inherent weakness in command-and-control systems in government and business, and the need for every developing nation to build a constitution of liberty and property rights.

If Austrian economists will recognize the powerful tools they have at their disposal to generate a new economic way of thinking, they will join the ranks of the Chicago economists as accomplished performers in modern economics. To do so will require Austrians to advance their model building and empirical work to a new level.

The Bridge Between Vienna and Chicago

On the back cover of this book is a draw bridge linking the Austrian and Chicago schools. In researching and writing this book over the past few years, I've often wondered if the draw bridge is going up, indicating a growing gap and less communication between the two schools, or coming down, llowing both schools to communicate more and gain from rade. I think you can now tell which way the draw bridge is going. It is coming down and integrating a dynamic prosperous community of scholars in both camps.

References

Bell, Daniel, and Irving Kristol, eds. 1981. *The Crisis in Economic Theory*. New York: Basic Books.

Blaug, Mark. 1997. *Not Only an Economist: Recent Essays*. Edward Elgar.

Boettke, Peter J. 1993. *Why Perestroika Failed*. New York: Routledge.

Boettke, Peter J. 2001. *Calculation and Coodination: Essays on Socialism and Transitional Political Economy*. London: Routledge.

Callahan, Gene and Roger W. Garrison. 2003. "Does Austrian Business Cycle Theory Help Explain the Dot-Com Boom and Bust?" *Quarterly Journal of Austrian Economics* 6:2 (summer), 67-98.

Colander, David, and Reuven Brenner. 1992. *Educating Economists*. Ann Arbor, MI: University of Michigan Press.

Colander, David. 1995. "The Stories We Tell: A Reconsideration of AS/AD Analysis." *Journal of Economic Perspectives* (summer), 169-88.

Drucker, Peter F. 1981. *Toward the Next Economics, and Other Essays*. New York: Harper & Row.

Garrison, Roger W. 2001. *Time and Money: The Macroeconomics of Capital Structure*. London: Routledge.

Heyne, Paul T., Peter J. Boettke, and David Prychitko. 2002. *The Economic Way of Thinking*. 10th ed. New York: Prentice Hall.

Hicks, John. 1973. *Capital and Time*. Oxford: Oxford University Press.

Horwitz, Steven. 2000. *Microfoundations and Macroeconomics: An Austrian Perspective*. London: Routledge.

Keeler, James P. 2001. "Empirical Evidence on the Austrian Business Cycle Theory." *The Review of Austrian Economics* 14:4, 331-51.

Mankiw, N. Gregory. 2004. *Principles of Economics*. 3rd ed. Ft. Worth, TX: Harcourt College Publishers.

Mulligan, Robert F. 2002. "A Hayekian Analysis of the Term Structure of Production." *Quarterly Journal of Austrian Economics* 5:2 (summer), 17-33.

Paqué, Karl-Heinz. 1985. "How Far is Vienna from Chicago? An Essay on the Methodology of Two Schools of Dogmatic Liberalism." *Kyklos* 38:412-434.

Rizzo, Mario. 1992. "Afterword: Austrian Economics for the Twenty-First Century," in Bruce J. Caldwell and Stephan Boehm, *Austrian Economics: Tensions and New Directions*. Boston: Kluwer Academic Publishers.

Selgin, George A. 1988. *The Theory of Free Banking*. Totowa, NJ: Rowman and Littlefield.

Selgin, George A. and Lawrence H. White. 1994. "How Would the Invisible Hand Handle Money?" *Journal of Economic Literature* 32:1718-49.

Skousen, Mark. 1990. *The Structure of Production*. New York: New York University Press.

Skousen, Mark. 2006 [2000]. *Economic Logic*. 2nd ed. Washington, DC: Capital Press.

Wainhouse, Charles E. 1984. "Empirical Evidence for Hayek's Theory of Economic Fluctuations," *Money in Crisis*, ed. By Barry N. Siegel. San Francisco: Pacific Institute for Public Policy Research.

White, Lawrence H. 1996. *Free Banking in Britain*. 2nd ed. New York: Routledge.

Yeager, Leland B., ed. 1962. *In Search of a Monetary Constitution*. Cambridge: Harvard University Press.

INDEX

ABOUT THE AUTHOR

Mark Skousen is a professional economist, financial advisor, university professor, and author of over 20 books. In 2004-05, he taught economics and finance at Columbia Business School and Barnard College at Columbia University. In 2001-02, he was president of the Foundation of Economic Education (FEE) in New York. From 1986 until 2003, Skousen taught economics, finance and history at Rollins College in Winter Park, Florida.

From 1972-75, Skousen was an economic analyst for the Central Intelligence Agency (CIA). Since then, he has been a consultant to IBM, Hutchinson Technology, and other Fortune 500 companies. He has a been a columnist for *Forbes* magazine (1997-2001), and has written articles for *The Wall Street Journal*, *Liberty*, *Reason*, and *The Journal of Economic Perspectives*.

Since 1980, Skousen has been editor in chief of *Forecasts & Strategies*, a popular award-winning investment newsletter published by Eagle Publishing in Washington, D. C.

He earned his Ph.D. in economics and monetary history from George Washington University in 1977. Since then he has written over 20 books, including *The Structure of Production* (New York University Press, 1990), *Puzzles and Paradoxes in Economics* (Edward Elgar Publishers, 1997), *Economic Logic* (Capital Press, 2000), *The Making of Modern Economics* (M. E. Sharpe, 2001), and *The Power of Economic Thinking* (Foundation for Economic Education, 2002).

In 2004, Grantham University named its business school "The Mark Skousen School of Business" in recognition of Skousen's work in economics, finance and management.

Websites:
www.markskousen.com
www.mskousen.com

OTHER BOOKS BY MARK SKOUSEN

THE MAKING OF MODERN ECONOMICS (M. E. Sharpe, 488 pages, $29.95 paperback; $74.95 hardcover). A bold new history of the great economic thinkers, from Adam Smith to Milton Friedman. Unlike other histories, Mark Skousen's book provides a running plot with a singular heroic figure, Adam Smith, at the center of the discipline. Skousen unites the great economists by ranking them for or against Adam Smith's "system of natural liberty," with complete chapters on the lives and ideas of Smith, Ricardo, Mill, Marx, Menger, Marshall, Fisher, Keynes, Samuelson, Mises, Hayek, Friedman and Schumpeter. Over 100 illustrations, portraits and photographs; provocative sidebars, humorous anecdotes, even musical selections reflecting the spirit of each major thinker. "Unputdownable!"— Mark Blaug. "Fascinating and infuriating."—*Foreign Affairs*

ECONOMIC LOGIC, 2nd edition (Capital Press, $29.95). An exciting new "logical" approach to economics. Unlike all other economics textbooks, which start with supply and demand, Skousen begins with the business profit-and-loss statement to demonstrate the dynamics of the global economy. In clear, crisp prose, he demonstrates how nations and individuals prosper by adopting the principles of entrepreneurship, savings and investment, marginal utility and cost control. The micro section includes chapters on profit and loss, supply and demand, the factors of production (land, labor, capital, entrepreneurship), and an entire chapter on financing capitalism (the stock and bond markets). This new updated version includes the much anticipated macro chapters, beginning with Skousen's unique 4-stage model of the macro economy. Other chapters include a better way to measure national output and employment, the history of money and central banking, inflation and monetary policy, taxes and the role of government, the national debt and deficit spending, government regulation, trade and protectionism, environmental economics, central planning and socialism, and globalization.

THE POWER OF ECONOMIC THINKING (Foundation for Economic Education, 334 pages, $19.95). Mark Skousen contends that economics is no longer the "dismal science" but an "imperial" science invading like an army the new frontiers of crime, politics, religion, history, and Wall Street, subjecting new economic analysis to gun rights, racial discrimination, drug abuse, professional sports, health care, grade-school education, and environmentalism. "In many ways, this is my favorite of your books ... I have earmarked several chapters to use in my classes."—Larry Wimmer, Brigham Young University

Mark Skousen's books are available from the publishers, Amazon.com, Laissez Faire Books (www.lfb.com), and local bookstores.